THE
MILLENNIUM
GUIDE

RICHARD KNIGHT

PARTIES, EVENTS & FESTIVALS AROUND THE WORLD

The Millennium Guide
First edition 1998

Publisher
Trailblazer Publications
The Old Manse, Tower Rd, Hindhead, Surrey GU26 6SU, UK
Fax (+44) 01428-607571
E-mail trailblazer@compuserve.com

British Library Cataloguing in Publication Data
A catalogue record for this book is available from the British Library

ISBN 1-873756-20-8

© **Richard Knight 1998**

The right of Richard Knight to be identified as the author of this work
has been asserted by him in accordance with the Copyright, Designs
and Patents Act 1988

Editor: Patricia Major
Layout: Bryn Thomas
Index: Jane Thomas

Every effort has been made by the author and publisher to ensure that
the information contained herein is as accurate and up to date as possible. However, they are unable to accept responsibility for any inconve-
nience, loss or injury sustained by anyone as a result of the advice and
information given in this guide.

Printed by
Kelso Graphics (☎ 01573-223214), The Knowes, Kelso TD5 7BH
Scotland

THE
MILLENNIUM GUIDE

RICHARD KNIGHT

PARTIES, EVENTS & FESTIVALS AROUND THE WORLD

For Maddy

Acknowledgements

Many thanks to: David Banford, Ric Birch, Philip Blain, Hilary Bradt, Dr Robin Catchpole, Neil Croak, Simon 'Colonel' Doody, Jeanne Golding, Tricia Hayne, Frankie Hendricks, Geraint 'Grunt' James, Professor Richard Landes, Yuka Makino, Midori Matsui, Michael Mitchell, Philip Owen, John Selman, Sandra de Sousa, Dr Martin West, and all the representatives of the various millennium organisations, tourist boards and travel companies who have helped in researching this book.

I'm grateful to Maggie Cameron and Bryn Thomas for coming up with the idea. Thanks also to my editor, Patricia Major, to Jane Thomas for the index, and to everyone else at Trailblazer for their enthusiasm and support.

As for my family, well, I couldn't have done it without you. Thanks!

The author

Graduating in journalism, Richard Knight left Cardiff University with two other attributes that well qualified him as author of *The Millennium Guide*: a strong desire to travel and a thorough understanding of what makes a great party. He has travelled widely in Africa, America and Europe and his articles have appeared in many newspapers and magazines in Britain and abroad. Before writing this guide, Richard was feature writer for *Holidays* magazine.

CONTENTS

THE MILLENNIUM

As the year 2000 approaches it seems that there are now two sorts of people – millennium-enthusiasts and millennium-cynics. It's true that the millennium is really only a date but it's a date which offers one very obvious reason to contemplate both the past and the future. The year 2000 marks a highly symbolic step in history and it should be celebrated for what it represents rather than for what it is. It represents a chance collectively to celebrate 1000 years of human endeavour. In other words: it represents an excellent excuse for the party of a lifetime.

When does the millennium begin?
This is something of a grey area. Clearly, the year 2000AD marks the 2000th anniversary of the birth of Christ. But if you consider this to be the sole significance of the millennium, you could be in for a shock. Academics claim that a 6th-century Scythian monk named Dionysus Exiguus miscalculated the date of Christ's birth. They claim He was born in what we would now call 4BC. That would make 1996 the year 2000 – so we've missed the real millennium! Christian leaders seem completely unruffled by this revelation, and, anyway, the fact that we have been keeping score for 2000 years is in itself something to celebrate even if we remove the Christian element completely.

Unfortunately, there is another problem. Most of the millennium-conscious world (with the notable exception of Switzerland) will treat the arrival of the year 2000 as the arrival of the third millennium. It isn't. Dionysus Exiguus was also the scholar who decided to use *Anno Domini* to label the years after Christ's birth. There was no year zero; he counted from 1BC to 1AD. As a result, the year 2000 will be the last year of the second millennium not the first of the third as is widely believed. If you do wait for 31 December 2000 before you celebrate, however, you will probably have missed the greatest party of all time and will have only the Swiss for company. Our advice: go with flow, forget accuracy, and celebrate on 31 December 1999.

Where will it all begin?

The Millennium Guide describes millennium celebrations across the world **in the order in which they will happen** – the order in which the sun comes up. Purists have other ideas about the big question of where the millennium really starts. An argument has developed between London and the South Pacific: both claim to be the first to see the year 2000.

For generations precision over time did not matter to the vast majority of people; there was always the sundial and, later in the West, the church clock while the wealthy and important

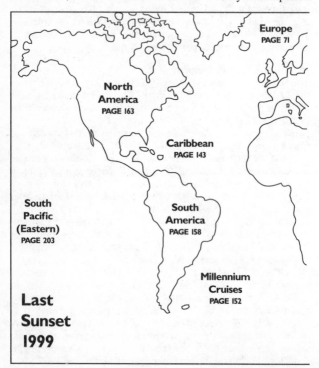

Last
Sunset
1999

had long-case clocks and watches. Until the Industrial Revolution, beginning in the second half of the 18th century in Britain and radiating across Europe and America, the need for accurate time was not apparent.

An industrial country, however, needed a nationwide transport network. This could not function efficiently without a timetable. In an attempt to ensure conformity the mean time at Greenwich Observatory was adopted by the transport system as the national norm: **Greenwich Mean Time** (GMT). Nevertheless, until the mid 19th century, because local time changes by

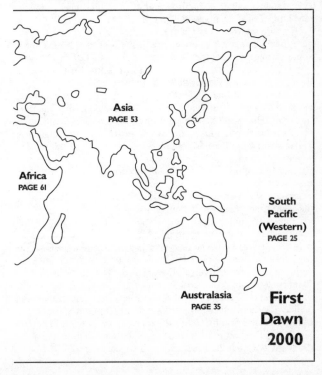

Asia
PAGE 53

Africa
PAGE 61

South
Pacific
(Western)
PAGE 25

Australasia
PAGE 35

**First
Dawn
2000**

about four minutes for every longitudinal degree, each town kept its own time. Tradition has it that the clock at Christchurch, Oxford, was kept four minutes behind GMT; this was known as Oxford Time.

In 1884 it was agreed at the International Meridian Conference in Washington DC that GMT should be the international standard or average time for the world. Greenwich was chosen because over 70% of the world's shipping at that time originated in London. The world was subsequently divided into 24 time zones. Each time zone has its own standard time which is a certain number of hours ahead of or behind GMT, making GMT the world's Universal Time. It was further agreed that the Universal Day should begin at midnight GMT.

In the same year an imaginary line was drawn. It runs north-south through the Pacific Ocean on or close to 180 degrees longitude and is called the **International Date Line**. East of this line the date is one day earlier than it is to the west.

The International Date Line has no legal definition and was adopted as a matter of convenience. At some point the date must tick over. That point is the Date Line, which was chosen because the 180 degree meridian touches land at few points. Islands on either side of the Date Line have similar local time but are one whole day apart.

Dr Catchpole of the Royal Observatory explains, 'the date-line is where it is because it appeared convenient. Bulges occur where an island group or country didn't want to be dissected by the Date Line. It's a social convention'.

These complex conventions have led to arguments which few delegates at the International Meridian Conference in 1884 could have foreseen. The new year begins at midnight GMT, or zero hours at zero degrees longitude, because that is the point at which each new Universal Day begins. The first dawn of 1 January 2000, however, will appear in the South Pacific close to the International Date Line. Serious millennium-celebrators must decide for themselves where the new millennium starts: either London or the South Pacific. If your choice is to head for the South Pacific, you must then contend with another debate about the point at which the first dawn will appear (see p29).

❏ KEEPING TIME

The desire to measure time is ancient. Mayans, Egyptians and Romans all devised calendars to support their advancing civilisations. Calendars are political as well as practical. Those great communities felt that quantifying time would somehow make them immortal or help them to command the future. More recent empire-builders such as Hitler have shown equal enthusiasm for implementing new calendars – but without the same success.

The Julian Calendar

Early calendars used the moon's cycle to determine days. But in the 1st century BC Sosigenes – an astronomer from Alexandria – advised Julius Caesar that the lunar calendar was inaccurate.

He proposed instead that a solar, or tropical, year be used as the yardstick for measuring time. According to Sosigenes, the tropical year lasted for 365.25 days. This was rounded down to 365 days a year and, to account for the missing quarter day, it was decided that an extra day would be added (or intercalated) every four years. Since the lunar calendar had been 10 months long, two new months were added between November and December to make the new calendar match the equinoxes. For the first 36 years that extra day was added too often because of a general misunderstanding of the rules among Roman officials. And who can blame them?

Emperor Augustus rectified this problem by missing out the intercalary day for 16 years. So, some 50 or more years after Sosigenes suggested the new system, the Julian Calendar was up and running properly.

The Gregorian Calendar

Sosigenes had done well to state that a tropical year lasted 365.25 days – but not quite well enough. The actual figure is 365.242199 days. It might not seem like much, but the Julian Calendar was out by 11 minutes and 14 seconds every year. After a thousand years this amounted to a whole week.

Matters were taken seriously when it was revealed that the vernal equinox – which determines Easter – was 10 days adrift from the prescribed date. Pope Paul III was keen to take action. Sadly for him, the solution wasn't agreed until after Gregory XIII became Pope; so denying Paul the privilege of naming the new calendar after himself.

The Gregorian Calendar (cont)

In 1582 Pope Gregory XIII tackled the immediate problem of the 10 day surplus with ruthless simplicity. He ordered that, for one year, October 5 was to become October 15 instead. The difference between Sosigenes' tropical year and the real figure amounted to 3.12 days every 400 years. To sort out this discrepancy Pope Gregory XIII ruled that centennial years divisible by four would be leap years. The year 2000, therefore, will be a leap year.

What a difference a day made

Most Roman Catholic countries obeyed the papal decree of 1582 but Britain was slow to accept it, not doing so until 1752 when the calendar needed not ten but eleven days removed from it. Because of complications over wages, leases and rents there was rioting in some areas of Britain as the cry went up: 'Give us back our eleven days!' People thought they had quite literally been robbed of a week and a half of their lives. Other European nations were even slower to accept the modified Gregorian Calendar; it was not recognised in Russia until 1918.

Doubts about the Gregorian System

The Gregorian calendar has, more or less, worked. As we approach the third millennium, however, time is our master more than ever before. Growing numbers of timekeepers are expressing doubts about the Gregorian system. They would like to see a system with months of equal lengths which would allow all significant days to fall on the same dates every year.

There are two proposals: the International Fixed Calendar (IFC) and the World Calendar. The IFC is a Gregorian calendar of 13 months, each of 28 days. The extra month (called 'Sol') would be inserted between June and July. An anonymous extra day falls after December 28 every year. Accountants are not keen; the IFC becomes messy when divided into business quarters.

Option two, the World Calendar, is made up of four quarters of 91 days with another incognito day intercalated after Christmas to bring the total number of days up to 365. The first month in every quarter has 31 days, the rest have 30.

One can't deny that tinkering with the system could lead to improvements. It does seem a shame, though, to reject a calendar that's taken so long to get right...well, nearly right.

Where is it all happening?

What could be worse than waking up on New Year's Day 2000 to realise that you have just squandered the biggest party of all time at your local bar or in front of the TV? To quote countless cheap commercials: '**Act now or risk missing out!**'

If you want to see the first rays of the future before anyone else, head for the **South Pacific**. Most sun-kissed South Pacific nations have made some attempt to claim the right to label their bash 'the first party of the next millennium'. Which one is right is hard to say – and, largely, irrelevant. Getting down and partying among the very first must be enough for all but the most pedantic reveller.

Fiji will hold an all-night dusk-'til-dawn party on the island of Vitu Levu. In Tonga, a month-long millennium festival will culminate in a Royal Banquet on New Year's Eve. Avarua City in the Cook Islands will host a Mardi Gras-style street party.

New Zealanders have been plotting their parties for years. The famously health-conscious Kiwis have devised several sporting events from a millennium marathon to a millennium golf tournament. More appealing to most, perhaps, will be a mega-party for 60,000 people in Gisborne – the easternmost city in New Zealand.

Australia has a natural advantage in the millennium stakes: Sydney will host the 2000 Olympic Games. Sydney-siders will also enjoy what will probably prove to be the biggest and best fireworks display in the world on New Year's Eve 1999.

Melbourne hopes to entice millennial travellers away from Sydney with a series of events throughout 2000. Those that hope to be nearer to nature when the Big Moment finally arrives might want to head for Ayers Rock which looks set to be a popular destination.

On the other side of the world, London will compete with Edinburgh for the best celebration in **Britain**. London might have the Millennium Dome, Millennium Wheel and a colossal party in Greenwich Park, but Edinburgh has hogmanay. Edinburgh's Hogmanay Festival has grown enormously in recent years and will probably be the best millennial street party in Europe.

Across the Channel, the **French** intend to greet the third millennium with a very Gallic mix of the elegant and the slightly bizarre. Elegant plans include a scheme to turn the Place de la Concorde into a giant sundial – with the Egyptian obelisk as the pointer. More bizarre will be the Eiffel Tower, the focus for French millennium celebrations, which will 'give birth' to a giant egg at midnight on 31 December 1999. The egg will then 'hatch' to reveal a bank of TV screens.

The **Viennese** will waltz into the next millennium in typically stylish fashion. Glamorous balls and concerts will take place at many of the Austrian capital's more opulent venues. In Germany a massive world fair, called Expo 2000, will act as a centrepiece for the country's very international contribution to the 'world party'.

This world party is nowhere more eagerly anticipated than in the **United States**. From the White House downwards, Americans want to mark the end of the 'American century' in style. New York City has long considered itself to be the New Year's Eve capital of America. Times Square will – as always – rival any other bash in the States with revelry on a massive scale. Other parties are planned all over the city, from the World Trade Center to the famous Rainbow Room. Millennium's Eve will go with a bang in the Big Apple. New Orleans will also play host to some major celebrations. A street party is planned around Jackson Square and there will be an upmarket celebration in Gallier House. The Big Easy is one of the world's true party capitals – on any night of the year. A three-day bash in southern California is expected to attract thousands.

Millennium planning is taken very seriously in **Canada**, where Vancouver looks set to lead the country with the best parties. Montréal will, of course, put on a better-than-ever jazz festival – and that's saying something.

Sadly, Africa, much of Asia and South America have been far slower to gear up for the surge in tourism which the millennium will surely bring. There are travel opportunities to these area – but few specific events. Of course, one must remember that the millennium only really applies to about one third of the world's population. The **independent traveller** will need to think ahead to get to some of the better-known of the world's 'exclamation marks' in time for 2000. More obvious places like the Pyramids will attract thousands, despite the fact that the authorities have so far refused to allow an organised party there.

Cruise and travel companies are putting together a range of exciting packages to the world's party capitals and to some of the more romantic sites in which to welcome the next millennium.

Now really is the time to contact these companies and make your own millennium plans. Choose carefully; you have only one chance to see in the third millennium...well, two at the most!

The Christian Millennium

Like Christmas, the real significance of the millennium is in danger of being eclipsed by commercial hype. Despite the fact that the actual year of the birth of Christ has been called into question, it is still true that the year 2000AD is the 2000th anniversary of Christianity. Christian leaders are planning celebrations and hope to make the world aware that the year 2000 is predominantly a religious event. See p53 for information on the millennium in the Holy Lands.

The Vatican is bracing itself for a millennial squeeze; over 21 million visitors are expected to descend on the 109-acre state over the Jubilee 2000 period. Normally, the Vatican's population is just one thousand. Pilgrims will be welcomed to the Vatican by a special organisation. A committee will be established to control price and quality in the region's hotels. Archbishop Sebastiani, Secretary-General of Jubilee 2000, said pilgrims should experience 'the extraordinariness of the Jubilee in a dimension of ordinary serenity'. The Vatican is keen to avoid what it calls 'religious tourism' and to promote 'true and proper pilgrimage'. Rome is also preparing for huge numbers of pilgrims.

In Britain the Church of England, Roman Catholics, Methodists, Baptists, the Evangelical Alliance and the United Reformed Church have set up a company to sell 25 million candles to be burnt for a minute at midnight on 31 December 1999. Religious celebrations are scheduled all over America. Southern Baptists are planning a massive New Year's Eve party called Youthlink 2000. Groups of young Baptists in Los Angeles, Denver, Tampa, Atlanta, Philadelphia, St Louis and Houston will be linked via satellite. The party will cover four time zones.

❑ THE END IS NIGH!

It's just possible that every millennium celebration in this book will be over-shadowed by a rather more pressing event: the end of the world. The ubiquitous Nostradamus, bearded America cult leaders and shadowy figures lurking on the edge of Christianity have all expressed doubt about our chances of reaching the third millennium in one piece. Let's deal with each of these doom-mongers in turn.

Nostradamus

Michel Nostradamus was a brilliant physician; he became a doctor at a very young age and led a crusade to help plague victims. He was not so good at prophecy. Modern interpretation of his verse – which is big business – has led to such useless predictions as: 'King Charles' coronation to occur in 1992' and 'America burns 1993-1996'.

Even Nostradamus could not have foreseen how seriously people would take his addled scribblings 400 years after his death. His work was highly incoherent and, of course, written in 16th century French. Those that do attempt to distil predictions from this scrawl run the risk of using their under-nourished imaginations to make Nostradamus' words fit their own pre-conceived ideas about the future.

Nostradamus has made a reference to the millennium. In Quatrain (verse) 72 of Century 10 he appears to predict that July 1999 will see the 'Great King of Terror ...bring the Great King of the Mongols back to life' and that 'pestilence, war and famine will rule'. So what? There is almost always disease, war and famine making life a misery somewhere. As for the return of Genghis Khan, he would probably find himself slightly less effective on today's battlefield.

Modern Prophets

Several more recent 'prophets' have attempted to warn the world of impending apocalypse. American evangelist Hal Lindsey is expecting global war to spread from the Middle East in 2000. His credibility suffered in the eighties, however, after he wrongly predicted that Christ would return to Earth one generation after the Jews had returned to their homeland. Another American, Edgar Cayce, has predicted that a world war in 1999 will lead to a tilt in the world's axis.

Other US psychics claim that aliens will steal the earth's oxygen in 1999, that the Antichrist will seize the US Presidency in 2000 and that a giant meteorite will collide with earth on 28 September 1999 with such force that all humanity will be wiped out. Slightly more convincing, but still unlikely, is New Zealander Michael Callagher's prediction that nuclear war will break out between Israel, Britain and the States on Christmas Day 1999.

Cults and Religious Groups

Lone prophets are often ludicrous and rarely worrying. How can any sane person believe these people when most have predicted Armageddon at regular intervals since the seventies? Cults are more alarming. Ted Daniels, a leading cult authority, claims that well over 1000 active cults use the threat of imminent doom as part of their recruitment pitch. The cult industry was dealt a blow in 1997, however, when the Heaven's Gate sect weren't plucked from earth by a spaceship travelling in the wake of Hale-Bopp as they had expected.

Religious groups such as Jehovah's Witnesses, Mormons and Seventh-Day Adventists are getting ready for the millennium. The Witnesses have not specified a date, having got it wrong eight times already, but expect their 144,000 most virtuous members to go to heaven while the world faces doomsday some time around the turn of the millennium.

The Second Coming?

Many Christians believe that 2000 will see the Second Coming of Christ. Millions of American Christians feel a need to convert others before He comes (see p181). An astonishing number of Italian Catholics thought the earthquakes which rocked their country in 1997 were signs of looming reckoning (see p76). If Jesus was planning to return to earth on the 2000th anniversary of His birth, he is probably already too late (see p7).

Why Worry?

Contrary to popular myth, Nostradamus rarely got it right. Most latter-day prophets can be written off as mad. If the world is hit by a cataclysmic event in the next millennium, it is far more likely to be caused by computer chaos (see p190) or environmental disaster than the resurrection of Mongol kings or alien oxygen thieves. Still, keep your fingers crossed!

Booking Hotel Rooms

Finding a place to stay could be the hardest stage in your millennial planning. Most hotels have yet to start taking reservations. Once they do open the books, rooms will go fast. Try to get onto a waiting list or offer a deposit. Prices will be high. If you do offer a deposit to a hotel which hasn't published its millennium rates, make sure it is refundable in case the final price is higher than you had anticipated.

Hotels listed in this guide are divided into budget, moderate and expensive price categories. The price band in each category is listed in local currency and is based on a standard double room for two at the time of going to press.

Prices could change substantially between now and the millennium; the prices listed here should be used as an approximate guide.

Flight Reservations

The following airlines have firm millennium policies:
- **Air New Zealand** (UK ☎ 0181-741 2299, USA ☎ 800-262 1234, Australia ☎ area code +13 24 76) are taking bookings, fares from the UK to NZ start at £1,700.
- **American Airlines** (UK ☎ 0345-789789, USA ☎ 800 433 7300) will accept bookings from 12 months in advance of travel.
- **British Airways** (UK ☎ 0345 222111, for USA and Australia contact local office) have begun to take bookings
- **Continental** (UK ☎ 0800-776464, USA 800-344 6888) will take reservations from 10 months in advance of travel.
- **Delta** (UK ☎ 0800-414767, USA ☎ 800-241 4141, Australia ☎ 800-500 992) will take bookings from eight months in advance of travel.
- **Qantas** (UK ☎ 0345-747767, USA ☎ 800 2274 500, Australia ☎ area code +13 12 11) will take bookings no more than 350 days in advance of travel
- **Virgin** (UK ☎ 01293 747747, USA ☎ 800-862 8621, Australia ☎ 800-646 747) won't decide routes or prices until early 1999.

Try to book your flight as early as you can, and don't forget to confirm your reservation 24-48 hours prior to departure.

General Advice for Millennium Travellers

Since many millennial travellers will be making short trips over long distances, jet lag could be a problem. There is also a pressing need to get things right first time – inoculations, visas etc – because this is one holiday you cannot postpone.

● **Jet lag** can be unpleasant and debilitating. There are literally hundreds of so-called cures on the market. In this writer's experience, however, the best cure is simply to try to sleep on the flight and to force yourself into the new regime as quickly as possible. Giving in to tiredness or hunger too early will just delay the effects.

● **Visas** Don't leave it to the last minute to check with your travel agent, tour operator or the relevant tourist authority/embassy to find which visas or entry documents you need for your chosen destination.

● **Travel Insurance** If your personal medical plans and household insurance don't cover you for foreign travel, make sure you buy adequate extra cover. The level of medical cover you need will depend on where you plan to go; for example, healthcare is more expensive in the States than it is in Europe. Remember to check that any possessions cover is at least equal to the value of the belongings you take with you, and look out for an acceptable level of cover for cancellation or curtailment. This is particularly important for millennial travellers, who are more vulnerable than most to cancellation due to the 'one-off' nature of their holiday.

● **Inoculations** are equally important. Consult your doctor to make sure you are fully 'jabbed-up' well before your departure. Some countries will demand proof of your having received certain inoculations (often yellow fever) before letting you in. Remember that anti-malarial pills usually have to be taken some time before your departure date – and for some time after you get back. It is also most important to avoid getting bitten; use plenty of mosquito repellent and a mosquito net.

If you are taking prescribed drugs, make sure you have enough to last for your entire trip. Don't remove any drugs from their bottles or packets – this can give customs officers cause for concern.

Useful Web Sites

The Internet is the preferred medium of millennium event organisers, perhaps because the millennium is about the future and the Internet is still seen as a futuristic channel. Already the web has been spammed by masses of millennium-related information ranging from the random ramblings of weirdy-beardies to some of the slickest sites on the net.

Here's our guide to the most useful millennium sites in cyberspace. (All addresses are prefixed by http://).

● **Events listings** For most people, the most interesting sites are those that list events. There are quite a few of these but none is comprehensive.

www.everything2000.com One of the first and still the best millennium site. Recently re-vamped. Sections on millennium resources, features, news, a competition and, of course, events.

www.futurecast.com/millenniumania/main.htm Regularly hosts interesting millennium-related articles from US newspapers. There's not too much here but what they do have is excellent.

www.greenwich2000.com/millennium/index.html One of the better listings sites which looks set to grow quickly. Not surprisingly, greenwich2000 is particularly good for events in Britain, but there are sections on other parts of the world.

www.igc.apc.org/millennium/events/index.html All sorts of sometimes pretentious but often interesting millennium projects are listed at this Millennium Institute site. Many of the ideas listed here are still just that: ideas.

www.jepa.co.uk/shopping/party.html A useful site to which you can add your own party details for free – not bad! The design is hardly inspiring, but if you want information rather than gimmicks it is well worth visiting.

www.newyrseve1999.com Will get there; still needs more info.

www.tour-eiffel.fr/an2000_uk/ Clicking on a world map takes you to a list of parties in that area. It's a good idea, but the information is thin in places. Clear bias towards France.

www.2000celebration.com Worth checking from time to time, but don't expect too much.

www.sentertainment2000.com Gives every impression of being created and then abandoned. Perhaps that's what happened. It could grow though, so check it out occasionally.

● **Year 2000 travel specialists** A small band of entrepreneurial cyber travel agencies specialise in millennium travel packages. Individually, they provide a smattering of interesting offers. Between the six you will find quite a lot of information.

www.carterstravel.ab.ca/2000.htm

www.destinations2000.com

www.ibtravel.com/millennium_2000.htm

www.rextravel.com

www.scotiasports.com/millennium.htm

www.2000travel.com

● **Destinations** This is a collection of particularly good (but not specifically millennium-related) travel and tourism sites which might help you to make your travel plans.

www.dfat.gov.au.home.html (Australia)

www.cookislands-tourism.com (Cook Islands)

www.fijifvb.gov.fj (Fiji)

www.germany-tourism.de (Germany)

www.gisborne2000.org.nz (Gisborne, NZ)

www.cum.qc.ca/octgm (Montréal)

www.quebec_region.cuq.qc.cq (Québec)

www.roma2000.com (Rome)

www.newasia-singapore.com (Singapore)

www.infocentre.com (South Pacific)

www.vatican.va (Vatican)

www.pise/-orbit/samoa/welcome.html (Western Samoa)

❏ How to Survive the Morning After

Hangovers follow New Year's Eve as surely as the third millennium follows the second. There is no all-conquering cure for the morning after blues, but here is a brief guide to the best advice:

There are a few ideas for preventing hangovers; don't worry, drinking less isn't on our list. A glass of milk before going on a binge and drinking a lot of water (at least a pint) before going to bed both help. The only problem is that if you can remember to do the latter, you probably aren't drunk enough for a real hangover anyway. Primrose oil is thought to encourage the liver to break down alcohol faster. Eating before drinking also helps; food lines the stomach and absorbs alcohol. That old adage 'beer on wine, feel fine – wine on beer, feel queer' works. It really is true, although it could be hard to avoid drinking champagne after beer on New Year's Eve 1999.

All of the above won't help big drinkers. When you wake up to find your head in a clamp, your tongue stuck to the roof of your mouth and your stomach pickled in vodka, you need to take action – fast. Nutritionists suggest drinking orange juice because the vitamin C neutralises the effects of alcohol. Bad idea – orange juice might help in the long run, but its most immediate effect is to induce nausea. An enormous, greasy fried breakfast is a time-honoured cure among students. It works; alcohol reduces blood sugar levels which leads to drowsiness and 'the shakes'.

There are a thousand and one hangover cocktails. Every self-respecting barman has a recipe of his own. They all work as long as they contain alcohol. Recent scientific research appears to prove that a small measure of alcohol on the morning after is the most efficient way to reduce the symptoms of a hangover. Anyone who has ever thrown down a Bloody Mary or Fernet Branca knows the scientists are right. If non-alcoholic cocktails like eggnog work, it's because they contain vitamin C or, simply, food.

Almost as soon as fermenting was invented, people across the globe began searching for hangover cures. The Greeks swore by cabbage, Mexicans eat stewed tripe and in India they add a pinch of cumin and a teaspoon of lime juice to a glass of orange juice.

It seems that if you want to lessen the pain on New Year's Day 2000, there are four things you should do: don't drink wine on top of beer, drink lots of water before going to bed and the next day eat a big breakfast. Follow this with the hair of the dog that bit you – ie another drink!

● **Specific events or projects** The following sites deal with particular millennial happenings. Most provide useful updates.

www.billennium.com (Billennium, USA)

www.celebration2000.com (Celebration 2000, New York)

www.celebration2000.gouv.fr (France)

www.emp2000.ukonline.co.uk (Electronic Millennium Project)

www.expo2000.de (Hanover Expo 2000)

www.firstlight2000.com (First Light)

www.firstnightintl.org (First Night, Boston)
  Thorough site which leaves few questions unanswered.

www.futurepacific.co.nz/odyssey.html
  (Odyssey's End, Gisborne)

www.hogmanay.co.uk (Glasgow Hogmanay)

www.mclellangroup.com/rhythmoftheearth/contents.html
  (Rhythm of the Earth Drumming Event)

www.millennia.org (Millennium Foundation of Canada)

www.mx2000.co.uk (Millennium Experience, UK)

www.party2000.com (Party 2000, California)

www.soulzone.com/millenum/index.html (All One Tribe Drum Festival) Fairly unhelpful site which hasn't changed in ages.

www.southafrica2000.com (Trance Party, Cape Town)
  Tantalising site which appears to be constantly on the verge of expanding on the few scraps of info which it has tossed out so far.

www.sydney.olympic.org (Sydney Olympics)

www.times-square.org/index2.html (Times Square, New York)

www.timevault-2000.co.nz (Time Vault Project, NZ)

www.tp2000.org.nz (Turning Point 2000, NZ)

www.whitehouse.gov/Initiatives/Millennium/
  (American Government Millennium Plans)

www.worldpeace2000.org (Peace Project)

www.yes2000.co.uk (The Millennial Foundation)

● **Millennium chat** If you can't keep your enthusiasm for the millennium to yourself, you can meet and chat to people with similar interests at either of the following sites. Talk2000 is the best, and you will find every aspect of the millennium discussed here. The only problem is that everyone's contribution to the group is sent to you via e-mail – it can be very time consuming trawling through the gibberish to find the good stuff. Be patient: it's there.

www.club2000.com

www.talk2000.org – This is a well-managed, useful and friendly millennium resource which makes it easy to air your views and to listen to the views of other – often specialist – contributors.

SOUTH PACIFIC (WEST)

The islands of the South Pacific have it all: wonderful beaches, friendly people, a great climate – and good rugby. Most people don't need an excuse to visit but in case you do here's one: despite the fact the New Year officially begins after midnight GMT, the position of the International Date Line means the dawn of the year 2000 will first be seen in the South Pacific. Since this book discusses destinations in the order in which the sun will come up on New Year's Day 2000, Western Samoa and the Cook Islands (which are to the east of the Date Line) start on p203.

Fiji

Fiji has won friends all over the world with its laid-back island life and welcoming population spread across three hundred won-

---

❏ **FIJI**
Contacts: South Pacific Millennium Consortium/Tourism Council of the South Pacific (☎ +679 304 177, fax: +679 301 995, e-mail: spice @is.com.fj), Level 3, FNPF Place, 343-359 Victoria Parade, PO Box 13119, Suva; Internet: http://www.infocentre.com.
Fiji Visitors Bureau (☎ +679 302 433, fax +679 300 970, e-mail: infodesk@fijifvb.gov.fj), Thomas St, PO Box 92, Suva; Internet: http://www.fijifvb.gov.fj.
Weather in Dec/Jan: Average maximum temperature 29°C
Capital: Suva on Viti Levu
Flight times: to Viti Levu from:
　　　　　LA: 11 hours (direct)
　　　　　London: 27 hours (via LA)
　　　　　Sydney: 4 hours (direct)
Approximate exchange rates: Fiji dollar (FJ$) FJ$2.53 = £1, FJ$1.54 = US$1, FJ$1.02 = A$1
Time difference: GMT plus 12 hours
Country dialling code: ☎ 679

derful islands. The same qualities are likely to make it a fantastic millennium destination. The South Pacific Consortium, formed to unite South Sea island celebration organisers, is based in Fiji – making it the millennium capital of the South Pacific.

There will be a strong **ecological flavour** to the Fijian celebrations. New 'green' ideas and products will be on show with several symposia dedicated to looking at the future of ecological management. FACE, the Foundation of Arts, Cultures and the Environment, is co-planning a pan-Fijian millennium party with the Fijian authorities. It will be themed 'A Celebration of Planet Earth, its Cultures and Environment', based on the Island of Viti Levu and will run from 28 December 1999 to 2 January 2000. During 1998 the **Fijian High Chiefs** are travelling around the world in a public relations exercise designed to get as many dignitaries and tribal leaders as possible to attend the Fijian festival of the new millennium.

VITI LEVU

At over 10,000 sq km Viti Levu is the largest island in Fiji. It's the seat of government and most of the country's industry is based there. A mountain range dissects the island. The drier western side has the city of **Nadi** (pronounced 'Nandi'), which is home to the international airport and a New Year's Eve concert in 1999. The wetter east boasts the capital, **Suva**, which will also host a concert on New Year's Eve 1999.

Nadi is a good place for accommodation. Its main industry is tourism making it a handy base. Suva is the most populous city in the South Pacific and as such can suffer from the sort of problems most big cities face. It is also one of the wetter spots in Fiji. That said, it sits in a delightful location and is well worth a visit.

❑ **Fiji – Where to Stay**
Accommodation is open to reservations through the Fiji Visitors Bureau (see **Contacts**, p25). Travellers can choose from hotels, resorts, campgrounds or bed and breakfast. Some dormitory facilities will be available and some villages will allow visitors to stay in traditional mbures (the local style of housing).

Divers and sun-seekers won't be disappointed. Fiji is one of best diving destinations in the world and has a consistent tropical climate with plenty of sun. The best beach is **Natadola,** between **Momi** and **Sigatoka**. Other activities include river trips, pleasure flights and cruises to outlying islands. One interesting attraction is the **Tavuni Hill Fort** where visitors can see cannibals' utensils such as a traditional head-chopping stone. Cannibalism was practised in Fiji until around one hundred years ago.

The FACE festival site will be established somewhere along the **Coral Coast** of Viti Levu which stretches along the south-western seaboard.

New Year's Eve Dusk 'til Dawn Concert: Viti Levu

The main festival and concert site will be on the Coral Coast of Viti Levu, with other concerts taking place in the cities of **Suva** and **Nadi**. A dusk 'til dawn concert will be the main event of the Fijian millennium festival. As other nations begin their New Year's Eve celebrations they will be linked to the Fijian festival site by satellite television.

A ceremony will precede the concert at approximately 6pm when drums will accompany the sun setting over the Pacific Ocean. A chain of bonfires will link the Date Line to the festival site. The concert proper will then kick off with ancient tribal music. Between 6.30-9pm world music and dance will be brought to the various stages which are to be built around the festival site. The period between 9-11.30pm will be given over to rock and pop artists. The world music feature of the festival is likely to be produced by WOMAD (the World of Music, Arts and Dance), formed by British recording star Peter Gabriel in 1982.

From 11.30-11.45pm millennium messages will be conveyed to the world. Children from different cultures will tell of their hopes for the future.

The countdown to midnight will start at 11.45pm. Choirs and percussion will help the tension to build as expectant onlookers watch the clock approach the year 2000. After the momentous moment, five hours of celebratory music and dancing will follow. Traditional music will be played, including Maori, Celtic and American-Indian styles. For those who last the whole night, a ceremony will mark the first light of dawn between 5.30-6am. Hundreds of canoes will be launched into the sea from Savialevu and Taveuni in a ritual which hasn't been seen in Fiji for a century. Television will connect the dawn ceremony with the festival site and the world.

A CD-ROM time capsule will be buried at the festival site where it is hoped it will remain for a further thousand years. On it will be messages from visitors, performers and participants.

World Village

A representative world community will be built close to the festival site. American-Indian teepees, Mongolian yurts, Bedouin tents and South Pacific mbures will be among the styles of accommodation on display from around the world.

The village will be designed for visitor participation with activities such as drumming and dancing.

Millennial symposia

FACE hopes to bring world leaders and experts to Fiji to present a series of symposia addressing the question of how living standards can be raised around the world.

❏ **Lighting the 180° Meridian**

It seems that every South Pacific Island which lies west of the International Date Line has made the claim that it will witness the first dawn of the new millennium. Fiji's claim is based on the fact that the 180° meridian passes through three Fijian Islands and that the International Date Line was drawn loosely around that meridian. It is a contentious argument; but Fiji has decided to make a feature of its much-loved meridian.

By New Year's Eve 1999 the length of the Date Line which cuts across the islands of Taveuni, Rabi and Vanua Levu will be illuminated by lights powerful enough to be seen from space. The time threshold will also be delineated by a wall. Each block in the wall will contain a sealed glass time capsule which will, in turn, contain a personal message to the future written by the capsule's owner. It will cost about US$500 to buy one. Future Fijian generations will be left strict instructions not to open the capsules until the year 3000.

❏ Problems in Paradise

Fourteen Pacific nations, including Western Samoa, Fiji, Tonga and Kiribati, have formed a South Pacific Consortium to capitalise on the enormous tourism potential of their 'first dawn' status. Since the International Date Line is mere convention and has no legal definition there is some confusion – and argument – about the exact point at which the new dawn will first appear.

After The Millennium Adventure Company (see p30) bought the rights to the highest point on Pitt Island in the Chathams, which was to have been the first place on land to see the sunrise on 1 January 2000, the Republic of Kiribati changed the Date Line. Now Caroline Island will be the first.

According to Dr Catchpole of the Royal Greenwich Observatory, Kiribati had every right to make the change. Philip Blain of the The Millennium Adventure Company disagrees, arguing that cartographers and navigators don't accept a sudden decision to reject the arbitrary line to which Kiribati had agreed since 1884. Blain is convincing; the Date Line has been accepted by so many for so long that the decision to fiddle with it should, perhaps, be ignored. He is putting his money where his mouth is by co-organising a millennium event on Pitt.

The Royal Geographical Society in London has published a scientific paper by Blain which makes a strong case for accepting that Pitt Island will see the first dawn of the next millennium. In any case, as Caroline is uninhabited, there can be no doubt that Pitt Island will be the first populated place to see the sunrise on 1 January 2000.

The King of Tonga is also annoyed. He had hoped to hold his own 'first dawn' party, but has now been forced to accept that Tonga is several minutes behind the front-runners. Fiji also plans to hold a 'first light' party despite rival claims, arguing that the true dateline is the 180 degree meridian which passes through three Fijian islands.

Dr Catchpole has further confused the situation by suggesting that, 'the very first year 2000 dawn will actually be at the Autumnal Equinox at the South Pole on 22 September 1999. The sun will rise for the first time and won't set until March the following year.'

The irony is that 1 January 2000 is not the genuine start of the new millennium; the first day of the third millennium and the 21st century is actually 1 January 2001 (see pp7-8).

New Year's Eve 1999 Parties and Tour:
Fiji and the Cook Islands (27 Dec 1999)

Millennium 2000 has devised what is likely to be a fantastic millennium holiday offer. Their idea is simple but highly appealing; why not skip over the International Date Line and celebrate the turn of the century twice? On 27 December 1999 the tour will leave from London and Los Angeles for Fiji. Accommodation will be at the Sheraton Royal Denarau or the Sheraton Fiji Resort. A New Year's Eve gala party will be laid on, with fireworks at midnight and a champagne breakfast on the beach the following morning. The party will be linked by television to 30 other party sites around the world which are part of a global celebration being planned by the Millennial Foundation in Scotland (see p137). Millennium 2000 is part of the Millennial Foundation. Having been among the world's first to see in the

---

❑ The Millennium Adventure Company

Norris McWhirter (of *Guinness Book of Records* fame) and Philip Blain formed the Millennium Adventure Company (MAC) to secure the rights to the highest points on Pitt Island in the Chathams. As we have already noted, McWhirter and Blain maintain that the first dawn of the new millennium will be seen from Pitt Island. The two could not have foreseen that rival claims would emerge from Kiribati, Tonga, Fiji and even Antarctica, but the MAC remains confident that Pitt Island will see the first sunrise of the year 2000.

Pitt is inhabited and it will be possible to visit the island to see in the new millennium. However, the high points – which are controlled by the MAC – will be reserved for a select few. TV companies are being invited to pay to film the first dawn of the third millennium. Apart from camera crews, the MAC hopes to fly 100 young people to Pitt to witness the great moment. As Blain explains: 'we will form a millennium foundation to find 100 youths from around the world who will be selected on merit in terms of their ideas for the future. They will go down in history as being among the first people in the world to see the new millennium'.

The Company will also produce a series of 'millennium packages' which will help people and families to record the moment when the millennium arrives. McWhirter plans to publish a *Millennium Book of Records*.

year 2000, the group will then be flown across the International Date Line to the Cook Islands where a second New Year's Eve Party has been planned and space reserved at the Rarotongan Resort. After lunch on New Year's Day (Cook Islands time) the group will be returned to Fiji where the holiday will continue until 6 January. Price: £5500. Add-on options to Australia, New Zealand and North America are available. Jetset Tours, First Dawn Celebrations and Travel Portfolio are also offering double millennium celebrations in the South Pacific (see pp33-4). **Contact:** Millennium 2000 (☎ +44 (0) 141-204 2000, fax +44 (0) 141-248 1591), 10 Sandyford Place, Glasgow G3 7NB, UK.

New Years Eve Parties and Tour: Fiji and the Cook Is, with Bangkok and Sydney (20 Dec 1999 – 4 Jan 2000)

A hectic end to the millennium is on offer from Travel Portfolio. This 15-day trip takes in Bangkok, with accommodation at the Shangri La Hotel, before moving on to the Renaissance Hotel in Sydney in time for Christmas. Next stop Fiji where a New Year's Eve party has been arranged. On 1 January 2000 the tour will skip back in time by crossing the Date Line to the Cook Islands for another New Year's rave-up. Travel Portfolio time travellers will stay at the Shangri La Fijian Resort on Fiji and the Raratongan Hotel in the Cook Is. The price is £3498 twin share. **Contact:** Travel Portfolio (☎ +44 (0) 1284 762255, fax 769011), 73 Churchgate St, Bury St Edmunds, Suffolk IP33 1RL, UK.

Millennium Cruises: Fiji and the South Seas
Fijian cruises: (23/25 Dec 1999 – 3/5 Jan 2000)

US tour operator Maupintour has announced two millennium cruises around Fiji, each lasting 11 days. The company plans to join the main celebrations on Fiji and to allow passengers time to explore some of the more remote parts of the islands including the Yasawa group. A longer **South Seas cruise (26 Dec 1999 – 10 Jan 2000)** will take in the islands of Fiji, New Caledonia and Vanuatu and will include a port of call at Cairns, Australia. Prices will be available in December 1998. A US$850 per person deposit is required to reserve a place on either of the above cruises. **Contact:** Maupintour (+1 800-255 4266).

Tonga

His Majesty King Taufa'ahau Tupou IV of Tonga is a millennium enthusiast. He was annoyed when astronomers pointed out that his bash might not be the first party of the year 2000. Undeterred, he has announced plans for a month-long festival from 1 December 1999 to 1 January 2000. The International Date Line Hotel in Tonga has been fully booked for a decade.

Most Tongan brochures claim the Kingdom to be 'the first land to see the dawn of each new day'. That might not be the case (see p29). But claims that it is the last remaining Polynesian monarchy, the only Pacific nation to avoid foreign rule and a genuine island paradise are certainly true.

Christianity is big, the climate is pleasant, time hardly matters and the people are friendly. The main island, Vava'u, offers good accommodation. Apart from taking it easy, the main pleasures are whale watching, diving and sailing. Tonga won't offer an action-packed start to the next millennium, but if you would prefer to relax then this is your place.

❑ **TONGA**

Contacts: Tonga Visitors' Bureau, PO Box 37, Nuku'alofa, Tonga (☎ +676 23-507/21-733, fax +676 22-129, telex 66269 PRIMO). **Internet:** http://www.infocentre.com/spt

Weather in Dec/Jan: Average maximum temperature 29°C

Capital: Nuku'alofa

Flight times: to Viti Levu from:
> New York: 17 hours, 30 minutes (via LA)
> LA: 11 hours, 30 minutes (direct)
> London: 27 hours (via LA)
> Sydney: 4 hours (direct)

Approximate exchange rates: Tongan Dollar or Pa'anga (T$) – take US dollars

Time difference: GMT plus 13 hours

Country dialling code: ☎ 676

Millennium Festival: Tonga (1 Dec 1999 – 1 Jan 2000)
Some unusual events have been planned in Tonga. The festival
starts with an **Inter-Cultural Fishing Week** and **Carving and
Dancing Expo**. Later highlights include the **Royal 2000 Golf
Classics** on 6th, the **New Millennium Music Festival** on 7th and
a **Brass Band Championship** on 8th December. Apart from the
Mr Tonga 2000 contest on 10th and the **Miss Tonga 2000** contest on 16 December, perhaps the most interesting display will be
the final of the **National Weight Loss Competition** which will
be held on 17 December. It's not clear whether contestants will
attempt to lose weight on the spot.

New Year's Eve Party: Tonga (31 Dec 1999)
New Year's Eve will see a large media-based festival featuring
cultural shows, a cruise ship gala and Royal Banquet. At midnight a millennium farewell ceremony will precede a mass millennial welcome – if not actually the first, then certainly one of
the first. There will also be a series of prayer ceremonies.

**New Year's Eve 1999 Parties and Tour:
Tonga and Western Samoa (26 Dec 1999 – 3 Jan 2000)**
London-based First Dawn Celebrations is offering a New Year's
Eve 1999 celebration – twice. There will be a party in Tonga
(where the Company has bought up a good deal of the island's
accommodation over the New Year period) and another in
Western Samoa after a 90-minute flight across the Date Line.
Both New Year's Eve events will feature gala dinners, sound and
light shows and fireworks.

The tour starts and finishes in London, but flights to and
from Tonga will go via either Los Angeles or Sydney, allowing
American and Australian tourists to join the trip. The cost is not
yet finalised, but Wayne Morris, Managing Director of First
Dawn, expects the final price to be an expensive US$8-9000.
Add-on tours to New Zealand, Australia or other Pacific Islands
can be arranged through First Dawn. Millennium 2000, Jetset
Tours and Travel Portfolio are also offering double millennium
celebrations in the South Pacific (see p30). **Contact:** Wayne
Morris (fax +44 (0) 0171 281 1786).

New Year's Eve 1999 Parties and Tour:
Tonga and Western Samoa (27 Dec 1999 – 9 Jan 2000)

Budget-conscious hedonists should contact Jetset Tours (☎ +44 0990 555 757). The long-haul specialists like the millennium so much, they've decided to celebrate it twice. This 12-day tour will take revellers to Tonga on 27 December 1999. On New Year's Eve a millennium gala dinner and party has been organised. On New Year's Day (Tongan time) the tour will move across the International Date Line to Western Samoa to party all over again. The group will have been among the first and last to see the sun rise on the year 2000. Millennium 2000, First Dawn Celebrations and Travel Portfolio are also offering double millennium celebrations in the South Pacific (see p30). Price: £2499.

❏ Kiribati and Caroline Island

The Republic of Kiribati (pronounced 'Kiribas') includes Caroline Island. Caroline is at the centre of a row over the point at which the first dawn of the year 2000 will be seen (see p29). Tourism in this attractive island nation is fairly low-key and Caroline Island is uninhabited. Akitara K of the Kiribati Visitors' Bureau says, 'There will be a celebration of the new millennium on 31 December 1999 on Caroline Island. Plans are under way to develop it in preparation for the witnessing of the historic sunrise in the year 2000'. Unfortunately, the speed at which things are done in Kiribati is, at best, leisurely. Neil and Melinda Croak are trying to organise a party on the island but have found the authorities to be particularly laid back. 'They don't do anything quickly', says Neil, 'which is why this will be such a great vacation'.

The Croaks recommend travelling from Hawaii to Kiritimati Island in Kiribati on Coral Pacific Airlines. Kiritimati is one of the closest islands to Caroline. Two hotels on Kiritimati are accepting reservations from millennial tourists. They are: the *Captain Cook Hotel*, Kiritimati Island, Republic of Kiribati (☎ +686-81230, fax +686-81425) and the *Mini Hotel Kiritimati*, Kiritimati Island, Republic of Kiribati (☎ +686-81225/201, fax +686-81336). Prices per night will be about US$60 for a double room, US$40 for a single plus US$40 for three meals daily. **Contact:** Kiribati Visitors' Bureau (☎ +686 28-287/28-288, fax +686 26-193), PO Box 261, Bikenibeu, Tarawa, Republic of Kiribati. For more information about the Croaks' party, fax Neil on (+1 770-234 9911).

AUSTRALASIA

New Zealand

There are events scheduled to take place all over New Zealand which is relatively advanced in its millennium preparations. A large number of those events have a sporting theme, and there is little doubt that NZ is the place to go if you hope to be in the throes of physical exertion when the new millennium arrives.

❏ **NEW ZEALAND**
Contacts: **Canterbury Tourism Council**, PO Box 2600, Christchurch (☎ 3-379 9629, fax 3-365 0787). **Destination Queens-town**, PO Box 353, Queenstown (☎ 3-442 7440, fax 3-442 7441). **Events Gisborne**, PO Box 2000, Gisborne (☎ 6-867 2049, fax 6-868 1368). **New Zealand Tourist Board**, PO Box 95, Wellington (☎ 4-472 8860, fax 4-478 1736). **Tourism Auckland**, PO Box 5561, Wellesley Street, Auckland (☎ 9-307 7999, fax 9-377 2154). **Tourism Rotorua**, Private Bag 3007, Rotorua (☎ 7-348 4133, fax 7-349 4133). **Tourism Wellington**, PO Box 10017, Wellington (☎ 4-499 9995, fax 4-499 9996).
Average maximum temperature °C

	Dec	Jan
Auckland	21	23
Christchurch	21	21
Wellington	19	21

Capital: Wellington
Flight times: to Auckland from:
    LA: 12 hours
    London: 28 hours
    Sydney: 3 hours
Approximate exchange rates: New Zealand Dollar (NZ$) – £1=2.8, US$1=1.7, A$=1.12
Time difference: GMT plus 12 hours
Country dialling code: ☎ 64

GISBORNE

Gisborne City, on the eastern edge of the North Island of New Zealand, will be the first city in the world to feel the warmth of the first dawn of the third millennium. Hastings has also laid claim to that title, but Gisborne has been planning how best to celebrate for longer and so will probably host the better parties.

Odyssey's End 2000: Gisborne (31 Dec 1999)

Club Odyssey's End, which describes itself as 'the world's most exciting millennium club', is to throw a 24-hour gala gathering in Gisborne. Thousands of revellers will enjoy a heady mix of 'Olympic style' ceremony and celebration. After a ceremony to mark the last sunset of the 20th century, a party featuring international entertainers and a laser and fireworks display will rage throughout the night. Participants will pause to observe a midnight ceremony and a first light ceremony before indulging in a millennium breakfast. A final ceremony will be preceded by club-members sealing a time capsule for future generations.

The party will take place on a waterfront festival site. Attendance is limited to 60,000 people. **Contact:** Bill Griffith (fax +64 9-358 3386 or Internet www.futurepacific.co.nz/odyssey.html).

❏ **Gisborne – What to See**

Gisborne overlooks the ill-named **Poverty Bay** on the east coast of New Zealand. Captain Cook gave the inlet its disparaging name when, in 1769, he claimed the country for King George III but was promptly forced to leave by local Maoris. Three rivers trisect Gisborne which is ringed with fertile agricultural land.

Kaiti Beach is the spot where Cook made his attempt to take New Zealand for his King. An obelisk marks the event. Other Cook memorabilia can be found on **Kaiti Hill**, where his statue looks across a great view of the city and bay, and the **Gisborne Museum** where Cook is given his own display.

The city's main beach is **Waikanae**. To the north are some good surfing beaches. **Te Urewera National Park** lies to the west of Gisborne. It is easily worth the journey – with wonderful views, some important areas of native forest and much wildlife.

New Year's Eve Party: Gisborne (31 Dec 1999)

A New Year's Eve party will be held under the Town and Millennium Clocks in Gisborne, with live entertainment provided while party-goers wait for that all-important first dawn.

More celebrations will take place on New Year's Day. Gisborne hopes to provide an event primarily for families to enjoy.

A First Light Music Festival, featuring local Maori music and contemporary bands, will be held at Muriwai throughout the night of 31 December 1999.

Servant 2000: Gisborne (27 Dec 1999 – 5 Jan 2000)

Gisborne's authorities haven't lost sight of the fact that the year 2000 is primarily a date of religious significance. 'Servant 2000' is a chance for Christians to welcome the year 2000 through a series of events including a Millennium Service and an evening concert.

Millennium Tour: Gisborne (27 Dec 1999 – 5 Jan 2000)

British long-haul specialist Jetset (☎ +44 0990-555 757) is offering a trip to Gisborne in time to join the celebrations on New Year's Eve 1999.

This all-inclusive holiday, which includes three nights in Auckland, will cost £2490 per person. A five-day extension with hire car and accommodation vouchers is available for an extra £484 per person.

OTHER AREAS IN NEW ZEALAND
Pacific Tall Ships Festival (26 Nov 1999 – 18 Jan 2000)

New Zealand plans to welcome tall ships from all over the world with crews and passengers sailing into the new millennium as part of an impressive regatta.

The voyage will start in Sydney in November 1999. From there the ships will sail to the New Zealand capital, Wellington. Christmas will be spent at Napier before the armada sets sail for Gisborne in time to see in the year 2000. The tall ships won't be alone in Gisborne's harbour where several cruise ships have already booked berths.

An onshore New Year's Eve party for the sailors will be followed by a cannon-fire salute to welcome the dawn. After various New Year's Day celebrations, the tall ships will head for Tauranga and then Auckland which they should reach by 12 January. Five days of events are lined up in Auckland for passengers and crew before the ships leave for their final destination, the Bay of Islands, on 18 January. **Contact:** Caroline Taylor (fax 6-868 1368, e-mail caroline@gdc.govt.nz).

First Dawn Party: Hastings (31 Dec 1999)

According to some calculations, Te Mata Peak to the south of Hastings will see the dawn sooner than Gisborne. There will be a party at the peak on New Year's Eve, and a first dawn celebration held the following morning.

America's Cup: Auckland (Nov 1999 – March 2000)

Having won the last America's Cup in 1995, New Zealand will host this 4-yearly event in 1999. The America's Cup is the most prized trophy on offer to the sailing world. In 1999/2000 a particularly fierce competition will be fought, as the event will be seen to straddle two millennia and it will be the thirtieth time the race has taken place.

Auckland's Viaduct Basin in the downtown area will form the hub of the activity and spectators will be able to follow the yachts on charter boats.

The competition will be fought in the Hauraki Gulf between the East Coast Bays and Rangitoto Island. The Challenger series of races starts in October 1999. **Contact:** Tony Thomas, race organiser (fax 9-300 3238).

Millennium 2000 Golf Tournament: Formosa

Although dates are still unavailable, plans are underway for an international golf tournament at the Formosa Golf Course, Auckland. The course is new, and was co-designed by top New Zealand golfer Bob Charles. Formosa hopes to welcome around forty star players to its immaculate greens. **Contact:** John Sutherland (☎ 4-293 1518).

The Millennium Marathon: Hamilton (1 Jan 2000)

What better way to start the new millennium than running? Some might say drinking or sleeping – but if you are a keen marathon-runner this event is likely to catch your imagination.

Andy Galloway is organising what he hopes will be the first marathon of the year 2000. The 42-kilometre run will circle the

---

❑ Millennium Time Vault Project

An ambitious group of New Zealanders, including sculptor Denis Hall, has been working on the TimeVault 2000 project for three years. Their idea is a good one: to build a lasting time capsule into which anyone can deposit items they would like their descendants to find hundreds of years from now.

The TimeVault project is still being developed and will not definitely go ahead. Hall has calculated that 1% of the population of New Zealand will need to contribute to the Vault if it is to pay for itself. Three types of deposit are planned: capsules which will be opened after 50, 100 and 1000 years. Prices are expected to be around NZ$180 for the short-term capsules and NZ$2000 for 1000-year deposits in the separate Millennium Vault.

Engineers have devised a pyramid-shaped structure which will use bank vault technology to make it impenetrable. It is, apparently, relatively easy to construct a building capable of lasting a thousand years. Security is more complex. As Hall says: 'I imagine that by the 25th century, the museum's curators will convince the authorities that the need to have the contents protected by 25th century technology will be greater than the need to honour the intention of the people of the year 2000. Another scenario could see a technologically destitute people regarding the TimeVault Pyramids with wonder and wishing they could find a way in.'

There is, as yet, no agreed choice of site for the pyramid. Hall would like to see the Vault built on Belmont Hill which overlooks the city of Wellington. However, earthquakes pose a serious threat to the survival of the Vault. Geologists have predicted that New Zealand will be hit by three cataclysmic earthquakes over the next 1000 years. Belmont Hill is one of the most stable points in New Zealand.

Hall and his team are confident their TimeVault will work, and even hope to export the idea to other countries. Interested parties have come forward from the States, Canada, Australia and Italy.

city of Hamilton which is south of Auckland on North Island.

Participants will enjoy mainly level terrain and fantastic views. The start-time is 6am, and the finish line is at the Te Rapa Racecourse. Alongside the more serious main event will be a 10-kilometre Millennium Fun-Run (sounds serious enough) and a five-kilometre Millennium Walk.

Before the race a New Year's Eve party is planned. A post-race awards luncheon is also scheduled. Race registration has already started. **Contact:** Andy Galloway (fax 7-849 1789).

2000 First To The Sun (30 Dec 1999 – Jan 2000)

Some 2000 cyclists are invited to join a 1000-kilometre millennium bicycle ride around North Island. From Auckland the route will wind along the beautiful Pacific Coast Highway before arriving at Gisborne; then it's on to the Raukumara Range.

Daily distances will be somewhere between 45 and 80 miles but most of the journey will be on well-surfaced roads. That said, the organisers do describe the ride as fit for 'moderately experienced cyclists and above'. Arrangements will be made for participants who wish to take non-riding partners with them.

Contact: 2000 First To The Sun, PO Box 266, 334 State Street, Suite 106-266, Los Altos, California 94022, USA or, in the UK, Chris Bradley (☎ +44 (0) 1903-242 518).

New Year's Eve 1999 Party and Six-Day Tour: Auckland

Scotland's Millennial Foundation, which is to use television to link party sites around the world, will broadcast the major celebrations planned at Auckland Harbour as part of this global event. It is also offering a six-day tour to Auckland which will coincide with New Year's Eve 1999. Accommodation has been booked at the Carlton Hotel and a day trip to Gisborne will be included. Price: £2500. **Contact:** The Millennial Foundation (☎ +44 (0) 141-204 2000, fax +44 (0) 141-248 1591, Internet: http://www.yes2000.co.uk), 10 Sandyford Place, Glasgow G3 7NB, UK.

Mardi Gras: Rotorua (31 Dec 1999)

In Australasia Mardi Gras means a carnival at any time – not just on Shrove Tuesday. That's why Rotorua is holding its own Mardi Gras on New Year's Eve 1999. **Contact:** Tourism Rotorua (see p35).

Millennium World Tour
Ex-New Zealand (Jan 2000-Dec 2001)

British-based adventure travel specialist Encounter (☎ +44 (0) 171-370 6845) is offering two year-long around-the-world trips to welcome the new millennium. Starting from New Zealand, the marathon journeys will make use of just about every form of transport. Both will be broken up into three or four sections so that people without a year to spare can join at various places.

The two trips will set off from New Zealand in opposite directions and will cross over on the other side of the world. The cost, itinerary and firm dates are still on the drawing board, but the land-only price will be about £180 per person per week.

❏ **Turning Point 2000: Canterbury**

Based in Christchurch, Turning Point 2000 is an umbrella organisation for millennium planning in the Canterbury area of the South Island of New Zealand. Several lasting projects are being developed to complement a number of events which are scheduled to take place throughout the year 2000.

Planned projects include: history and heritage trails, tree planting, environmental regeneration, a commemorative bridge over the Avon, a year 2000 song and the linking of schools via the Internet.

Year 2000 events include: a series of Summer Theatre special performances organised by Christchurch City Council (including *Opera by Candlelight*, *Summer Rock* and a *Teddy Bear's Picnic*), a science and technology exhibition at the Westpac Trust Centre, a live portrayal of the impact of the year 2000 on Pacific cultures, a seven-day mini-Olympics for schoolchildren, the inaugural International Dance and Music Festival in October, *Solutions* – an international children's summit at the Christchurch Convention Centre and a ceremony to welcome the third millennium on 31 December 2000. **Contact:** Turning Point 2000 (☎ 3-379 2008, fax 3-379 7131, Internet http://www.tp20 00.org.nz), PO Box 237, 1st Floor, Old Railway Station, 392 Moorhouse Avenue, Christchurch.

New Year's Eve Parties: Christchurch and Queenstown
After a New Year's Eve party at North Hagley Park in **Christ-church**, revellers will re-group at Godley Heads for a dawn ceremony. An open-air free party has also been confirmed at **Queenstown**. There will be a picnic and fiesta on **Brighton Beach** to witness the sun rise on the year 2000.

Australia

Australians are thought by many to be a party-going people. But when it comes to the millennium, Australia appears to be taking a fairly restrained approach. One reason is the fact that Sydney has won the competition to host the 2000 Olympic Games. As a result, much of Australia's millennium fever seems to be focused on that prestigious event to the detriment of other celebrations. Another reason is Prime Minister John Howard's announcement that Australia should celebrate on 31 December 2000 – the correct eve of the new millennium and the centenary of Federation in Australia.

SYDNEY
Sydney has been in party mood since Captain Cook sailed into Botany Bay in 1770 and celebrated his discovery of one of the finest natural harbours in the world. Few visitors could argue that Sydney is one of the world's most energetic and engaging cities. It will be just that on 31 December 1999.

New Year's Eve Party: Sydney (31 Dec 1999)
Spectak, the company which has been chosen to produce the Sydney 2000 Olympic ceremonies, is to stage a giant party around Sydney Harbour on New Year's Eve 1999. There are plans to launch fireworks from 18 barges on the water and from six firing positions to the east and west of the harbour. Twenty buildings will be illuminated to enhance the effect. Spectak will produce a similar event – but on a smaller scale – on New Year's

Eve 1998. Ric Birch, President of Spectak, says 'we expect as many as two million people on 31 December 1999 – if isn't the biggest fireworks display in the world it'll certainly be the best'.

New Year's Eve Party: Sydney Opera House
Sydney is to join a string of 30 venues for a linked global party organised by the Millennial Foundation (see p137). A New

---

❏ **AUSTRALIA**

Contacts: Canberra Tourism (☎ 6-205 0666, fax 6-205 0629) Level 8 CBS Tower, Cnr Akuna & Bunda Streets, Canberra City ACT 2600. **Queensland Tourist and Travel Corporation** (☎ 7-3406 5400, fax 7-3406 5436), Riverside Centre, 123 Eagle Street, Brisbane QLD 4000. **Northern Territory Tourist Commission** (☎ 8-9999 3900, fax 8-9999 3888), 3rd Floor, Tourism House, 43 Mitchell St, Darwin NT 0800. **South Australian Tourism Commission** (☎ 8-8303 2222, fax 8-8303 2269), Floors 7/8, Terrace Towers, 178 North Terrace, Adelaide SA 5000. **Tourism New South Wales** (☎ 2-9931 1111, fax-2 9931 1424), Levels 5 & 6, 140 George Street, The Rocks NSW 2000. **Tourism Tasmania**, Trafalgar Building (☎ 02-6233 8011, fax 02-6230 8353), 110 Collins Street, Hobart TAS 7000. **Tourism Victoria** (☎ 02-6233 8011, fax 02-6230 8353), 55 Swanston Street, Melbourne VIC 3001(☎ 02-6233 8011, fax 02-6230 8353). **Western Australia Tourism Commission** (☎ 9-220 1700, fax 9-220 1702) , Floors 5/6, St George's Ct, 16 St George's Terrace, Perth WA 6000 **Internet:** http://www.d fat.gov.au.home.html.

Average maximum temperature °C

	Dec	Jan
Cairns	32	32
Sydney	25	26

Capital: Canberra

Flight times: to Sydney from:
- LA: 12 hours
- London: 22 hours
- Auckland: 3 hours

Approximate exchange rates: Australian dollar (A$) – £1=2.4, US$1=1.51

Time difference: (Sydney/Melbourne) GMT +10

Country dialling code: ☎ 61

❏ SYDNEY – A BRIEF GUIDE

Perhaps the second most enduring icon in Sydney (the first being the **Opera House**) is the **Sydney Harbour Bridge**. Built in 1932, the bridge – known locally as the 'coathanger' – is one of the longest single-span bridges in the world at 550 metres. It connects the well-to-do northern suburbs with the city centre which wraps itself around the southern side of the harbour.

Since its completion in 1973, the **Sydney Opera House** has come to be seen as one of the most remarkable buildings of this century. Whether you love it or hate it (it's impossible to be indifferent) the Opera House is definitely worth visiting. For a great view of it, stop at the Park Hyatt Hotel.

The **Rocks** is the oldest part of Sydney. From here, you can enjoy stunning views across the city while relaxing in a lively café atmosphere. This is also an area of historical importance although, sadly, large chunks of the Rocks disappeared under the foundations of the Sydney Harbour Bridge. In more recent years, Sydney has proved itself to be a city capable of impressive regeneration. **Paddington** and **Darling Harbour** – both run-down right up until the 1970s – are now stylish centres of entertainment, shopping and desirable homes. Incredibly, Sydney's city limits contain seven national parks and several wildlife sanctuaries. **Garigal National Park** offers hiking and boat rentals, while **Waratah Park** nature reserve is home to such quintessential Australian creatures as kangaroos, wallabies and wombats.

On a sunny day – and there are many – Sydney comes into its own with 32 sandy beaches beckoning sun-seekers. The most famous is **Bondi**, south of the Harbour, which is surrounded by rather ugly development but is a haven for surfers and travellers. Within the harbour itself are some lovely beaches such as **Watsons Bay** (home of Doyle's, the famous seafood restaurant) and **Neilson Park**. North of the Harbour are more sandy stretches including **Manly** which can be reached by ferry from Circular Quay. **Narrabeen** and **Newport** are near legendary surfspots and **Curl Curl** – also beyond Manly – is a pleasant place for families to visit.

Where to Stay

There are 30,000 hotel rooms in Sydney and a further 5700 are on the way before 2000. The organisers of the Olympics are negotiating to regulate hotel prices during the year 2000.

● **Expensive** (over A$250) *Regent of Sydney* (☎ 02-9238 0000),

199 George Street, which includes Kables – one of the best restaurants in the city – has some fast-disappearing Opera House-view rooms left; the *Hotel Inter-Continental* (☎ 02-9230 0200), 117 Macquarie Street, which is partly formed by the 1849 Treasury Building, has some harbour-view rooms available for a A$2000 2-night package which includes the hotel's own 'party of the century'. Rooms with city-side views are available without the party. The *ANA Hotel* (☎ 02-9250 6000), 176 Cumberland Street, has a long waiting list but might be worth trying; *Quay West* (☎ 02-9240 6000, fax 02-9240 6060), 98 Gloucester Street; *Observatory Hotel* (☎ 02-9256 2222, fax 02-9256 2233), 89 Kent Street; *Park Hyatt Sydney* (☎ 02-9241 1234), 7 Hickson Road; *Ritz Carlton* (☎ 02-9362 4455, fax 02-9362 4744), 93 Macquarie Street; *Sheraton on the Park* (☎ 02-9286 6000, fax 02-9286 6686), 161 Elizabeth Street; *Sydney Marriott* (☎ 02-9362 8400), 36 College Street.

● **Moderate** (between A$100-250) *Castlereagh Inn* (☎ 02-9264 2281), 169 Castlereagh Street; *Sydney Travellers Rest Hotel* (☎ 02-9281 5555), 37 Ultimo Road; *Park Regis Hotel* (☎ 02-9267 6511), 27 Park Street; *Oxford Koala Hotel* (☎ 02-9269 0645), Cnr of Oxford and Pelican Streets; *Harbour Rocks* (☎ 02-9251 8944), 34 Harrington Street; *Hyde Park Inn* (☎ 02-9264 6001), 271 Elizabeth Street; *Kingsview Motel* (☎ 02-9358 5599); and the *Manly Paradise Beach Plaza Apartments* (☎ 02-9977 5799), 49 North Steyne; *Royal Garden International* (☎ 02-9281 6999), 431 Pitt Street.

● **Budget** (under A$100) *Barclay* (☎ 02-9358 6133), 17 Bayswater Road; *Beverley Hills Benelong* (☎ 02-9570 1455), 427 King Georges Road; *Orwell Lodge* (☎ 02-9358 1745), 18 Orwell Street; *YWCA* (☎ 02-9264 2451), 5 Wentworth Avenue; *Pension Albergo* (☎ 02-9560 0179), 5 Day Street; *Pittwater YHA Hostel* (☎ 02-9999 2196) in the Ku-ring-gai Chase National Park which can only be reached by boat; *Westend* (☎ 02-9211 4822), 412 Pitt Street; *Wynyard Hotel* (☎ 02-9299 1330), Cnr Clarence and Erskine Streets.

Party Places

There are plenty of places to party in Sydney. One of the best ways to find out what's happening is to buy Friday's *Sydney Morning Herald* with its *Metro* listings section. The better nightclubs include: *Sugareef* on Bayswater Road, a club which prides itself on its exclusivity and does attract some famous faces to its VIP room.

Party Places (cont)
There's also *Sublime* at 252 Pitt Street; *Juliana's* at the Sydney Hilton for a more up-market crowd; *Club Apia* at 92-94 Parrametta Road; *Metropolis* at 99 Walker Street with cheap drinks and no cover; *Icebox* at 2 Kellett Street; and *Palladium* on Roslyn Street. *JD's Ministry of Dance* at 54 Darlinghurst Road is popular with backpackers.

Kings Cross is Sydney's lively but seedy red-light district. But it's not just the dirty-mac brigade who find fun in the area. There's a high concentration of restaurants, great bars and live music venues.

Festivals in Sydney in December and January
Sydney celebrates itself in January with the **Festival of Sydney**. Hyde Park will host outdoor movie shows and contemporary music concerts. In the Domain area, open-air concerts will entertain crowds under the stars while the Opera House will, of course, present performances by international stars.

One of Sydney's last great events of the year 2000 will be the annual **Sydney Harbour Yacht Race** held on Boxing Day. This is one of the most enjoyable occasions in Sydney-siders' diaries with dozens of yachts racing across the Harbour.

Smaller vessels line up alongside competitors to form an extraordinary armada and a wonderful sight. If you can find your way on to one these boats then do so: you can't beat a front-row seat.

Year's Eve Mask Party will be held in the Sydney Opera House and will be hosted by the Mayor of Sydney.

Dinner and dancing will be followed by fireworks over the Harbour which will be watched from the grounds of the Opera House – probably the best seat in Sydney. It has become a tradition for Sydney-siders to don masks on New Year's Eve to symbolise the many faces of the famously diverse nature of their city.

New Year's Eve 1999 Party and Six-Day Tour: Sydney
The Millennial Foundation (see p137), which is to link the Mayor's party at the Sydney Opera House to 30 other parties worldwide, is offering a six-day millennium tour to Sydney

which will include access to the gala celebration. For £2500, the trip includes accommodation at the ANA Hotel in the Rocks district. **Contact:** The Millennial Foundation (☎ +44 (0) 141-204 2000, fax +44 (0) 141-248 1591, Internet: http://www.yes20 00.co.uk), 10 Sandy-ford Place, Glasgow, G3 7NB, UK.

2000 Olympic Games: Sydney (16 Sep – 1 Oct 2000)

While the world dreams up ways to celebrate the new millennium, Sydney has the ideal answer: the Olympic Games. The 2000 games are particularly important, marking the end of a century which has seen sport rise to the very forefront of popular imagination.

The games will be based at the **Olympic Park** at Homebush Park, a once disused industrial area. Homebush Park is 14 kilometres from the centre of Sydney. By 16 September 2000, there will be venues for 15 sports and a 110,000-seat Olympic stadium on the site. This will be the largest Olympic stadium in the world. Next to the site will be a Sydney Showground which will showcase sports and provide an indoor training arena.

Most Olympic organisers adopt a theme around which to stage the games. Australia has christened the 2000 Olympics *The Athletes' Games.* With this in mind, Sydney has promised to give to the athletes the 'most technically excellent and athlete-orientated' games possible.

To make those words reality, Sydney's bid budgeted for A$1.8 billion to run the scheme. On top of that the Federal Government and host State, New South Wales, have promised a further A$3 billion for structural improvements to Sydney's international airport and road and rail networks.

After the Olympics come the Paralympic Games from October 14-24. Five thousand athletes will compete in the games which will include archery, powerlifting, shooting, basketball and tennis. **Internet Info:** http://www.sydney.olympic.org

Millennium Tour: Sydney (23/26 Dec 1999 – 3/7 Jan 2000)

This is good value: Travel Portfolio is offering five nights at the Renaissance Hotel in Sydney, a gala New Year's Eve 1999 party and return flights from London with Qantas or British Airways for £1999. A Cairns extension is available for an added £396. That includes transfers to Cairns, accommodation at the Colonial Club Resort and a day at the Great Barrier Reef. It's also possible to leave London on 23 December to spend Christmas at the Shangri La Hotel in Bangkok before flying to Sydney for New Year's Eve. The Bangkok and London tour costs £2355. The full trip, to Bangkok, Sydney and Cairns from 23 December 1999 to 7 Jan 2000, will cost £2598. All prices are twin share.

Contact: Travel Portfolio (☎ +44 (0) 1284 762 255, fax +44 (0) 1284 769 011), 73 Churchgate Street, Bury St Edmunds, Suffolk IP33 1RL, UK.

Millennium Tour: Sydney (29 Dec 1999 – 2 Jan)
US tour operator Maupintour is offering a four-day trip to Sydney to see in the year 2000. A US$850 per person deposit is required to secure a place. Maupintour have yet to announce the price. This is one way to book a room at a high-end hotel in a city which is attracting a lot of competition for its New Year's Eve 1999 bed-space. **Contact:** (☎ +1 800-255 4266).

Millennium Tour: Sydney (28 Dec 1999 – 6 Jan 2000)
(With optional Northern Queensland extension, 8-16 Jan 2000). This Jetset (☎ +44 0990-555 757) trip to Sydney appears to be well priced. For £1952 per person, you'll get flights from Britain, transfers, accommodation and a New Year's Eve party. A harbour cruise and trips to the Blue Mountains and Jenolan Caves are also included. A Northern Queensland extension is available for an extra £369 per person.

MELBOURNE
Victoria State Premier Jeff Kennett plans to make Melbourne the 'City of the Third Millennium'. A series of events is being organised, starting with a giant party on 31 December 1999, and closing with a better-than-ever Melbourne Festival in October 2001.

Melbourne was developed on the proceeds of a frantic 19th century goldrush. Its growth has been rapid and the city is now the second largest in Australia. It's still improving, however, with an immense city-centre redevelopment scheme planned to be complete by October 2000. British architects Lab Architecture Studio have won the contract to re-build some 45,000 square metres in the heart of Melbourne. This ambitious project will include decking-over a railway, creating exhibition and shop space and linking the central business district with the Melbourne Opera House. A new gallery of Australian art will also be built.

The scheme has been designed to mark both the Federation of the States of Australia and the new millennium.

Melbourne Millennium Festival: Melbourne (Oct 2001)

The Melbourne Festival is widely considered to be the best arts festival in the Australian calendar. Organisers plan to create a better than ever event in the year 2001 to confirm Melbourne as

---

❏ **Melbourne – Where to Stay**

● **Expensive** (over A$250): the *Grand Hyatt* (☎ 03-9653 4444), 123 Collins Street, which is to hold two parties, has vacancies available; the *Hotel Sofitel* (☎ 03-9653 0000), 25 Collins Street, is taking inquiries; *Le Meridien Melbourne* (☎ 03-9620 9111), 495 Collins Street; *Melbourne Hilton on the Park* (☎ 03-9419 3311), 129 Wellington Parade; *Rockmans Regency Hotel* (☎ 03-9662 3900), Cnr of Exhibition and Lonsdale Streets; *Sebel of Melbourne* (☎ 03-9629 4088), 321 Flinders Lane; *Sheraton Towers Southgate* (☎ 03-9696 3100), 1 Brown Street; *Windsor Hotel* (☎ 03-9653 0653), Cnr of Spring Street and Little Collins Street.

● **Moderate** (A$100-250): *Adelphi* (☎ 03-9650 7555), 187 Flinders Lane; *Bayview on the Park* (☎ 03-9243 9999), 52 Queens Road; *Eden on the Park* (☎ 03-9820 2222), 6 Queens Road; *Holiday Inn Park Suites* (☎ 03-9663 3333), 333 Exhibition Street; *Novatel Melbourne* (☎ 03-9650 5800), 270 Collins Street; *Rydges on Flinders* (☎ 03-9629 4111), Cnr of Spencer Street and Flinders Lane; *Savoy Park Plaza* (☎ 03-9622 8888), 630 Little Collins Street.

● **Budget** (under A$100): *Batmans Hill Hotel* (☎ 03-9614 6344), 66 Spencer Street; *City Centre Hotel* (☎ 03-9654 5401), 22 Little Collins Street; *Exford Hotel* (☎ 03-9663 2697), 199 Russell Street; *Hotel Ibis* (☎ 03-9639 2399), 15 Therry Street; *Hotel Y* (☎ 03-9329 5788), 489 Elizabeth Street; *Toad Hall* (☎ 03-9600 9010), 441 Elizabeth Street; *Victoria Hotel* (☎ 03-9653 0411), 215 Little Collins Street.

'the City of the Third Millennium' and to bring the its millennium events to an extravagant climax. There will be more venues, events and performance companies than ever before. A group of other Melbourne festivals, including the International Film Festival, Next Wave and Fringe festivals, are to merge with the Melbourne Festival to form this 'super-event'.

Contact: (☎ 03-9662 4242, fax 03-9663 4141, e-mail melfest@ibm.net).

New Year's Eve Celebration: Melbourne (31 Dec 1999)

The Melbourne Millennium Committee has promised a spectacular (and free!) family-orientated party on New Year's Eve 1999. Fireworks, street parties and outdoor performers will be positioned around three party centres: the Old Exhibition Building, the Museum of Victoria and Carlton Gardens.

New Year's Eve Parties 1999 and 2000: Melbourne

The *Grand Hyatt Hotel* is to hold two New Year's Eve parties: one on 31 December 1999 to celebrate the last year of the second millennium and one on 31 December 2000 to usher in the third. The Grand Hyatt is one of very few party venues to recognise the fact that the new millennium starts in 2001. **Contact:** Grand Hyatt (☎ 03-9653 4444).

Expo 21C: Melbourne (January 2001)

To celebrate both the new millennium and the centenary of Federation, Melbourne will host Expo 21C. The display will examine the future and the four themes which the Expo organisers consider to be of most relevance to Australia at the start of the third millennium: technology, the environment, communications and identity.

❏ **Australia Day (26 Jan 2000)**
Millennium party-goers might want to stay on for the **Australia Day** celebrations on January 26. It's a national public holiday which sees concerts, parties and entertainment put on all over the continent.

OTHER AREAS IN AUSTRALIA

Millennium Tour: Australia (13 Dec 1999 – 3 Jan 2000)

This three-week trip includes a New Year's Eve 1999 party by the roof-top pool at the 4-star Old Sydney Park Royal Hotel. Revellers will get a great view of the New Year's Eve fireworks over Sydney Harbour. Price: approximately £4895 (a £200 refundable deposit will secure a place until the full itinerary and price are announced during early summer 1998).

Contact: Allways PacificTravel (☎ +44 (0) 1494-875757, fax +44 (0) 1494 874747, e-mail sales@all-ways.co.uk), 4 The Green, Chalfont St Giles, Buckinghamshire HP8 4QF, UK.

Millennium Party and Diving Tours: Sydney and the Great Barrier Reef (28 Dec 1999 – 9/11 Jan 2000)

American tour operator Ozdive (☎ +1-972-818 1575, fax +1-972-818 1576) is offering two millennium scuba-diving trips and a land-based holiday – all of which start from Sydney. Divers will spend New Year's Eve in Sydney at the Astor Goldsbrough Apartment Hotel before setting off for the Palm Royal Hotel in Cairns. The tours start from US$1850 and go up in price to US$3600. Flights are not included in those prices.

Millennium Tour and Party at Ayers Rock: (20 Dec 1999 – 10 Jan 2000)

The highlight of this three-week tour to Australia will be an outdoor Sounds of Silence millennium celebration and dinner at the beautiful Ayers Rock in the centre of Australia. Price: approximately £4895 (a £200 refundable deposit will secure a place until the full itinerary and price are announced during early summer 1998). **Contact:** Allways PacificTravel (☎ +44 (0) 1494-875757, fax +44 (0) 1494 874747, e-mail sales@all-ways.co.uk), 4 The Green, Chalfont St Giles, Buckinghamshire HP8 4QF, UK.

South Pacific Millennium Tours: Sydney/Hayman Island

(From 23 Dec 1999-2 or 8 Jan 2000 with NYE in Sydney, or 20 Dec 1999-6 Jan 2000 with NYE on Hayman Island, Great Barrier Reef). Travcoa, an American travel company, is offering two South Pacific millennium tours. The first is an 11- or 17-day millennium tour to Papeete, Bora Bora (both in French Polynesia), Sydney (for New Year's Eve), Melbourne and Hayman Island. The land-only price is likely to be around US$5995 or US$8195 (depending on the length of stay). The second tour is an 18-day trip to Auckland, Mount Cook, Christchurch, Melbourne, Hayman Island (for New Year's Eve) and Sydney. The land-only price will be at least US$8195. **Contact:** Travcoa (☎ +1 714-476 2800 or 800-992 2003 for a toll-free call from within the US).

New Millennium Celebration: Mount Warning (31 Dec 1999)

Mount Warning (the Aboriginal name for which means 'first light') on **Byron Bay** is the easternmost tip of Australia. As such it will be the first place on the continent to see the year 2000, and it is the venue for a new millennium celebration. Sydney claims its fireworks will be visible from Mount Warning – giving visitors the best of both celebrations.

New Year's Eve on the Wharf: Stokes Hill Wharf, Darwin (31 Dec 1999 and 31 Dec 2000)

Amid confusion over the right time to welcome the new millennium, Darwin is hedging its bets. Two parties have been planned – one each on New Year's Eve 1999 and 2000. The parties, which are to be family events in Darwin's Wharf Precinct, will include dancing and fireworks. **Contact:** Jan Young (☎ 0889-99 3849).

❑ **The Centenary of Federation**

Australia will be 100 years old on 1 January 2001. The Centenary of Federation will be celebrated across the country throughout 2001 as the national spotlight moves from one area to the next. Several major events have already been agreed: a ceremony in Centennial Park, Sydney, and a street parade with floats from every State and Territory, a five-day celebration in Melbourne with a re-enactment of the first sitting of the Commonwealth Parliament, a National Museum of Australia to open in Canberra, centenary celebrations for the Australian Army and Australia's hosting of the 2001 Commonwealth Heads of Government Meeting.

Contact: Secretariat for the Centenary of Federation Council (☎ 02-6270 8173, fax 02-6270 8188).

ASIA

So far, few celebrations have been planned in Asia, but there are several attractive millennium tours on offer. For ideas for independent travellers see p55.

The Middle East

ISRAEL
Megiddo
According to the Book of Revelation, Armageddon will be the final battleground in the fight between good and evil. Armageddon is now known as Megiddo, which is in Israel. Thousands plan to visit Megiddo on New Year's Eve 1999 in the hope of witnessing this ultimate and apocalyptic bout for themselves.

Megiddo has attracted so much attention that entrepreneurs now plan to transform it from the dusty locale of a maximum security prison to a sort of biblical theme park. The promoters are said to be expecting some four million visitors over the course of 2000.

Nazareth
In Nazareth, plans are underway to re-develop infrastructure and prepare millennium celebrations. Half of all visitors to Israel see Nazareth, but the City has had limited funds for maintaining its many places of religious significance. These include *Mensa Christi* and the cave which was Joseph's workshop. Israel's Government is supporting the scheme to improve Nazareth. With its beautiful Old City, Suq and Basillica of the Annunciation, Nazareth is set to attract an enormous number of tourists on the eve of the new millennium.

Bethlehem

Other events are scheduled in Bethlehem on the West Bank. The Palestinian Authority, UNESCO and the Municipality of Bethlehem are developing plans to restore the town and to celebrate the 2,000th anniversary of the Nativity under the title 'Bethlehem 2000'. UNESCO is behind an international campaign to raise funds for the project. An Emergency Master Plan has been devised for the re-development of the Old Town. Major international celebrations will take place on 24 and 31 December 1999. Events are also planned throughout the year 2000. Well-wishers see the millennium as a chance for a much needed boost to Bethlehem's fortunes.

Jerusalem

Jerusalem will also benefit from a millennial lick of paint and a useful injection of funds. The Franciscans have been asked by the Holy See to restore and develop key parts of this Holy place. Auditoriums will be built to allow religious, cultural and educational workshops and functions. Silence will be imposed at some of the most significant of Jerusalem's landmarks.

Two sister organisations, Holy Land 2000™ and Magi 2000™ are hoping to offer 10-, 12- and 14-day millennium tours to the Holy Land and a re-enactment of the **Journey of the Magi**. The latter is a 5-month commemorative pilgrimage to Bethlehem. The organisers hope up to 10,000 people will join the Journey on its last leg from Jerusalem to Bethlehem over the twelve days of Christmas 1999. Don't try to contact these organisations direct; both will sell the tours through travel agents only. Contact the Holy Land travel specialist Christian Tours USA Inc (☎ +1 516-867 5052 or, from within the States, 800-887 9988, fax +1 516-867 1514, e-mail ctusa@ix.netcom.com) which will take tours to the Holy Lands throughout 2000.

Millennium Tour: Middle East (15 Dec 1999 – 2 Jan 2000)
Christmas in Lalibela, New Year's Eve in Muscat. Price: US$8495. Prices are estimated and land-based only. **Contact:** Travcoa (☎ +1 714-476 2800 or, from within America, 800-992 2003), 2350 S E Bristol, Newport Beach, Ca 9266, USA.

❏ ASIA FOR THE INDEPENDENT TRAVELLER

Since the year 2000 is a Christian milestone, it is not surprising that there has been little millennial planning in Asia. This section will outline only those few sites of particular interest where there has been a strong rumour that an event might take place. If you do decide to find your own way to one of the following destinations, you may not find an organised party, but you will find other independent revellers.

Australians in particular will head for **Bali** in time to greet the next millennium. Despite being less than 100 miles across at its longest point, Bali has become the epicentre of Indonesian tourism. Beautiful sandy beaches interrupt a jagged coastline. Inland Bali is characterised by terraced paddy-fields, lush hills, temples and the extravagant festivals for which the Balinese are famous. There is no doubt that Bali will be inundated with millennial revellers come 1999, and that, should you wish to join the fun, planning ahead is essential. Bali is easy to reach by air. The international airport is at Ngurah Rai which is about two miles south of Kuta. Buses and minibuses (*bemos*) serve the island well. There are no trains.

The Great Wall of **China** will attract a good number of visitors on 31 December 1999, despite the fact that the Chinese New Year falls later in January. There has been much talk about the possibility of a party at the Great Wall, probably near Beijing. No plans have been set in stone, but it does seem likely that independent revellers will congregate at Badaling or Mutianyu (both fully restored sections of wall) even if no properly-organised party materialises. If you hope to avoid other travellers on the Big Night, head for Simatai which is far quieter. The Great Wall will be an apt place to see in 2000; it took more than two millennia to build and is one of the most impressive sights the world has to offer. The best way to reach Badaling or Mutianyu is by bus from Beijing. Simatai is best reached by train (to Gubeikou) and taxi.

Agra in **India** is one very obvious millennial destination. This is the city of the Taj Mahal and the equally impressive Red Fort. The latter is a sixteenth-century fortress and palace which was built to mark the authority of Mughal power in India and was the template for the Red Fort in Delhi. More familiar to most visitors, perhaps, is the magnificent Taj Mahal. Shah Jehan built the towering Taj Mahal over the grave of his wife, Mumtaz Mahal, who had died in childbirth. It is a moving and inspiring building which rates as one of the man-made wonders of the world.

❏ **ASIA FOR THE INDEPENDENT TRAVELLER (cont)**
Japan
At least one Internet site claims to have details of a millennium celebration at the foot of beautiful Mount Fuji in Japan. There appears to be some confusion as to whether this is a legitimate event or simply someone's wishful thinking. Still, the idea is an appealing one, and there is no doubt that many travellers will head for Kawaguchiko, the most popular starting point for treks up the mountain, in time to see the new millennium dawn over one of the most impressive mountains in the world. Regular buses serve Kawaguchiko from Tokyo's Hamamatsuch and Shinjuku stations.

South Asia

INDIA
Millennium Ski Tour: The Himalaya (dates flexible)
The Ski Club of Great Britain (☎ +44 (0) 181-410 2000) plans to take groups heli-skiing in the Himalaya over 31 December 1999. Skiers will travel in groups of three with Himachal Helicopters. Accommodation will include a health club, sauna and jacuzzi. All trips will be tailor-made but a starting price of around £4000 should be anticipated.

Millennium Tour (28 Dec 1999 – 5 Jan 2000)
This busy tour through Moghul and Rajasthan includes visits to Old and New Delhi, Agra, Fatehpur Sikri and Jaipur. Price: £1496 (B&B). Abercrombie & Kent (see Contacts, p59).

SRI LANKA
Millennium Tour (23 Dec 1999 – 3 Jan 2000)
Accommodation at one of Sri Lanka's best beach resorts, the Triton at Ahungalla, will make this trip good value. Price: £1025 (B&B). Abercrombie & Kent (see Contacts, p59).

MALDIVES
Millennium Tour (22 Jan 1999 – 4 Jan 2000)

Again, A&K are offering two tours over the same dates. One can choose either the Banyan villas – price: £2724 (full-board) – or the Soneva villas on Kunfunadhoo Island – price: £2136 (B&B).

Abercrombie & Kent have calculated these per person prices for a similar trip from London in December 1996. The actual cost in 1999 is likely to be between 25-40% more. Final prices will be announced in September 1998. A £600 refundable deposit is required to reserve a space on an Abercrombie & Kent millennium trip. Another **non**-refundable deposit of £400 is required on 1 October 1998. The outstanding cost of the trip must be paid in full by 1 October 1999. (See Contacts, p59).

BURMA (MYANMAR)
Road to Mandalay Millennium River Cruise

The Orient-Express-owned *Road to Mandalay* river-cruiser will make a millennial voyage on the Irrawaddy River. After a stay in Rangoon (Yangon), passengers will be taken to Mandalay – the cultural capital of Burma – to meet the boat. Ports of call will include: Mount Popa, Ava and Sagaing Hills. New Year's Eve will be celebrated in Pagan (Bagan). With over 2000 Buddhist shrines and temples spread over a vast plain beside the Irrawaddy, Pagan will provide a remarkable backdrop to this millennium celebration. While the itinerary has been fixed, the dates and prices have not. A deposit will secure a place on the cruise. (See Contacts, p59).

THAILAND
Eastern & Oriental Express Millennium Journey
Bangkok to Singapore (29 Dec 1999 – 4 Jan 2000)

On 29 December 1999 the wonderful Eastern & Oriental Express will pull out of Bangkok station to take its passengers on a journey through Chiang Mai, Phitsanoluk, Kanchanaburi, over the River Kwai and on to Penang and Singapore. New Year's Eve 1999 will be celebrated in the ancient Thai city of Sukhothai. Prices will be agreed in June 1998. Deposits will be accepted before then. (See Contacts, p59).

Millennium Tours: Thailand

British travel operator Explore Worldwide (+44 (0) 1252-319448) will offer an 18-day trekking trip to Thailand over New Year's Eve 1999. Prices have not been decided but a similar tour cost £835 per person in 1998. The itinerary will include: Bangkok, Chiang Mai, Mae Hong Son, Sukhothai and Ayudhya.

Abercrombie & Kent (see Contacts, p59) have a Thailand tour (28 Dec 1999 – 5 Jan 2000) with a millennium celebration at The Chedi on Pansea Bay on the island of Phuket. The Chedi resort is an attractive collection of traditional-style Thai cottages. Price: £1499 (B&B). A&K are also selling a Thailand and Hong Kong tour (30 Dec 1999 – 10 Jan 2000). This includes: Hong Kong, Bangkok (for New Year's Eve) and Chiang Mai. Price: £2450 (room only).

SINGAPORE

World's Longest Street Party (30 Oct 1999 – 11 Feb 2000)

Singapore will tie its millennium celebrations into the World's Longest Street Party – a three-month string of festivals and events to welcome the Gregorian, Lunar and Chinese New Years. Highlights include: the DisneyFest, the Christmas Light-Up, Lunar New Year Celebrations and Chingay Parade. The Chingay Parade takes place in early February and is a magnificent street procession and party designed to welcome the Lunar New Year. **Contact:** Singapore Tourist Board (☎ +65 736-6622, Internet http://www.newasia-singapore.com), Tourism Court, 1 Orchard Spring Lane, Singapore 247729.

MALAYSIA

Millennium Tour (23 Dec 1999 – 4 Jan 2000)

A 12-day trip to the luxurious Datai Hotel on Langkawi Island in north-west Malaysia. Price: £1647 (room only). Abercrombie & Kent (see Contacts, p59).

INDONESIA

Millennium Tours: Bali

Abercrombie & Kent (see Contacts, p59) have an eight-day tour from 28 Dec 1999 to 5 Jan 2000 based near Ubud – the colourful cultural centre of Bali. Price: £1361 (room only). Travcoa also has a Bali tour (from 20 Dec 1999 to 3 Jan 2000). It includes: Bangkok, Singapore and Bali (for New Year's Eve at the Four Seasons Resort). Price: US$9995 (estimated and land-based only). **Contact:** Travcoa (☎ +1 714-476 2800 or, from within America, ☎ 800-992 2003), 2350 S E Bristol, Newport Beach, Ca 9266, USA.

Asia Millennium Tours from Maupintour

Maupintour (☎ +1 800-255 4266) are offering millennium tours to India (20 Dec 1999-3 Jan 2000), including Jaipur, Varanasi and Agra, Thailand (26 Dec 1999-2 Jan 2000) and Hong Kong (28 Dec 1999-2 Jan 2000). A deposit of US$850 is required to secure a place. A further US$350 is required on 15 Jan 1999 and half the final balance by 15 July 1999. Final prices are not yet available.

North Asia

HONG KONG
New Year's Eve Party and Tour (28 Dec 1999 – 3 Jan 2000)

Another party site to be filmed by the Millennial Foundation (see Contacts, below) on New Year's Eve 1999 is the fabulous Deluxe Ballroom at the Regent Hotel in Hong Kong. The Deluxe Ballroom has fine views of the harbour which will be the back-

---

❑ **Contacts**

● **Abercrombie & Kent** (☎ +44 (0) 171-730 9600, fax +44 (0) 171-730 9376), Sloane Square House, Holbein Place, London SW1V 8NS, UK.

● **Travcoa** (☎ +1 714-476 2800 or, from within America, 800-992 2003), 2350 S E Bristol, Newport Beach, Ca 9266, USA.

● **The Millennial Foundation** (☎ +44 (0) 141-204 2000, fax +44 (0) 141-248 1591, Internet: http://yes2000.co.uk).10 Sandyford Place, Glasgow, G3 7NB, UK.

● **Orient-Express** (☎ (US) +1 800-524 2420, (UK) ☎ +44 171-805 5100, (Singapore) ☎ +65 392-3500).

drop for a fireworks display at midnight. The Foundation is offering a six-day stay at the Regent Hotel, which includes tickets to the party, for £2500. The Hong Kong Cancer Fund (HKCF) is responsible for planning this Millennial Foundation event. With the help of the Hong Kong and Greater China Governments, the HKCF hopes to create another glittering spectacle: lighting up the **Great Wall of China** by laser from satellites in space. The project has yet to be officially confirmed but looks likely to go ahead.

Millennium tour (20 Dec 1999 – 2 Jan 2000)

Includes: Bangkok, Singapore and Hong Kong (for New Year's Eve). Price: US$8995. Prices are estimated and land-based only. **Contact:** Travcoa (☎ +1 714-476 2800 or, from within America, 800-992 2003), 2350 S E Bristol, Newport Beach, Ca 9266, USA.

JAPAN
New Year's Eve 1999 Party and Tour: Tokyo
(28 Dec 1999 – 3 Jan 2000)

The Millennial Foundation will use TV to link a millennium celebration at the Four Seasons Hotel in Tokyo to 30 other party sites around the world on New Year's Eve 1999. The Foundation is also offering a six-day stay at the Four Seasons – including access to the party – for £2500. (See Contacts, p59).

AFRICA

Africa has been – and still is – desperately slow to capitalise on its millennial appeal. Countries like Zimbabwe, Tanzania, Kenya and Egypt could attract thousands of travellers looking for somewhere magnificent to see in the next millennium. Egypt has rejected several high-profile attempts to turn the pyramids into a one-night party venue. Travel firms have been quicker to see the potential.

SEYCHELLES
New Year's Eve Party (31 Dec 1999)
London party-planners Capital VIP are to hold a star-studded Millennium's Eve party at a secret location in the Seychelles. The trendy team have invited countless big names including Tom Cruise, Nicole Kidman, Bruce Willis, Demi Moore and Piers Brosnan. How many will turn up is, of course, another matter. A limited number of all-inclusive tickets will be made available to mere mortals for a staggering £8500. **Contact:** Capital VIP (☎ +44 171-495 7070, fax +44 171-495 1020).

MAURITIUS
Millennium Tour (22 Dec 1999 – 7 Jan 2000)
Abercrombie & Kent are offering two tours to Mauritius over the same dates. One trip is to the opulent Le Saint Geran resort-hotel. Price: £5185 (half board). The other is to Le Touessrok which provides complimentary watersports. Price: £4232 (half-board). Both resorts are in great locations on the east coast of the island. Abercrombie & Kent (see Contacts, p59).

NAMIBIA
Millennium Tour (20 Dec 1999 – 8 Jan)
UK-based Sunvil Discovery (☎ +44 (0) 181-232 9777) has a 19-night millennium fly-drive tour on offer. Price: approximately £2800; a £300 deposit is required.

❑ AFRICA FOR THE INDEPENDENT TRAVELLER

The millennium is not yet big news in Africa. Only a few travel firms and a handful of entrepreneurial promoters are currently preparing to acknowledge the event by escorting tourists to the more dramatic party backdrops the continent has to offer. Independent travellers will also head for these places where they will be able to see in the next millennium surrounded by some of the most stunning landscapes in the world and in the company of others hoping to mark the moment in a similar fashion.

Egypt

Several party-planners have approached the Egyptian authorities in the hope of holding events at the **Pyramids**. Amazingly, and – perhaps – stupidly, the Egyptians have so far rejected every advance. At the time of going to press, no events were organised at the Pyramids (despite what some Internet sites would have us believe). Whether the Egyptians hope to stage their own event, are holding out for a better offer or simply don't want drunken revellers let loose among their most marketable assets is still unclear. It will be possible for independent revellers to get to the Pyramids under their own steam. There are, in fact, 97 pyramids in various locations across the desert from Cairo to Fayoum. However, it is the Great Pyramids of Giza which will – as always – attract the most attention. The site is just over seven miles from Cairo and getting there is straightforward: take a bus or minibus from Midan Tahrir (30-40pt) or take a taxi (£E15 each-way) from the city-centre.

One of the most enjoyable and hassle-free ways to see Egypt is from a **Nile cruise**. River cruises are no longer reserved for stiffly-starched colonial types and Agatha Christie characters. Indeed, Nile cruises have never been more accessible. Egypt has suffered from a sharp drop in visitor numbers over the past few years, and prices reflect this. Pre-booked cruises can cost as little as US$250 for a week's excursion. It can cost half that to book a cruise from within Egypt – but your chances of finding a last-minute bargain for the millennium are slim.

Kenya

With crime in Kenya perceived by many to be real problem, and with Uganda and Tanzania becoming increasingly wise to tourism, Kenya has been forced to make extra effort in recent years to hold on to its reputation as the place to go for safaris. The **Masai Mara**

National Reserve is the most popular highlight Kenya has to offer. While it easy to see why – this is the Kenyan part of the wonderful Serengeti plains which boast incredible wildlife – the well-trodden atmosphere of the area might be off-putting to some. Masai Mara's status as the biggest draw in Kenya means that it is easy to get to and there are a number of places to stay. There are two flights a day to Masai Mara from Nairobi ($90 each way).

A less obvious but equally attractive millennium destination is the ancient town of **Lamu**. Lamu is the oldest inhabited town in Kenya and, in many ways, one is tempted to believe that it has changed very little for hundreds of years. The mainly Muslim population still wears traditional dress, and the streets are congested not with battered Mercedes taxis but with donkeys and people. To reach Lamu, fly to Manda Island from Mombasa ($90-95). From Manda, take a ferry to Lamu (KSh55). Buses run to Lamu from Mombasa via Malindi.

Tanzania

To many travellers, Tanzania is the 'real' East Africa. One can hardly fail to find beauty in every corner of the country. There are, however, three clear highlights which will stand out above all others as obvious millennium destinations: Mount Kilimanjaro, Serengeti National Park and Ngorongoro Crater.

Mt Kilimanjaro is the highest mountain in Africa. Its perfectly-formed and snow-capped peak is visible from miles around and is one of the most enduring sights on the continent. Despite its height, Kilimanjaro is relatively easy to climb. The mountain provides several distinct habitats which change with altitude. A belt of rainforest gives cover for monkeys, leopards, rhinos and elephants. Most visitors find accommodation in Marangu, Moshi or Arusha (all of which can be reached by minibus from Dar es Salaam). These are the most convenient bases from which to trek up the mountain. Marangu is the start point for the easiest and most popular trek.

With endless bush and a massive animal population, it's no surprise that north Tanzania's **Serengeti National Park** is considered by many to be the most beautiful corner of East Africa. There are around 30 campsites in the Serengeti ($25-50 per person) but some have no facilities beyond more or less flat ground. There are also a good number of lodges and tented camps which range in price enormously. You'll need to book well in advance for the millennium.

Tanzania for the independent traveller (cont)

More impressive still is the **Ngorongoro Conservation Area** which lies just south of the Serengeti. The views from atop this 12.5-mile-wide crater are stunning. Ngorongoro is a haven for animals which rely on the permanent water supply on the crater floor. Every species found in East Africa can be found here. There are several lodges and camp-sites on the crater rim. If you are quick enough to find a place to stay here, you will see in the next millennium surrounded by some of the most incredible views anywhere in the world. By far the easiest way to get to Ngorongoro is by 4WD from Arusha. Otherwise, try to join a private bus from Arusha or hitch with one of the many trucks which regularly pass through the area. Visitors must be accompanied by a ranger.

Zimbabwe

Nearly 15% of Zimbabwe is protected wildlife habitat. Hwange and Zambezi/Victoria Falls National Parks are the best-known parks and will be popular millennial destinations. There are many other reserves and parks, some of which are little visited. Travellers hoping to see in the millennium in relative peace will find plenty of stunning but secluded spots in Zimbabwe.

Hwange National Park is wildlife-packed and relatively easy to reach. But it is quiet compared to, say, Kruger, the Serengeti or any park in Kenya. Human interference forced animals into this area which was considered to have too unfriendly a climate for human colonisation. Hwange is not as immediately beautiful as many of the other parks mentioned in this chapter, but it is a great place to go to watch wildlife. There are a lot of camp sites and lodges in Hwange which has boomed over the last few years thanks in part to its accessibility. The park has its own airfield served by flights from Harare and Victoria Falls. Frequent buses service the park from Bulawayo and Victoria Falls. There is also a train service from Bulawayo and Victoria Falls which stops at Dete on the edge of the park.

Everyone has seen pictures of **Victoria Falls**. Everyone should see the real thing. If you're looking for somewhere truly magnificent to be when the millennium arrives, come here. Over a mile wide and 100-metres-deep, the awesome falls are justifiably one of the world's biggest attractions. There is little choice but to stay at the over-touristy Victoria Falls Town which can be reached by air from Harare, Namibia and Botswana. Buses frequently arrive from

Hwange ($8) and Bulawayo ($12). A train link connects Victoria Falls to Bulawayo and Livingstone in Zambia. Sadly, the much-loved steam engine which served this route until recently has now been replaced by a more modern locomotive.

Botswana

While Botswana does not figure on most travellers' itineraries, there are two very good reasons to visit: Chobe National Park and the Okavango Delta. In **Chobe National Park** you can see Botswana's most diverse wildlife; the reserve is all the more attractive for its relatively low profile. There is a booming elephant population and plenty of crocodiles. Accommodation around the park is reasonably well-developed. For big bucks you could stay at the opulent Chobe Game Lodge where Richard Burton and Elizabeth Taylor spent one of their honeymoons. There are many good-value cheaper options. The busy town of Kasane is a major gateway to Chobe with regular flights to and from Victoria Falls ($125), Gaborone ($180) and Maun ($115). Buses are less reliable but there are services between Kasane and Victoria Falls ($20) and Nata ($12).

The Okavango Delta is the largest inland delta in the world. Expect to see plenty of giraffes, hippos, zebras and elephants. The Okavango is a spectacular habitat which is, perhaps, most impressive in and around the Moremi Wildlife Reserve. Most travellers reach the Okavango through Maun which is connected by air to Harare ($200), Gaborone ($180) and Victoria Falls ($150). Buses depart daily for Francistown ($15). There are plenty of game lodges, camps and hotels. The tour industry in the Okavango is quite well developed.

South Africa

The millennium will be celebrated in South Africa, but the country has, so far, been slow to decide exactly how. **Cape Town** has traditionally been the place to be on New Year's Eve, and that won't change in 1999. With a fortnight-long New Year's festival a regular fixture in the Cape Town calendar and a reputation for being the good-time capital of South Africa, the city will lead the country's millennium celebrations. Cape Town occupies a spectacular bay sheltered under the magnificent Table Mountain. There are few finer settings anywhere in the world. Cape Town International Airport is well served by international and domestic carriers.

South Africa for the independent traveller (cont)
(Cape Town). Regular shuttle buses (R20) and taxis (R130) run between the airport and the city-centre. National coach operators run services between Cape Town and Pretoria and Johannesburg (R320), Port Elizabeth (R130) and Springbok (R180).

Away from the cities, **Kruger National Park** is the biggest draw in South Africa. Bigger than Wales, it is one of the most (if not *the* most) stunning and varied reserves in Africa. Kruger has consistently been the best-managed and protected park on the continent. The legacy of that attention is an incredible animal population which includes over 2000 lions and nearly 8000 elephants. Park-run rest camps are dotted all over the park and are your best bet for reasonably-priced accommodation. Daily flights connect Johannesburg to Skukuza and Phalaborwa. A cheaper but inconvenient option is to take a bus or car to Nelspruit where connections are available to three park entrances.

Kruger's immense size will easily absorb millennium travellers. Competition will be keener for a room in one of the many up-market hotels in the breathtaking **Drakensberg Mountains**. This formidable range rises up out of the Natal grasslands to form a colossal natural fortress and one of the most staggering sights in Africa. Several lovely hotels sit perched in the mountains, and most will put on special entertainment on 31 December 1999. Try the Cathedral Peak Hotel, The Nest or Champagne Castle. These are among the best-located party venues in South Africa. Most resorts will pick up guests from the coach stations at Estcourt, Ladysmith or Swinburne.

TANZANIA
Millennium tour (dates flexible)
Luxury Tanzania specialists Mashado are offering a tailor-made millennium safari. The itinerary is flexible, but will be based on a 14-day tour to Kilimanjaro, Ngorongoro Crater and the Tarangire and Serengeti National Parks. Accommodation will be at high-quality lodges and camps. Christmas and New Year's Eve celebrations are to be included in the price. The price is not yet definite – and depends on the exact details of the tour one chooses – but is likely to be approximately US$8500. That doesn't include international flights. **Contact:** Mashado Central

Reservations and Head Office (☎ +255 57-6585/4398, fax +255 57-8020/4409, e-mail mashado@habari.co.tz), PO Box 14823, Arusha, Tanzania, East Africa

SOUTH AFRICA
New Year's Eve Trance Party (31 Dec 1999)
Trance music promoters in South Africa are organising a live millennium trance concert on Table Mountain, above Cape Town. The organisers are hoping to attract major trance DJs from around the world. Information is slowly unfolding at: http://www.south africa2000.com

New Year's Eve Party (31 Dec 1999)
'Nellie', as the Mount Nelson Hotel is known, is the best place to stay in Cape Town and occupies one of the most admired sites in the world. It is set in nine acres of gardens with great views of Table Mountain. Nellie will be celebrating her centenary in 1999. There will be a gala party and dinner on New Year's Eve 1999. Prices and a full itinerary will be available from June 1998. Over the Millennium's Eve period the hotel will accept bookings only for a minimum stay of 14 nights.

    Contact: Mount Nelson Hotel (☎ +27 21-231000, fax +27 21-247472 or, from within the UK, ☎ 0181-568 8366 or, from within the States, ☎ 804-522 5022), 76 Orange Street, Cape Town 8001, South Africa.

Millennium Tour: South Africa
British-based Thomas Cook Holidays (+44 (0) 1733-417000) has a six-night millennium tour to Cape Town on offer with accommodation at the Cape Sun Intercontinental Hotel. Price: approximately £3195.

MILLENNIUM TOURS (ABERCROMBIE & KENT)
● **Great Africa Air Cruise (27 Dec 1999 – 10 Jan 2000)** Space is limited to just 75 guests on this whistle-stop tour of Africa. A specially chartered aircraft will leave London for Luxor on 27 December 1999. After three nights at the Winter Palace Hotel, it's on to the Victoria Falls Hotel at Victoria Falls (for New Year's

Eve), the Serena Hotel in Zanzibar, the Ngorongoro Crater and the Serengeti in Tanzania, Nairobi and finally the Masai Mara or Mount Kenya. Price: £11,500 (all-inclusive).

● **Morocco (29 Dec 1999 – 4 Jan 2000)** A five-night stay at the famous La Mamounia in Marrakech. Price: £1386 (bed and continental breakfast).

● **Egypt (28 Dec 1999 – 4 Jan 2000)** Three days in Cairo followed by a Nile cruise to the ancient sites at Luxor and Aswan. Price: £2141 (bed and full breakfast in Cairo and full board on Nile cruise).

● **Egypt (30 Dec 1999 – 3 Jan 2000)** This long millennial weekend in Cairo makes use of the Mena House Hotel which is set in 40-acres of gardens at Giza, not far from the Great Pyramid and the Sphinx. Price: £954 (bed and full breakfast).

● **Kenya (21 Dec 1999 – 4 Jan 2000)** Groups of six will see in the millennium in the Masai Mara Game Reserve as part of this 14-day safari. Accommodation will be at permanent lodges and camps. Price: £2842 (full board).

● **Kenya (24 Dec 1999 – 6 Jan 2000)** The highlight of this contrasting safari is the chance to spend New Year's Eve 1999 under Mount Kilimanjaro. Accommodation will be at luxury camps, with one night at the Mt Kenya Safari Club. Price: £3142 (full board)

● **Tanzania (27 Dec 1999 – 4 Jan 2000)** Includes: Lake Manyara, Ngorongoro Crater and Serengeti National Park. Price: £2126 (full board).

● **Zimbabwe (27 Dec 1999 – 4 Jan 2000)** There is only space for 18 couples on this exclusive trip to the Matetsi Water Lodge near Victoria Falls. Price: £2860 (full board/B&B)

● **Botswana (27 Dec 1999 – 5 Jan 2000)** Abercrombie & Kent have reserved Jack's Camp in the Makgadikgadi National Park, which can accommodate just eight couples. It is the only permanent camp in the Kalahari. Price: £3215 (full board on safari, B&B).

● **South Africa (27 Dec 1999 – 5 Jan 2000)** A nine-day safari at the 10,000-hectare Makalali Private Game Reserve by the Makhutswi River. The Reserve is reached by 'plane from Johannesburg. Price: £3376 (full board/B&B).

● **South Africa (27 Dec 1999 – 5 Jan)** This tour includes a week at the 5-star Tswalu Game Lodge in Tswalu Game Reserve – which is the largest privately-owned game reserve in South Africa. Price: £3110 (full board/B&B)

● **Namibia (21 Dec 1999 – 3 Jan 2000)** A striking desert backdrop to an outdoor New Year's Eve 1999 party is on offer to a very limited number. Price £2540 (full board/B&B)

Abercrombie & Kent have calculated these per person prices for a similar trip from London in December 1996. The actual cost in 1999 is likely to be between 25-40% more. Final prices will be announced in September 1998. A £600 refundable deposit is required to reserve a space on an Abercrombie & Kent millennium trip. Another **non**-refundable deposit of £400 is required on 1 October 1998. The outstanding cost of the trip must be paid in full by 1 October 1999. **Contact:** Abercrombie & Kent (☎ +44 (0) 171-730 9600, fax +44 (0) 171-730 9376), Sloane Square House, Holbein Place, London SW1V 8NS, UK.

AFRICA MILLENNIUM TOURS (MAUPINTOUR)

Maupintour (☎ +1 800-255 4266) have arranged millennium tours to **South Africa** (20 Dec 1999-1 Jan 2000), **Kenya** (26 Dec

---

❑ **Luxury lodges for hire**

Richard Bonham Safaris have two African lodges for hire over 31 December 1999. Ol Donyo Wuas Lodge in the Chyulu Hills of Kenya has fantastic views of Mount Kilimanjaro and exclusive access to some 250,000-acres of bush. It has seven double cottages, two of which have extra rooms for families.

Sand Rivers Lodge in Tanzania occupies a prime position in the Selous with views over the Rufiji River. It has eight double bedrooms and its own airstrip (a 40-minute flight from Dar-es-Salaam).

Both lodges must be wholly booked by one party and are available for a minimum of four nights over the New Year's Eve 1999 period. Price: US$1000 per person, per night.

Contact: Richard Bonham Safaris (☎ +254 2-882 521, fax +254 2-882728, e-mail bonham.luke@swiftkenya.com), PO Box 24133, Nairobi, Kenya

1999-3 Jan 2000) with New Year's Eve at The Ark game lodge and two tours to **Egypt** (dates not yet announced). A deposit of US$850 is required to secure a place. A further US$350 is required on 15 Jan 1999 and half the final balance by 15 July 1999. Final prices are not yet available.

AFRICA MILLENNIUM TOURS (TRAVCOA)

● **South Africa (21 Dec 1999 – 4 Jan 2000)** Christmas in Mala Mala, New Year's Eve in Cape Town. Also includes Rovos Rail Garden Route and Victoria Falls. Price: US$7995
● **South Africa (22 Dec 1999 – 3 Jan 2000)** Christmas in Cape Town, New Year's Eve in Sun City. Price: US$6995
● **East Africa (26 Dec 1999 – 9 Jan 2000)** Includes: Nairobi, Masai Mara (for New Year's Eve), Serengeti and Ngorongoro Crater. Price: US$6995
● **Egypt (22 Dec 1999 – 2 Jan 2000)** Christmas in Cairo, New Year's Eve on the Nile. Price: US$5495

Prices are estimated and land-based only. **Contact:** Travcoa (☎ +1 714-476 2800 or, from within America, 800-992 2003), 2350 S E Bristol, Newport Beach, Ca 92660, USA.

EUROPE

Millennium celebrations across Europe are as varied as one would expect from such a diverse continent. Revellers can waltz into the future in Vienna, party under the giant Millennium Dome in Britain or join the French at a spectacular celebration by the Eiffel Tower.

Italy

Pope John Paul II has declared the year 2000 to be a Jubilee, or Holy Year (see p73). Rome and the Vatican are expecting some 21 million visitors over the Jubilee 2000 period (see p72). With such an extraordinary number of pilgrims and tourists anticipat-

---

❏ **ITALY**
Contacts: Rome Tourist Authority (☎ 6-488 991, fax 6-481 9316) Via Parigi 11, Rome 00185. **Vatican Information Service** (☎ +39 6-6989 2425, fax +39 6-6988 3053) 00120 Vatican City.
Internet: Rome: http://www.roma2000.com; **Vatican:** http://www.vatican.va
Average maximum temperature °C

	Dec	Jan
Rome	13	11

Capital: Rome
Flight times: to Rome from:
      LA: 15 hours, 30 minutes
      London: 2 hours
      Sydney: 25 hours
Approximate exchange rates: Lira (L) – £1=2944, US$1=1802, A$1=1195
Time difference: GMT +1
Country dialling code: ☎ 39

ed, Italy is concentrating its millennium preparations on the capital by improving its infrastructure and restoring churches.

ROME

Rome will attract millions on New Year's Eve 1999. Visitors will come for the Vatican and its atmospheric New Year's Eve ceremony as well as for Rome itself – a city rich in history, and whose architecture alone spans the last two thousand years. For a brief guide to Rome and where to stay, see p74.

Jubilee 2000: Vatican City (Year 2000)

The Vatican's *Peregrinato ad Petri Sedem* is to welcome pilgrims to the Vatican throughout the year 2000. Officials are intent on preserving true pilgrimage and will not encourage religious tourism. Most visitors are expected to congregate on Wednesdays

---

❑ **Vatican City**

With its own currency, postal service and police force, the Vatican has been the world's smallest state since the Lateran Treaty recognised its independence in 1929.

St Peter's Square is an enormous piazza with **St Peter's Basilica** at its head and an obelisk brought to Rome by Caligula at its centre. Standing in the piazza gives one a useful sense of the layout of the Vatican and is a good reference point from which to explore the gems of this capital of Roman Catholicism. The Basilica itself is stunning. It took 150 years to build, and enjoyed the attention of some of the finest artists and architects alive at the time, including Michelangelo and Raphael. One of the best views in Rome is from the top of the dome of the Basilica.

Nestled next to the north wall of St Peter's Basilica is the **Sistine Chapel**. The ceiling of the chapel, painted by Michelangelo, depicts the *Creation* and other scenes from the *Old Testament*. The west wall is decorated with the *Last Judgement*. Over the last decade both have been meticulously restored. Other parts of the chapel, which was built in 1484 to be the private chapel of Pope Sixtus IV, are painted by Renaissance masters such as Botticelli.

Successive Popes have amassed a remarkable collection of art and riches which are displayed to full effect in the **Vatican Museums**.

when the Pope often gives a morning audience (10-11am) in the Papal Audience Hall. Tickets are required. They can be obtained from the *Prefettura della Casa Pontifica* in the Vatican.

New Year's Eve Ceremony: Vatican City (31 Dec 1999)

The Pope will preside over a traditional High Mass in the Church of Saint Ignatius Loyola on the afternoon of New Year's Eve 1999. The *Te Deum* will be sung to give thanks for the year, century and millennium just ended.

Millennium Landmark: Rome (31 Dec 1999 – 1 Jan 2000)

While Rome is not well prepared for millennium celebrations, it will provide a fantastic backdrop to private parties and street celebrations which will take place across the city. Hotels will soon be accepting reservations, and several will offer their own New Year's Eve parties.

Italy's capital is not known for efficiency. It is judged by many to be both chaotic and poorly managed. The year 2000 might be a chance for Rome to dispel that image and to silence those critics who have not forgotten the 1990 World Cup. Italia 90 promised much but delivered little except the Three Tenors. In fact, if Rome is not properly prepared for Jubilee 2000 visitors, the city could actually be damaged by the sheer volume of tourists. An ambitious programme of development has been proposed. It includes: a new underground between the Colosseum and St Peter's, new parks, a city-wide policy on museum-opening times, an escalator joining the Basilica to the Vatican Museums, improved public transport and a facelift for the Colosseum.

❏ **What is a Holy Year?**

A Holy Year is a Roman Catholic tradition, ordered by the Pope at times of great religious significance. There have been two Holy Years this century. Pope Pius XI made 1933 a Holy Year to mark the 1900th anniversary of redemption. The 1950th anniversary of the redemption was also proclaimed a Holy Year by Pope John Paul II in 1983.

❏ ROME – A BRIEF GUIDE

What can one say about Rome? This is a city of style and striking beauty. There are few more appropriate places to see in the new millennium. After all, the ancient Romans invented the calendar system which is still in use today.

What to See

Rome is rich in buildings, fountains and statues which reflect either the Roman Empire or the Roman Catholic Church. It is the impact of these two forces which has shaped the city. There is so much to see in Rome that this short passage is wholly inadequate. Like most cities, however, there are some sights which really must be seen. While Rome sprawls for miles, many of the really exciting landmarks are in a relatively small area around the Roman Forum. It's also true that for many people Rome is best discovered by accident wandering from one piazza to the next.

The **Roman Forum**, which is still being excavated, was the political and cultural hub of ancient Rome. Today, there is a lot to see although a good imagination helps to fill in the gaps.

South-east of the Forum is the **Colosseum**, perhaps the most familiar structure in Rome. Time and traffic have done their best to defeat this giant arena, but it is still most impressive.

One of the better preserved buildings in ancient Rome is the **Pantheon**. The Pantheon is an ancient temple – built on the site of an even older one – which is one of the most significant architectural feats of the Roman Empire.

More recent but equally beautiful are Bernini's **Fontana dei Quattro Fiumi**, the **Spanish Steps**, the **Fontana de Trevi** and – of course – the **Vatican** (see p72).

Above all, Rome is a city for living – provided you avoid being hit by a Fiat Bambino! It's full of magnificent restaurants, bars and clubs. The combination of ancient relics, renaissance beauty and now a vibrant night life makes Rome a great place to be when the new millennium comes along.

To find out **what's on** in Rome look for the *Trovaroma* section in Thursday's *La Repubblica* newspaper.

Where to Stay

● **Expensive** (over L300,000): the *Excelsior* (☎ 06-47081, fax 06-4826205), Via Vittorio Veneto 125, Rome's most sumptuous hotel.

Where to Stay (cont)

Hassler Villa Medici (06-699340, fax 06-6789991), Piazza Triniti dei Monti 6; the *Plaza* (☎ 06-69921111, fax 06-69941575), Via del Corso 126, attracts celebrities; *Eden* (☎ 06-478121, fax 06-4821584), Via Ludovisi 49; *Bernini Bristol* (☎ 06-4883051, fax 06-4824266), Piazza Barberini 23; *Majestic* (☎ 06-486841, fax 06-4880984), Via Vittorio Veneto 50; *Commodore* (☎ 06-485656, fax 06-4747562), Via Torino1; *Holiday Inn Eur* (☎ 06-65581, fax 06-6557005), V. le Castello della Magliana 65; *Ritz* (☎/fax 06-8083751), Via Chelini 41; *Sheriton Roma* (☎ 06-54531, fax 06-5940689), Viale del Pattinaggio; *The Regency* (☎ 06-4819281, fax 06-4746850), Via Romagna 42.

● **Moderate** (between L150,000-300,000): *Alexandra* (☎ 06-4881943, fax 06-4871804), Via Vittorio Veneto 18; *Amalfi* (☎ 06-4744313, fax 06-4820575), Via Merulana 278; *Caprice* (☎ 06-4880779, fax 06-484812), Via Liguria 38; *Corona* (☎ 06-4880080, fax 06-4823614), Via Napoli 3; Donatello (☎ 06-7010833, fax 06-7011656), Via di Porta Maggiore 83; *Firenze* (☎ 06-6797240, fax 06-6785636), Via Due Macelli 106; *Laurentia* (☎ 06-4450218, fax 06-4453821), Largo degli Osci 63; *Luxor* (☎ 06-485420, fax 06-4815571), Via Agostina Depretis 104; *Mozart* (☎ 06-36001915, fax 06-36001735), Via dei Greci 23; *Oxford* (☎ 06-42828952, fax 06-42815349), Via Boncompagni 89; *San Silvestro* (☎ 06-6794169, fax 06-6791105), Via del Gambero 3; *St Moritz* (☎ 06-4743068, fax 06-4740097), Via Nazionale 51; *Tiziano* (☎ 06-6865019, fax 06-6865019), Corso Vittorio Emanuele 110; *Villa Torlonia* (06-4402630, fax 06-4402637), Via B Eustachio 5.

● **Budget** (under L150,000): *Bixio* (☎ 06-70497327), Via Bixio 46; *Capri* (☎ 06-491367), Via Magenta 13; *Delle Rose* (☎ 06-4819339, fax 06-4744707), Via Principe Amedeo 62; *Fatima* (☎ 06-4454201), Viale Castro Pretorio 25; *Navona* (☎ 06-6864203, fax 06-68803802), *Via dei Sediari* 8; Porta Pia (☎ 06-44249911, fax 06-44249924), Via Messina 25; *Villa Maria Regina* (☎ 06-3294293, fax 06-36308225), Via della Camilluccia 687; *YWCA* (☎ 06-4880460), Via Cesare Balbo 4.

Millennium Landmark: Rome (cont from p73)

It has also been suggested that an old gasometer which overlooks the Tiber should be turned into a giant viewing platform.

Sceptical Romans, who have heard it all before, were impressed in 1996 when the Piazza dei Cinquecento was beautified in a record five months. It remains to be seen whether the city can continue with its improvements in such a successful fashion.

Millennium Tour: Rome (27 Dec 1999 – 2 Jan 2000)

This six-day trip from US operator Maupintour will include accommodation at a top hotel, an historical tour of the Eternal City and a New Year's Eve 1999 party. A US$850 per person deposit is requires to reserve a place. **Contact:** (☎ +1 800-255 4266).

❏ Earthquakes signal The End

Towards the end of 1997 Italy was rocked by a series of earth tremors which damaged important cultural landmarks and works of art. Thousands were forced to leave their homes and the total cost of the disaster ran into hundreds of millions of dollars.

Some Italians began to fear that these pre-millennial tremors signalled the End of the World. Many believed an apocalyptic prophecy from Nostradamus (see pp18-19) was being realised. Others maintained that the tremors were a prelude to doom predicted in the Three Secrets of Fatima.

The Secrets of Fatima are messages which are believed to have been delivered by the Virgin Mary to three peasant children in Portugal in 1917. Consecutive Popes have kept the secrets to themselves, but they are said to be messages of doom brought about by the world's failure to repent its sins.

The Vatican became so alarmed by the increasingly frantic mood of many Roman Catholics in Italy that it took the unusual step of issuing a statement on the matter. Loris Francesco Capovilla, former secretary to Pope John XXIII and one of very few people to have read the Secrets of Fatima, said: 'The secrets are not linked to the end of the millennium. You can exclude this'. Believers will have to keep on guessing.

Millennium Walk: Rome (16 Dec 1999 – 2 Jan 2000)
In 1976 Christopher Whinney walked from London to Rome. He then set up the specialist British tour operator **Alternative Travel** (☎ +44 (0) 1865-310399, fax +44 (0) 1865-310299). To celebrate the millennium, Whinney has organised a 156-mile walk from Siena to Rome in time to spend New Year's Eve 1999 in the Eternal City.

This 18-day trip, of which 13 days are spent walking, departs from Siena on 16 December 1999. All sorts of roads are followed – from Etruscan roads to footpaths – based on Whinney's carefully researched route which he discovered over 20 years ago. The walkers will remain in open countryside until within 10 miles of Rome. The cost of the trip will be around £5000. A deposit of £500 is required to reserve a place. Alternative Travel suggest that 'initial fitness will allow maximum enjoyment'. Similar tours are available throughout the year 2000.

GENOA
Tall Ships 2000 Starting Point: Genoa (20-23 April 2000)
Genoa will give a stylish send-off to crews competing in the Tall Ships 2000 trans-Atlantic millennium race (see p150).

From Genoa, the great square riggers – and some smaller vessels – will head for Cádiz before tackling the long sea crossing that will take them to Bermuda.

As the starting point of a one-off millennium race, Genoa will host a series of maritime events and parties. Genoa is a beautiful city, with a proud seafaring history, which together make it the perfect port from which to launch the first leg of Tall Ships 2000.

Germany

Expo2000 in Hanover will be the main millennial event in Germany and possibly the biggest in the world. This world exposition is a hugely ambitious project and is something of an umbrella organisation for millennial activity in Germany.

Another long-awaited event is the Passion Plays season in Oberammergau. These plays have been performed since 1633.

❑ **GERMANY**

Contacts

● **Expo2000 Hannover GmbH** (☎ 511-8404 0, fax 511-8404 130, e-mail info@expo2000.de), D-30510 Hannover

● **Hannover Tourist Information** (☎ 511-30 14 25, fax 511-30 14 14, e-mail hcc@hannover.de), Ernst-August-Platz 2 (Am Hauptbahnhof), D-30159, Hannover

● **Oberammergau Tourist Information** (☎ 08822-10 21, fax 08822-73 25), Eugen-Pabst-Strasse 9a, Oberammergau

● **Berliner Festspiele GmbH** (☎ 30-25 48 90, fax 30-25 48 91 11), Budapester Strasse 50, D-10787, Berlin

● **Berlin Tourismus Marketing GmbH** (☎ 30-26 47 480), Am Karlsbad 11, D-10785, Berlin

● **Internet:** http: //www.germany-tourism.de

Average maximum temperature °C

	Dec	Jan
Berlin	3	2

Capital: Bonn/Berlin

Flight times: to Berlin from:
LA: 11 hours, 45 minutes
London: 1 hour 45 minutes
Sydney: 25 hours, 30 minutes

Approximate exchange rates: Deutschmark (DM) – £1=2.9, US$1=1.8, A$1=1.2

Time difference: GMT +1

Country dialling code: ☎ 49

The last were in 1990 and they are performed every ten years, the cast made up entirely of the villagers. Some half a million visitors are expected in the year 2000.

HANOVER

Hanover hides its half a million strong population in a city of wide open spaces and parks. It will need all the space it can get between June and October 2000 when 40 million people are expected to visit Expo 2000.

Expo2000: Hanover (1 June-31 Oct 2000)

German Chancellor Helmut Kohl has invited 185 countries and nine international organisations to the world exposition in Hanover between June and October in the year 2000. Expo2000 will champion the theme 'Humankind – Nature – Technology.'

World fairs have traditionally been used to display the cutting edge of technology. Germany plans to use the fair to argue that technology should now be put to better use. In the words of the Expo organisers: 'The hope is that Expo2000 will generate optimism for the new millennium'.

Expo2000 aims to create a microcosm of the world in a 100,000 square metre exhibition space. Life in the third millennium will be portrayed under several sub-themes, including: Health and Nutrition, Living and Working, Communication and

---

❏ **Hanover – Where to Stay**

Competition for a bed in Hanover will be stiff over the Expo2000 period. There are 9000 hotel beds in the city, 23,000 in the region but 100,000 visitors are expected daily.

There is a solution – of sorts. Visitors will find a bed if they are prepared to stay in one of several cities within two hours of Hanover by train. Overflow cities include Berlin, Cologne and Frankfurt. An alternative is to stay with a family in a private house. There are 16,000 such rooms available ranging from 75-190DM per night.

To be assured of a bed close to the exposition site, either in a hotel or with a family, try booking in advance on the Hanover accommodation hotline (☎ 511-81 13 500, fax 511-81 13 541).

Information and Education and Culture. The first world exposition, or Great Exhibition, was held in London in 1851. Since then 61 expositions have been staged around the world. Expo2000 will be Germany's first and is designed to appeal to a very broad audience and to promote international collaboration. **Internet Info:** http://www.expo2000.de

LEIPZIG
Bach-Fest 2000 (21-28 July 2000)
Leipzig will mark the 250th anniversary of Bach's death in 2000. More than 60 events are scheduled. For one week, from 9.30am to 11pm each day, internationally acclaimed orchestras and soloists will celebrate Bach's music.

    Contact: Sabine Martin (☎ 341-964 4166-69, fax 341-964 4195).

OBERAMMERGAU
The Passion Plays: (May-Sep 2000)
During the Thirty Years War in the 17th century, Black Death became widespread across Europe. In 1632 it reached Bavaria. Guards were posted to prevent plague victims from carrying the killer disease into villages. But a farmer from Oberammergau, Kaspar Schisler, contracted the fatal illness while working the surrounding land and somehow entered his village unnoticed. Within a year, one fifth of the population of Oberammergau had died.

    In 1633 Oberammergau Council ruled that every 10 years the villagers, in an attempt to appease the plague, would perform a play of Christ's suffering and death. No one has died of Black Death in Oberammergau since 1633. In 1680 it was agreed that the plays should be enacted at the beginning of every decade. The plays were therefore last seen in 1990.

    The 2000 Passion Plays will be performed daily from May to September from 9am to 5.30pm with a three hour lunch break. **Tickets:** In Britain: DER Travel Service (☎ +44 (0) 171-290 1111), German Travel Centre (☎ +44 (0) 181-429 2900) or Moswin Tours (☎ +44 (0) 116-271 9922).

❑ **Fifty Years of the Federal Republic of Germany and Ten Years of Unification**

For Germans, the last years of the Twentieth Century bring two significant anniversaries: 50 years of the Federal Republic will be celebrated in 1999, while the year 2000 marks 10 years of unification.

After Germany's defeat in 1945, the victorious allies divided the country into four zones. Tension between the Western and Soviet conquerors grew, however, leading to the USSR blocking Western access to Berlin in 1948. A series of air lifts sustained the besieged western zones but the Cold War had started. In 1949 two separate States were created: the German Federal Republic to the west and the German Democratic Republic (GDR) to the east.

Over 40 years later communism collapsed across Eastern Europe and, indeed, the Soviet Union. A right-wing government took power in the GDR and economic union with West Germany soon followed. Helmut Kohl and Mikhail Gorbachev then began to work out a formula for complete unification. That unification began on 3 October 1990.

BERLIN

A mood of reflection is likely to surround New Year's Eve celebrations in Berlin in 1999. Dr Ulrich Eckhardt, Director of the Berlin Festival Organisation, explains: 'The world has been radically changed by events which had Berlin as their epicentre. Nowhere else in the world is it so easy to comprehend how lessons for the future can be drawn from this tragic century'.

Another sobering thought for Berlin is that during 1999 and 2000 the Government will reclaim the city as Germany's capital. With such weighty issues in mind, Berlin has organised some thoughtful events to run alongside more lively parties for which the city is famous.

New Year's Eve Parties (31 Dec 1999 – 1 Jan 2000)

Two distinguished Berlin hotels have announced New Year's Eve parties. The *Hotel Brandenburger-Hof* (☎ 30-21 40 50) and the *Kempinski* (☎ 30-88 43 40) are both working on extravagant plans. The Kempinski's entertainment may include a night flight across Berlin.

❑ BERLIN – A BRIEF GUIDE

Berlin is an extraordinary city. Although the wall which divided the city for 40 years was pulled down in November 1989, there is still a sense of separation. The East is characterised by sombre Soviet-style architecture and grandiose monuments; the West suffered heavy war damage in 1945 but has been extensively redeveloped. Today further development is gradually uniting the city and preparing it for its role as the home of German government in 1999.

What to See

Berlin's most enduring landmark is the **Brandenburg Gate**. The triumphal arch was built in 1788, but in this century came to be seen as a symbol of Nazi Germany and, later, characterised a divided Germany because of its position in 'No Man's Land' between East and West. For a glimpse of life with The Wall, go to the **House at Checkpoint Charlie** which has been turned into a fascinating museum.

Another building to feature strongly in Germany's recent history is the **Reichstag**. This parliament building was set on fire in 1933 in a Nazi propaganda stunt and was bombed in the war. More recently it has been restored and internally re-designed by British architect Norman Foster.

For a great view across Berlin, head for the **TV Tower** in Alexanderplatz which has a viewing platform some 350 feet up.

Where to Stay

● **Expensive** (over DM350): The *Kempinski Hotel Bristol Berlin* (☎ 30-88 43 40, fax 30-883 60 75), Kurfürstendamm 27, and the *Brandenburger Hof* (☎ 30-2 14 05-0, fax 30-2 14 05-100), Eislebener Strasse 14, are organising New Year's Eve 1999 parties; *Alsterhof Ringhotel* (☎ 30-21 24 20, fax 30-2 18 39 49), Augsburger Strasse 5; *Grand Hotel* (☎ 30-20 27-0, fax 30-20 27 34 19), Friedrichstrasse 158-164; *Inter-Continental* (☎ 30-260 20, fax 30-260 28 07 60), Budapester Strasse 2.

● **Moderate** (between DM200-350): *Hotel Avantgarde* (☎ 30-882 64 66, fax 30-882 40 11), Kurfürstendamm 15; *Concept Hotel* (☎ 30-884 26 0, fax 30-884 26 500), Grolmanstrasse 41-43; *Best Western Hotel Euro-Consul* (☎ 30-61 38 20, fax 30-61 38 22 22), Sonnenallee 6; *Hotel Unter den Linden* (☎ 30-23 81 10, fax 30-23 81 11 00), Unter den Kinden 14; *Holiday Inn Berlin-Kurfürstendamm* (☎ 30-88 09 30, fax 30-88 09 39 39) Bleibtreustrasse 25.

Where to Stay (cont)
Hotel Sylter Hof Berlin (☎ 30-21 200, fax 30-21 42 826),
Kurfürstendamm 114-116; Residenz Berlin (☎ 30-88 44 30, fax 30-882 47 26), Meinekestrasse 9.
● **Budget** (up to DM200)*Hotel-Pension Schöneberg* (☎ 30-781 88 30, fax 30-21 30 3-160), Hauptstrasse 135; *Hotel-Pension Dittberner* (☎ 30-881 64 85, fax 30-885 40 46), Wielandstrasse 26; *Hotel Belvedere* (☎ 30-82 60 010, fax 30-826 00 1-63), Seebergsteig 4; *Karl-Renner-Haus* (☎ 30-833 50 29, fax 30-833 91 57), Ringstrasse 76-77; *Haus Vier Jahreszeiten* (☎ 30-873 20 14, fax 30-873 82 23), Bundesallee 31; *Studentenhostel* (☎ 30-784 67 20, fax 30-788 15 23), Meiniger St. 10.

Party Places
There's a clear difference between clubs in west Berlin and those to the east; the best are in the west but often the most interesting are to the east. Clubs usually get going late – around 11pm or midnight – and are generally cheaper than Londoners or New Yorkers might expect. For listings buy the unfortunately-named *Zitty* magazine or the English-language *Checkpoint*.

City Celebrations: Berlin (31 Dec 1999)
An outdoor spectacular is planned around the city-centre, with fireworks and street parties leading the celebrations. Live bands and DJs will perform from stages around the Brandenburg Gate.

New Year's Eve 1999 Party and Tour: Berlin
A Gala Party will be held on 31 December 1999 at the Charlottenburg Palace in Berlin. The Millennial Foundation (see p137) will connect the event to 30 other party sites around the world as part of a global millennium telecast. Charlottenburg Palace was built in 1695 for Queen Sophie Charlotte. It is a magnificent and fitting place in which to welcome the year 2000.

A six-day tour of Berlin – including tickets for the celebration at Charlottenburg – is available from the Millennial Foundation. Visitors will experience both East and West Berlin. The first three nights will be spent at the Cecilienhof Castle at Potsdam made famous as the site of the 1945 Potsdam

Conference when Churchill, Stalin and Truman met at the centre of the destroyed Third Reich to stamp their authority on the post-war decisions made at Yalta. The last three nights will be spent at the Four Seasons Hotel in Friedrichstadt. Price: £1750.

Contact: Millennial Foundation (☎ +44 (0) 141-204 2000, fax +44 (0) 141-248 1591, Internet: http://www.yes2000.co.uk), 10 Sandyford Place, Glasgow, G3 7NB, UK.

'Heritage of our Age' Lecture Cycle: Berlin (14 May 1996 – 2001)

Together with the Einstein Forum, the Festival Organisation has arranged a five-year lecture cycle to 'do the groundwork for crossing the threshold of the 21st century'. The main theme is the contribution science has made to social development.

Seven Hills Exhibition: Berlin (16 April-15 Oct 2000)

This *Theatrum Mundi* will map out the future and form Berlin's central millennium exhibition. Visions of the future will be projected through new media, creating what the Seven Hills organisers hope will be a 'festival of the senses'.

It's hoped the festival will be staged at Schlossplatz – the midpoint between the former East and West blocks of Berlin.

Open Season: Berlin (Summer 2000)

All state and state-funded institutions will stay open 24-hours a day throughout the summer of 2000. It is hoped that this ambitious programme will boost Berlin's cultural life at the outset of its new role as the capital of Germany.

DRESDEN
Millennium Tour to Dresden and Prague (26 Dec 1999 – 2 Jan 2000)

US millennium-specialists Maupintour (☎ +1 800-255 4266) are offering a two-centre trip to Dresden and Prague to see in the year 2000. New Year's Eve will be spent in Prague. This choice of cities is an interesting one; both have played significant roles in 20th century history. Dresden was a centre of art and culture and one of the most beautiful cities in Germany until it suffered heavy bombing during 1945. It is still one of the most interesting cities in Eastern Europe and, after reunification, again became the capital of Saxony. Also part of this tour, Prague (capital of the Czech Republic) is one the most beautiful cities in Europe. Unlike Dresden, Prague survived World War Two with very little physical damage. In winter, when snow is common , Prague is a fairytale city. It will be a wonderful setting for New Year's Eve 1999, and it is also a European City of Culture in the year 2000.

MUNICH
Millennium Tour (27 Dec 1999 – 2 Jan 2000)
Maupintour is also offering a six-day millennial tour to Munich which will include a New Year's Eve 1999 streetcar party. This is a good trip to take if you plan to wash the second millennium down with plenty of beer; Munich is the third largest producer of beer in the world, and there will be plenty of it on offer at the New Year's Eve party.

A US$850 per person deposit is required to reserve a place on any of these tours. **Contact:** Maupintour (☎ +1 800-255 4266).

❏ **Swiss Accuracy**

OK, so the third millennium really starts on 1 January 2001. Most countries have decided to ignore that because the change from 1999 to 2000 *feels* more significant. This global error has annoyed two countries which have formed an unlikely alliance in their desire to wait until 31 December 2000 before the big party: Australia (see p50) and Switzerland.

Australians have been asked by their Prime Minister to wait for the real millennium before they let rip. Few are expected to heed that advice, however, and several events are being planned for New Year's Eve 1999.

The Swiss, on the other hand, are sticking to the rules – and so they should. Switzerland has an enviable reputation for accuracy which would surely be damaged by premature partying. There is a price to pay: on 31 December 2000 Switzerland will be partying alone.

Austria

For centuries, Austrians have waltzed their way into the New
Year through a series of balls and concerts. This is the place to go
for a stylish start to 2000.

VIENNA

Vienna has developed a reputation for being one of the world's
New Year's Eve capitals, drawing thousands of visitors from less
celebratory climes.

The Imperial Ball: Vienna (31 Dec 1999)

Vienna's Hofburg Palace, once the winter residence of Austrian
Emperors, is the setting for an opulent New Year's Eve Imperial
Ball every year. This event will be one of the more sophisticated
Millennium's Eve parties in Vienna

On arrival, guests can watch the changing of the guard while
ladies are presented with gifts by footmen clad in full imperial

---

❑ **AUSTRIA**
Contacts
● **Vienna Tourist Board** (☎ 1-211 14 0, fax 1-216 84 92), Obere
Augartenstrasse 40, A-1025, Vienna
Average maximum temperature °C

	Dec	Jan
Vienna	3	1

Capital: Vienna
Flight times: to Vienna from:
      LA: 13 hours
      London: 2 hours 15 minutes
      Sydney: 23 hours
Approximate exchange rates: Austrian Shilling (ATS or Sch) –
£1=21, US$1=12.8, A$1=8.5
Time difference: GMT +1
Country dialling code: ☎ 43

regalia. A gala banquet or buffet then takes place. The actual ball is in the magnificent State Apartments. Bands and orchestras will entertain guests in the Festival Hall. Midnight will be marked by the sound of the bell from St Stephan's Cathedral. This being Vienna, stars from the State Opera will then perform Viennese operettas into the New Year.

Tickets: Prices are likely to range from between 2000 and 6000 ATS and will be available from: Hofburg Congress Centre (☎ 1-587 36 66 23, fax 1-587 55 71 249), Heidenplatz, PO Box 113, A-1014, Vienna.

New Year's Trail

Downtown Vienna really is a great place to be when the clock strikes midnight on 31 December. The **New Year's Trail** is a two-kilometre stretch of celebrations through the city centre.

Every year the streets are packed with stalls, stages and, of course, waltzers. There are even **waltzing lanes** set aside specifically for twinkle-toed frolickers. You can have free waltz lessons on **Neuer Markt**.

Younger party-goers, however, can easily avoid Strauss; every type of musical taste is catered for among the numerous stages in the trail area.

❏ **Vienna's Ball Season (Jan-Feb 2000)**
The Ball Season is a well-established tradition in Vienna. It dates back hundreds of years. All sorts of balls take place during January and February, ranging from the Flower Ball to the Physician's Ball – in fact there are over two hundred in the Ball Calendar. One of the more promising is the Magician's Ball. There doesn't appear to be a Secret Policemen's Ball.

Keen ball-goers might want to wait around after the Imperial Ball for the equally impressive **Opera Ball**, held in February in the Vienna State Opera House. More information about this notable society event can be found from: Opernball-Büro (☎ 1-514 44 26 06, fax 1-514 44 26 24), Goethegasse 1, A-1010 Vienna.

There will also be Viennese Balls in both the **Bristol** and **Imperial** luxury hotels (see Where to Stay, p88).

❏ VIENNA – A BRIEF GUIDE

For generations Vienna has been one of the great capitals of Europe as the economic, cultural and political centre of the **Habsburg Empire**. It is rich in historical associations and the striking monuments reflect its importance. Yet Vienna has a warmth and liveliness that promises well for the millennium celebrations to be held here.

What to See

Some better-known attractions include: the **Opera House**, a magnificent neo-renaissance complex, the **Winter Riding School**, home of the world-famous **Lipizzaner horses**, and **Karlskirche**, a stunning baroque church built in gratitude for deliverance from the plague in the 18th century.

An air of grandeur surrounds Vienna, nowhere more so than at the **Belvedere**. Two palaces face each other across a stately garden which is full of intriguing references to classical mythology.

The **Burgtheater**, one of the world's most impressive auditoriums, is a star attraction. The splendour betrays little of its troubled past. It began life in 1741 but was rebuilt in 1888. Some 11 years later it was revealed that several seats had no view and the theatre was forced to close. In 1945 it was bombed.

The **Museum of Applied Arts** is one of Vienna's most respected museums. It maps Austrian art and design through the centuries. To relax after pounding the Viennese pavements, head for the **Prater** woods and parkland. Prater includes a fair and giant Ferris Wheel (see p90).

Where to Stay

Several top hotels have close links with, or are recommended by, the Imperial Ball organisers. These include the *Bristol*, *Imperial* and less expensive *Alpha*.

● **Expensive** (over 1500 ATS): the *Bristol* (☎ 1-515 160, fax 1-515 16 550), Kärntner Ring 1, is one of Vienna's most sumptuous hotels; *Imperial* (☎ 1-501 100, fax 1-501 10 410), Kärntner Ring 16, is *the* place to stay if you can afford it. Both hotels are operated by ITT Sheraton and have adopted a policy of accepting only 7-11 night stays around New Year's Eve 1999 owing to the high demand for rooms; *Inter-Continental Wien* (☎ 1-711 22 0, fax 1-713 44 89), Johannesgasse 28.

Where to Stay (cont)
Radisson SAS Palais Hotel (☎ 1-51 51 70, fax 1-51 22 216),
Parkring 16; *Vienna Hilton* (☎ 1-717 00, fax 1-713 06 91), Am
Stadtpark; *Ambassador* (☎ 1-51 46 6, fax 1-51 3 29 99), Kärntner
Strasse 22; *De France* (☎ 1-313 68 0, fax 1-319 59 69),
Schottenring 3; *Holiday Inn Crowne Plaza* (☎ 1-727 77, fax 1-727
77-199), Handelskai 269.
● **Moderate** (between 800-1500 ATS): *Arenberg* (☎ 1-512 52 91,
fax 1-513 9356), Stubenring 2; *Altsadt Vienna* (☎ 1-526 33 990,
fax 1-523 4901), Kirchengrasse 41; *Alpha* (☎ 1-319 16 46, fax 1-
319 42 16), Doltzmanngasse 8; *Capri* (☎ 1-214 84 04, fax 1-214 27
85), Praterstrasse 44-46; *Müllner Landgasthof* (☎ 1-774 27 26, fax
1-774 27 26-21), Esslinger Hauptstrasse 82; *Stasta* (☎ 1-865 97 88,
fax 1-865 97 88-35), Lehmanngasse 11; *Viktoria* (☎ 1-877 55 36,
fax 1-87 804 3220), Eduard-Klein-Gasse 9; *Zur Stadthalle* (☎ 1-
982 42 72, fax 1-982 41 05), Hackengasse 20.
● **Budget** (under 800 ATS): *Am Operneck* (☎ 1-512 93 10),
Kärnter Strasse 47; *Felicitas* (☎ 1-405 72 12), Josefsgasse 7;
Mozart (☎/fax 1-587 85 05), Theobaldgasse 15; *Orient* (☎ 1-533 73
07, fax 1-535 03 40), Tiefer Graben 30-32; *Stadt Bamberg* (☎ 1-
893 42 87, fax 1-892 78 51), Mariahilfer Strasse 167; *Wild* (☎ 1-
406 5174, fax 1-402 2168), Lange Gasse 10.

Party Places
The area in 1st District around St Rupert's Church is packed with
bars, clubs and restaurants. It's called the Viennese Bermuda
Triangle because it sucks in party-goers. On New Year's Eve 1999
you can be sure this area will be fantastic.

Some of the city's more fashionable clubs include: *Metropol* at
17 Hernalser Hauptstrasse 55; *Szene Wien* at 11 Hauffgrasse 26;
Arena at 3 Baumgasse 80 and *Rockhaus* at 20 Adalbert-Stifter-
Strasse 73. Other good dance clubs are: *P1* at 1 Rotgasse 9;
Nachtwerk at 23 Dr-Gonda-Gasse 9 and *Atrium* at 4 Schwind-
gasse 4.

The better bars include: *Los Tequilas* at 7 Kirchengasse 35
which boasts over 50 types of the Mexican liquor; *Andino* at 6
Münzwardeingasse 2 with a Latin American feel; *Oskar* at 1
Concordiaplatz and *Trabant* at 4 Schleifmühlgasse 13 for an East
German experience.

New Year's Eve Party: Vienna (31 Dec 1999)
ITT Sheraton are planning a grand millennium party in the **Palais Ferstel** conference centre. **Contact:** Andreas Bienenstein, Marketing Manager, Imperial Hotel (☎ 1-501 100, fax 1-501 10 410).

New Year's Concerts: Vienna (31 Dec 1999)
Perhaps the most celebrated aspect of Vienna's festivities are the **New Year Concerts**. These take place on New Year's Eve and New Year's Day as the illustrious Vienna Symphony and Vienna Hofburg Orchestras perform Strauss to see out the old year – or millennium – and Beethoven's Ninth Symphony, the *Ode to Joy*, to welcome the new. The two orchestras perform separately, and it should be possible to see both.

    Contact: Vienna Symphony Orchestra (☎ 1-712 12 11, fax 1-712 28 72); Vienna Hofburg Orchestra (☎ 1-587 52 09, fax 1-587 43 97).

Millennium Tour: Vienna (29 Dec 1999 – 2 Jan 2000)
Goodwood Travel (+44 (0) 1227-763336) is offering a three-night trip to Vienna by Concorde, with accommodation at the Marriott Hotel. Tickets to the Imperial Ball (see p86) are included. Price: £2695 (in 1998 – will be higher in 1999).

❑ **Wheels of Time**

Even before Vienna's Giant Ferris Wheel, or *Riesenrad*, was immortalised in the film of Graham Greene's *The Third Man*, it had become one of the city's most familiar landmarks. It was built at the end of the last century to a design by Englishman Walter B Basset, and is still highly popular one hundred years on.

    A giant British Airways Millennium Wheel will create a similar feature in London (see p117). It's hoped the Millennium Wheel will give Londoners the chance to admire a complete panorama of their city, a pleasure which is regularly enjoyed in Vienna.

    The last hundred years have seen fast progress in the heady world of wheels, however, and London's attraction, at 150 metres, will dwarf the 65-metre wheel in Vienna. In fact, Britain's Millennium Wheel will be the tallest in the world.

Millennium Tour: Vienna (21 Dec 1999 – 3 Jan 2000)
The American travel firm Travcoa is offering this two-week tour to Geneva, Zermatt, St Moritz and, in time for New Year's Eve, Vienna. Tickets to the famous Imperial Ball at the Hofburg Palace (see p86) will be included. The land only price – which could change – will be at least US$9995. **Contact:** (☎ +1 714-476 2800 or 800-992 2003 for a toll-free call from within the States).

❏ UNESCO 2000

The United Nations Educational, Scientific and Cultural Organisation, based in Paris, is backing several major millennial initiatives as well as naming Avignon, Bergen, Bologna, Brussels, Cracow, Helsinki, Prague, Reykjavik and Santiago de Compostela European Cities of Culture in the year 2000.

Education for the 21st Century
This is a project which aims to encourage member states to adopt the education principles of the International Commission on Education for the 21st Century. UNESCO hopes governments will use the new millennium to renew and revise education methods.

World Conference on Science for the 21st Century
The conference will be held in 1999 with the help of the International Council of Scientific Unions. The conference will analyse the contributions and impact of science and will promote scientific cooperation between nations. Delegates will also discuss the environment and the future of natural resources.

Heritage 2000
Heritage 2000 is an international network of universities which will work to protect heritage on a national and international level. A cultural festival and symposium will be produced by Heritage 2000 in the year 2000.

Other projects
UNESCO is also joining forces with other organisations to produce millennium events. These include the **Valencia Third Millennium Project** (see p110), **Yes 2000** from the Millennial Foundation (see p137), **Bethlehem 2000** (see p54) and **Santiago de Compostela 2000** (see p108). **Contact:** UNESCO, 7 Place de Fontenoy, 75352 Paris 07SP, France

Russia

MILLENNIUM TOURS TO RUSSIA

Scotland's Millennial Foundation (see p137) is offering tours to millennium celebrations in **St Petersburg** and **Moscow** – both will be part of a 24-hour global telecast planned by the Foundation for New Year's Eve 1999.

The St Petersburg tour includes accommodation at the imposing Grand Hotel on Nevsky Prospect and admission to a gala party and dinner which will feature a performance by the Kirov Ballet. Moscow's celebrations will headline a performance by the Bolshoi Ballet. Guests will stay at the Hotel Metropol. Both tours last six-days and cost £1750. **Contact:** Millennial Foundation (☎ +44 (0) 141-204 2000, fax +44 (0) 141-248 1591, Internet: http://www.yes 2000.co.uk), 10 Sandyford Place, Glasgow G3 7NB, UK.

Maupintour (☎ +1 800-255 4266) have a tour to St Petersburg from 27 Dec 1999-2 Jan 2000. Admission to a Czar's New Year's Eve Ball is included. No price has been announced yet but a US$850 per person deposit will secure a place. Steppes East (+44 (0) 1285 810267) has a four-night trip to St Petersburg with a black-tie New Year's Eve event at a royal palace and accommodation at the Grand Hotel Europe. Price: £1500.

❑ **Party in the Wilds of France**

Years ago a group of friends agreed to meet at a café in Florac (a small town in Southern France) at 8pm on New Year's Eve 1999 to see in the new millennium together. But their idea has grown – considerably. There will now be a music festival and New Year's Eve party out in the wilds near Florac with several stages and a state-of-the-art sound and light system. Revellers will still meet at the Café du Commerce in Florac at 8pm on 31 December 1999.

Contact: Internet http://home.worldnet.fr//jjeee/JEE.htm or e-mail jjeee@ worldnet.fr.

France

A group called Célébration 2000 has been formed to plan millennium events outside Paris but so far millennium celebrations in France are heavily focused on the capital. The approach of the next millennium has highlighted a light-hearted rivalry between Paris and London. Both cities want to greet the year 2000 with more flair than the other.

PARIS

The climax of French millennium celebrations will be the birth of a giant egg from the Eiffel Tower while the Place Charles de Gaulle, with its 12 converging avenues, is transformed into a

---

❏ **FRANCE**
Contacts
● **Office de Tourisme** (☎ 1-49 52 53 54), 127 avenues des Champs-Elysées, 8e, Paris
● **Mission Paris 2000** (☎ 1-42 76 73 90), 32 quai des Célestins, 75004 Paris
● **Celebration 2000** (☎ 1-53 71 20 00, fax 1-53 71 20 01, **Internet** http://www.celebration2000.gouv.fr), 36 rue Lacépède, 75005 Paris
Average maximum temperature °C

	Dec	Jan
Paris	7	6

Capital: Paris
Flight times: to Paris from:
　　　　LA – 15 hrs
　　　　London – 1 hr 10 mins
　　　　Sydney – 25 hrs
Approximate exchange rates: French Franc (FF) – £1=9.8, US$1=6.2, A$1=4.1
Time difference: GMT +1
Country dialling code: ☎ 33

giant clock face. This unusual mix of the bizarre and the subtle will make Paris an interesting millennium destination. See p97 for a brief guide to Paris and where to stay.

New Year's Eve Party: Paris (31 Dec 1999)

Thousands will gather in the Parc du Champ de Mars for the best millennium party in France. The **Eiffel Tower**, which stands at the north-west end of the park, is to be the centre of millennium celebrations in Paris. The Tower will also be the focus of a massive *son et lumière* spectacle leading up to midnight on 31 December 1999.

Before midnight, a colossal **egg** will be delivered from the belly of the Tower in an act of rather obvious imagery. It will then hatch to reveal a bank of TV screens which will show footage of other millennium celebrations from across the globe. The egg-birth is to be accompanied by 2000 drummers beating a 'millennial rhythm'. At precisely seven minutes before midnight, the entire area will be bathed in light so powerful it will appear to be day. After midnight, the party will continue, and the egg will be used to send and receive friendly e-mails to and from other countries.

Millennium Countdown Clock: Paris (31 Dec 1999)

When it comes to lighting up buildings, the French are past-masters. On New Year's Eve 1999, a highly imaginative scheme will transform the Place Charles de Gaulle into a colossal clock face.

Twelve avenues converge on the square in a regular pattern. Paris is the only city in the world to have such a useful feature with which it can create the most impressive countdown clock in the world.

The second hand will be a powerful laser light which will sweep the city from the top of the Arc de Triomphe. The hour hand will be one of the twelve avenues, lit up to 300 metres from the centre. The second hand will be marked by whichever avenue is lit to 500 metres in a different colour. At midnight, the countdown will climax with a sensational light show and party around the Arc de Triomphe.

The Book of Capitals: Paris (1 Sep 1999 – 1 Sep 2000)

An enormous book is to be built in front of the City Hall in Paris. *Le Livre Capitales* will sit on a slowly revolving plinth. Its 200 square metre pages will address weighty issues in the worlds of art, science and philosophy – a different theme tackled each day. The book will be written in French and English.

Millennium Sundial: Paris (21 June – 22 Sep 2000)

In 1913, the founder of the Astronomical Society of France, Camille Flammarion, attempted to turn the Place de la Concorde into a giant sundial. The First World War prevented him, but the project has now been revived.

Between the summer solstice and the autumn equinox 2000, the great Egyptian obelisk in the the Place de la Concorde will form the gnonom (pointer) of a massive sundial which will be marked out around the square.

This is a particularly appropriate project, since the sundial was probably man's first clock.

Tower of the Earth Millennium Project: Paris

When Monsieur Eiffel presented his plans for an enormous tower, he was no doubt greeted by a certain amount of suspicion. Architect Monsieur Normier will face similar scepticism with his plans for the Tower of the Earth.

The idea behind the 650-metre tower is to create a landmark for Paris which represents the city's modernity – as did the Eiffel Tower when it was built in 1889. In 1889 modernity meant indus-

---

❏ **Pollution by Perfume**

There is an element of the bizarre in the way the French plan to welcome the next millennium. One can (just) understand why the Eiffel Tower should lay an egg – and why a gargantuan tree should be built. But perfuming the Seine? During an international celebration of perfume in 2000, eau de toilette will be poured into the Seine. That should go down well with the 2000-strong shoal of brightly-lit plastic fish which is to be introduced to the river. There are even plans to tip the contents of an over-sized perfume bottle into space.

try. Now, it's argued, the environment is the great theme of our age. The tower will be built from wood and mock-pine and will resemble a tree. There will be four levels for exhibitions, concerts, restaurants, meeting places and broadcasting. At the top will sit a flower-like structure which will have five petals, each some 700 square metres.

It is hoped the tower will be a symbol of the need for conservation. Let's hope they don't use too many trees to make it! An annual Earth Prize will be awarded to make sure the meaning of the tower is not lost on future generations.

Other millennium celebrations in Paris

Giant eggs and trees have taken attention away from several other worthwhile millennium projects planned for Paris. These include: the beautifying of the banks of the River Seine, which will also be made more accessible to pedestrians; an immense hour-glass will be built; a city-wide parade called Hello 2000 is planned to launch the celebrations; three tethered balloons will sit 150 metres above the city; anyone who's 20 in 2000 is to receive a card entitling them to various perks around Paris and a music festival in the style of Woodstock will be held in 1999.

Millennium Tour: Paris (21 or 26 Dec 1999 – 3 Jan 2000)

Travcoa has devised a 9- or 14-day millennium tour to Vienna and Prague which will reach Paris in time for New Year's Eve 1999. For those on the longer trip, Christmas will be spent in Vienna. The estimated land-only price is US$6395 or US$9995. That price could go up.

Contact: (☎ +1 714-476 2800 or 800-992 2003 which is toll-free in America).

Millennium Tour: Paris (27 Dec 1999 – 2 Jan 2000)

As part of its extensive millennium brochure, US tour operator Maupintour is offering a six-day holiday in Paris which will include accommodation at the Hotel Scribe and a New Year's Eve 1999 party. The price has not been announced, but a US$850 per person deposit will secure a place. **Contact:** (☎ +1 800-255 4266).

❏ PARIS – A BRIEF GUIDE

Paris is divided into 20 *arrondissements*, or districts, each with a distinct character of its own. Wandering along the banks of the Seine from the 4er arrondissement to the 1er is, perhaps, the best way to appreciate the infinite variety that is the French capital.

What to See

The 4er arrondissement includes much of **Le Marais** (the Swamp), which is crowded with galleries and cafés. This area has traditionally been the haunt of artists, writers and architects. The Musée Picasso is nearby in the 3er arrondissement.

The real jewels of the 4er are the two islands in the Seine. **Notre-Dame**, the **Sainte-Chapelle** and **Conciergerie** are on the wonderful **Ile de la Cité**. This is also a great place to go to eat. On both banks of the river, and on the Ile de la Cité, there are hundreds of restaurants. Some are tourist traps – allowing their great location to make up for not-so-great food. But most are excellent; food in France is seldom poor.

Townhouses and boutiques occupy the other island, the **Ile St-Louis**. This former cow pasture is now home to 6000 Louisiens who enjoy what must be the best address in Paris. Also in the 4er is the **Centre Georges Pompidou** which has unexpectedly become the third most visited attraction in France. This famous inside-out structure houses a fine collection of modern art. Equally engaging are the many street performers in the square in front. A brightly-lit clock sits behind the Centre counting down to the year 2000.

Following the Seine west, one arrives in the 1er arrondissement, which is the cultural epicentre of Paris. The enormous **Musée du Louvre** is here, sitting at the head of **Les Jardins des Tuileries**. These formal gardens provide a much-needed haven from the rather intense atmosphere which surrounds the Louvre. So many people come to see this world-famous art gallery that it can be quite a battle just getting in.

The **Musée d'Orsay**, formerly a railway station, contains an impressive collection of art from the mid 19th to the early 20th centuries, including works by Delacroix, the Impressionists, Van Gogh, Cézanne and Matisse.

Shoppers should head for **Les Halles**, the old meat market of Paris which is now home to hundreds of upmarket boutiques.

Hackneyed it may be, but no trip to Paris would be complete without taking in the view from the top of the **Eiffel Tower** in the

Paris – What to See (cont)

7e arrondissement. This extraordinary landmark is strangely beautiful, and the panorama stunning. You do need a head for heights; the elevator ride to the top is rather alarming.

The **8e arrondissement** is impressive in a sort of grand and imperial way, but not as entertaining as other less self-conscious parts of Paris. The **Place de la Concorde**, with its giant Egyptian obelisk/sundial pointer, sits at one end of the elegant but expensive **Champs-Elysées** which extends as far as the **Arc de Triomphe**. Crossing the road to the Arc de Triomphe is the most exhilarating lottery in Europe – but the stakes are high!

A seedier but livelier time can be had in the **Opéra Garnier**, **Pigalle** and **Montmartre** area in the 9e and 18e arrondissements. Between the strip clubs and dark bars of Pigalle there are glimpses of a grander past. This area also has great restaurants and nightlife. Once the picturesque home of a thriving artists' community, Montmartre is now over-populated with both tourists and caricaturists. But only the most jaded traveller could fail to love it. Where else could the **Basilica of Sacré-Coeur** and the **Moulin Rouge** be near neighbours? A word of warning: the restaurants here might offer some of the most romantic settings in town, but the food is always over-priced and often inferior. A few steps away from the centre of Montmartre takes one to quieter streets where fewer francs will buy much more.

Paris is a fruitful city for those who harbour a morbid fascination with dead celebrities. The grandiose **Père-Lachaise Cemetery** in the 20e arrondissement counts such illustrious figures as Wilde, Proust, Balzac, Molière and Jim Morrison among its residents.

Where to Stay

● **Expensive** (over 1400FF) *Hôtel Costes* (☎ 01-42 44 50 00, fax 01-42 44 50 01), 239 rue St-Honoré; *Hôtel Concorde St-Lazare* (☎ 01-40 08 44 44), 108 rue St-Lazare; *Hôtel de Crillon* (☎ 01-44 71 15 00), 10 place de la Concorde; *George V* (☎ 01-47 23 54 00), 31 av. George V; *Lancaster* (☎ 01-40 76 40 76, fax 01-40 76 40 00), 7 rue de Berri; *Hôtel de Louvre* (☎ 01-44 58 38 38), place André-Malraux; *Hôtel Meurice* (☎ 01-44 58 10 10), 228 rue de Rivoli; *Le Montalembert* (☎ 01-45 49 68 68, fax 01-45 49 69 49), 3 rue de Montalembert; *Paris Marriott Hôtel Champs-Elysées* (☎ 01-53 93 55 00, fax 01-53 93 55 01), 70 av. des Champs-Elysées; *Plaza Athéné* (☎ 01-47 23 78 33), 23-27 av. Montaigne.

Paris – Where to Stay (cont)
Prince de Galles (☎ 01-47 23 55 11), 33 av. George V; *La Raphaël* (☎ 01-44 28 00 28, fax 01-45 01 21 50), 17 av. Kléber; *Hôtel Regina* (☎ 01-42 60 31 10), place des Pyramides; *Ritz* (☎ 01-43 16 30 30), 15 place Vendôme; *Westminster* (☎ 01-42 61 57 46), 13 rue de la Paix.

● **Moderate** (between 550-1400FF) *Hôtel Baudelaire Opéra* (☎ 01-42 97 50 62, fax 01-42 86 85 85), 61 rue Ste-Anne; *Hôtel Belle-Epoque* (☎ 01-43 44 06 66, fax 01-43 44 10 25), M Ledru-Rollin; *Hôtel Burgundy* (☎ 01-42 60 34 12, fax 01-47 03 95 20), 8 rue Duphot; *Hôtel Caron de Beaumarchais* (☎ 01-42 72 34 12, fax 01-42 72 34 63), 12 rue Vieille-du-Temple; *Hôtel l'Horset Opéra* (☎ 01-44 71 87 00, fax 01-42 66 55 54), 18 rue d'Antin; *Résidence Lord Byron* (☎ 01-43 59 89 98), 5 rue de Chateaubriand; *Hôtel de Lutèce* (☎ 01-43 26 23 52), 65 rue St-Louis-en-L'Ile;*Hôtel Relais Médici La Villa* (☎ 01-43 26 60 00, fax 01-46 34 63 63), 29 rue Jacob; *Grand Hôtel de Turenne* (☎ 01-42 78 43 25, fax 01-42 74 10 72), 6 rue de Turenne.

● **Budget** (under 550FF) *Hôtel Amiral Duperré* (☎ 01-42 81 55 33, fax 01-44 63 04 73), 32 rue Duperré; *Auberge de Jeunesse Le d'Artagnan* (☎ 01-40 32 34 56, fax 01-40 32 34 55), 80 rue Vitruve; *Brittanique* (☎ 01-42 33 74 59), 20 av. Victoria; *Hôtel Henri IV* (☎ 01-43 54 44 53), 25 pl Dauphine; *Mars Hôtel* (☎ 01-47 05 42 30, fax 01-47 05 45 91), 117 av. de la Bourdonnais; *Hôtel Montpensier* (☎ 01-42 96 28 50, fax 01-42 86 02 70), 12 rue de Richelieu; *Hôtel Pratic* (☎ 01-48 87 80 47, fax 01-48 87 40 04), 9 rue d'Ormesson; *Hôtel Regyn's Montmartre* (☎ 01-42 54 45 21, fax 01-42 23 76 69), 24 rue Lamarck; *Hôtel du Quai-Voltaire* (☎ 01-42 61 50 91), 10 quai Voltaire; *YWCA* (☎ 01-45 22 23 49), 22 rue Naples.

Party Places
The best way to find out what's going on in Paris is to buy the *Officiel des Spectacles* entertainment manual or *Pariscope* magazine. Clubs in Paris have suffered recently at the hands of police raids and bad press. Don't worry, there are plenty of cool clubs and late-night bars around. Try: *Les Bains*, 7 rue du Bourg-l'Abbe; *Bartók*, 64 rue de Charenton; *Le Divan du Monde*, 75 rue des Martyrs; *Elysée Montmartre*, 72 bd. Rochechouart; *La Locomotive*, 90 bd. de Clichy; *Le Néo*, 21 rue Montorgueil; *Le Palace*, 8 rue du Faubourg; *What's Up Bar*, 15 rue Daval.

❏ Will there be enough bubbly?

Since Dom Pérignon perfected the art of champagne making in the 17th century, bubbly has been the stuff of celebrations and a symbol of extravagance. But champagne can only come from the Champagne region of France, so production is limited. With the biggest bash of all time fast-approaching, people are starting to wonder...will the party run dry?

The answer: probably not. The Champagne Information Bureau is keen to point out that something like 1000 million bottles are currently rolling around in storage. In fact, champagne companies have been over-producing for some years. Around 400 million bottles will probably go down the world's collective hatch on New Year's Eve 1999. Rumours of champagne shortages may well have been circulated by rogue businesses trying to sell champagne as an investment opportunity.

Most champagne is non-vintage; that means made by blending the most recent year's harvest with some reserve wines from previous years. For many, though, the new millennium will warrant 'a drop of the good stuff'. Vintage champagne comes from an especially good year and is made from wines only of that year.

While it seems extremely unlikely that revellers will run out of champagne altogether, certain exceptional vintages may well dry up. A series of disappointing years during the early nineties, together with the fact that most good producers allow their wines three years to mature before release, means that serious champagne drinkers must look to 1990 for a classic bottle. Some experts have hailed 1990 as the best year for a decade. Such accolades will, of course, push up the price. 1989 and 1988 were also vintage years. Going back further, wines from 1985, 1982 and 1979 are all well worthy of the occasion.

If your palate, and wallet, will accept only the most exclusive bubbly, then several champagne houses offer *cuvées de prestige* – their very best. The sale of these wines was once limited to special clients, but is now much wider. Whether they really do taste better than a good vintage, however, is debatable.

There's a right way and a wrong way to open a bottle of champagne. Tip the bottle to a 45 degree angle – pointing it away from your guests – and remove the wire muzzle. Then take hold of the cork with one hand, resting your thumb on the top, and gently twist the bottle with your other hand. Allow the pressure to push the cork out slowly.

VULCANIA

Former French President Valéry Giscard d'Estaing is behind the construction of a volcano theme park which he hopes will provide the 'media event of 2000' and an apt way to mark the millennium.

Vulcania will boast a fake crater and underground auditorium in which visitors will be caught in a mock eruption. The park is being built in the Auvergene area which already has real – but dormant – volcanoes.

ROUEN
Armada 1999

The port of Rouen will host a major maritime millennial festival from 9-18 July 1999 which will bring ships to the town from all over the world.

Contact: Armada du Siècle (☎ 2-35 52 94 94, fax 2-35 15 45 45).

OTHER AREAS IN FRANCE

A Space City and planetarium are being built to mark the millennium in **Toulouse**. The new complex will host a convention on space in 2000.

Nantes will remember Jules Vernes, its most famous son, in its celebrations. Vernes-related events and exhibitions will take place throughout 2000. There are also plans to create a huge time capsule in which citizens of Nantes will be able to deposit messages and gifts for future generations. **Mont St Michel** will benefit from an ambitious millennium project to improve access to the mainland and to halt the threatening advance of salt marshes.

Avignon is one of nine European Cities of Culture in 2000. A string of cultural events will take place throughout the year. In spring the theme will be gardens, in summer the theatre, and cuisine in the autumn.

VFB Holidays (☎ +44 (0) 1242-240340) has several **country houses** and **châteaux** for hire over the Millennium's Eve period.

Monaco

Everyone knows that Monaco is the playground of the rich and famous. It's less widely appreciated that one doesn't really need Bond-like luck or Grimaldi-style wealth to enjoy this tiny territory – although it would help!

The sumptuous **Monte Carlo Casino** costs just 50FF to enter and, once inside, slot machines start at 1FF. Admittedly, food and accommodation in the world's most glamorous 1.25 square miles can cost fortune. But there are several budget one-star hotels and relatively inexpensive restaurants and cafés. In fact, prices in Monaco are about the same as those in other Riviera resorts. There's no doubt that partying into the third millennium in Monaco would be exciting. Events are planned in most of the Principality's more exclusive and expensive venues (the Casino, the Hotel Hermitage and the Hotel Loews Monte-Carlo). For those that fail to live it up at the Hotel Hermitage, there will be fireworks over the beautiful harbour and smaller parties at several clubs. A more permanent celebration of the new millennium is planned in the form of a state-of-the-art exhibition centre which is being built in time for the year 2000. It will be called the **Forum Grimaldi** after Monaco's ruling dynasty.

Two US travel companies have organised **millennium tours** to Monaco. Maupintour (☎ +1 800-255 4266) have planned a six-day trip from 27 December 1999 to 2 Jan 2000. The company has yet to announce a full itinerary or a definite price but guests can expect a good hotel and a New Year's Eve party. A US$850 per person deposit is required to secure a place on the trip. **Travcoa** (☎ +1 714-476 2800 or 800-992 2003 toll-free from within America) have arranged a European millennial tour between 21 Dec 1999 and 3 Jan 2000. The trip will take in Geneva, Zermatt and St Moritz before reaching Monte Carlo in time for New Year's Eve. The land only cost of this 2-week jaunt is expected to be at least US$9695. Travcoa are keen to point out that that price could rise.

Scandinavia

There will be two **European Cities of Culture** in Scandinavia in the year 2000: **Bergen** in Norway and **Helsinki** in Finland. Bergen (☎ +47 5555 2000, fax +47 5555 2001, e-mail bergen.2000@online.no) hopes to create 'the largest cultural celebration in Norway ever'. Bergen is to build the biggest information centre in Norway which will be called the Frescohall – so named because it will be decorated by the frescoes of Alex Revold.

Shows, exhibitions and theatre will be staged at the Frescohall throughout the year 2000 and beyond. Year 2000 events will start on 17 February. Tickets and event details will be available from 17 February 1999. Special year 2000 holiday packages will also be on offer. Helsinki 2000 (☎ +358 9-169 3208) has yet to make any plans.

If you're in **Denmark** on New Year's Eve 1999, the best place to go is Raadhuspladsen in Copenhagen where an annual street party is held.

MILLENNIUM TOURS TO SCANDINAVIA
Tauno Salo Tours (fax +358 3-653 3544) in Finland have organised two Millennium Tours.

The first, to **Kuusamo**, lasts from 28 December 1999 to 2 January 2000. Kuusamo is a real winter wonderland. The area around the town, 800 kilometres from Helsinki and close to the Russian border, has deep snow and dense forests. Various Lapland activities will be on offer, from skiing to reindeer lassoing. After a New Year's Eve dinner, guests will be taken to a camp in the wilderness where, apparently, shamans will 'declare you free from all the bad things of the nineties'. At midnight the cold night sky will be illuminated by fireworks and laser lights. Price: FLM 6454 or approximately £750 or US$1200. (International flights not included).

The second tour, to **Saariselkä**, lasts from 29 Dec 1999 to 2 Jan 2000. Saariselkä is 300 kilometres beyond the Arctic Circle and is famous for its untouched scenery and clear air. This tour is similar to the last, with activities like sled safaris and snow mobile excursions on offer. Again, the New Year's Eve party will take place outside after a celebratory meal. The outdoor venue will be illuminated by fires and the guests serenaded by a traditional Lapp choir. Champagne will be served from a bar built of ice. Fireworks will mark the arrival of 2000. Price: FLM 6454 (International flights not included).

New Year's Eve Party: World's largest igloo
On New Year's Eve 1999, the world's largest igloo – the Ice Hotel – will host a cold but unique millennium party in Swedish Lapland. An ice-bar will dispense Absolut vodka to help warm revellers. Arctic party-goers will sleep in heavy-duty sleeping bags on beds chiselled from solid ice. The hotel is built during autumn and melts the following spring. Scantours (☎ +44 (0) 171-839 2927) will offer a four-day trip to Lapland, including one night at the Ice Hotel. Prices are expected to start at around £800 per person.

Spain

Spain has a lot to celebrate. In the last decade alone, the country has seen its confidence grow in a spectacular way. Events like the Olympics – which Barcelona hosted in 1992 – have confirmed its position as a cultural centre both in Europe and beyond. As the year 2000 approaches, there is a feeling that the new century will bring further success to this sun-soaked nation.

MADRID
A series of cultural events and anniversaries is set to fall either side of what should be a great party in the centre of the capital on New Year's Eve 1999.

New Year's Eve Party: Madrid (Puerto del Sol)

Thousands turn up every New Year's Eve – or *Noche Vieja* – to hear Spain's most famous clock strike 12 in the Puerto del Sol in Madrid. On 31 Dec 1999, Puerto del Sol will be the venue for a better-than-ever party. The square will be swamped with confetti and streamers and illuminated by a spectacular fireworks display. A popular but strange Spanish custom is that of eating a grape at each stroke as the clock strikes midnight.

New Year's Eve 1999 Party: Madrid City Hall

The Mayor of Madrid is to host a major millennial party at the City Hall on New Year's Eve 1999. Scotland's Millennial Foundation will use television to link Madrid to other party sites around the world which are to form a global telecast. The party will also be linked to most of South America. Fireworks and a street party for all Madrid's citizens to enjoy will follow outside City Hall.

❑ **SPAIN**
Contacts
● **Madrid Tourist Office** (☎ 91-429 49 51, fax 91-429 09 09), Duque de Medinaceli 2, 28014-Madrid
● **Santiago de Compostela Tourist Office** (☎ 981-58 40 81), Rúa del Villar 43, 15705-Santiago de Compostela
● **Seville Tourist Office** (☎ 95-422 14 04, fax 95-422 97 53), Avenida de la Constitución 21, 41004-Sevilla
Average maximum temperature °C

	Dec	Jan
Madrid	9	9

Capital: Madrid
Flight times: to Madrid from:
    LA – 13 hrs
    London – 2 hrs
    Sydney – 29 hrs
Approximate exchange rates: Peseta (pta) – £1=254, US$1=155, A$1=103
Time difference: GMT +1
Country dialling code: ☎ 34

Millennium Anniversaries: Madrid (1998-2000)

Madrid will mark several important anniversaries towards the end of the millennium. During 1998 the 400th anniversary of King Philip II (1527-1598) will be commemorated by a series of exhibitions, concerts and theatre in Madrid, Escorial and Aranjeuz.

From 30 May-20 October 1998 the *Philip II: A Monarch and his Era* exhibition will take place at the El Escorial monastery. From June-July '98 *The Private Life of the King* exhibition will be held at the Royal Palace of Aranjuez. Madrid's Prado Museum will host the *Prince of Renaissance* exhibition from 1 October 1998-19 Jan 1999.

The Prado will then have four exhibitions to commemorate the 400th anniversary of the birth of Velázquez (1599-1660). Velázquez was a highly influential Spanish painter responsible for such works as *Pope Innocent X* (1650).

Finally, in the year 2000, the 500th anniversary of the birth of Charles V will be celebrated across Madrid. Charles V took the throne of Spain at a critical time and became a key figure in Renaissance Europe.

New Year's Eve 1999 Party and Tour: Madrid

The Millennial Foundation, which is to link the Mayor of Madrid's New Year's Eve party at City Hall to festival sites across the globe, is offering a six-day millennium tour to the Spanish capital. Price: £1750, which includes entrance to the gala celebration and accommodation at the up-market Palace Hotel. **Contact:** Millennial Foundation (☎ +44 (0) 141-204 2000, fax +44 (0) 141-248 1591, Internet: http://www.yes2000.co.uk), 10 Sandyford Place, Glasgow G3 7NB, UK.

❏ **Clock On**

The most popular New Year's Eve custom in Spain is to gather around the town or village clock at midnight. All over the country, communities will see in the new millennium together in this way.

In Madrid, thousands will welcome the year 2000 in the Puerto del Sol (see previous page).

❏ MADRID – A BRIEF GUIDE
What to See

The **Puerto del Sol**, a great place to be on New Year's Eve, is also the centre of both old Habsburg Madrid and, today, the city's transport system. This is a good place to start.

Palacio Real (the Royal Palace), to the west of Puerto del Sol, is one of the real jewels of Madrid. Built for the Bourbon Philip V, the Palace was completed in 1764 for Charles III. It is magnificent. Guided tours are available and are well worth it. Between the Palace and the Puerto del Sol is **Plaza Mayor**, the city's most impressive main square.

To the east of the Puerto del Sol are three world-class galleries which form an art triangle popularly called the **Boulevard of the Arts**. The Boulevard starts with the **Museo Thyssen-Bornemisza** next to the Plaza Canovas del Castillo. Baron Heinrich Thyssen moved his collection to Spain in the early nineties, giving Madrid one of the world's most extensive private collections.

Continuing down the Paseo del Prado one arrives at the celebrated **Museo del Prado**. The Prado is one of the richest art museums in the world and is – arguably – the most important neoclassical building in Spain. The art triangle is completed by the **Museo Nacional Centro de Arte Reina Sofía** which displays Picasso's *Guernica* among other great works by Spanish artists such as Miró and Dalí.

Where to Stay

● **Expensive** (over 19,000 ptas per room): The *Ritz* (☎ 1-521-28 56/57, fax 1-532-87 76) Plaza de la Lealtad 5 competes with the imposing *Palace* (☎ 1-360-80 00, fax 1-360-81 00) Pza. de las Cortes for celebrity clientele; *Wellington* (☎ 1-575-44 00, fax 1-576-41 64) C/ Velazquez 8; *Santa Mauro* (☎ 1-319-69 00, fax 1-308-54 77) C/ Zurbano 36; *Carlton* (☎ 1-539-71 00, fax 1-537-85 10) P Delicas 26; *Holiday Inn Madrid* (☎ 1-456-80 00, fax 1-456-80 01) Pza. Carlos Trías Beltrán; *Santo Domingo* (☎ 1-547-98 00, fax 1-547-59 95) Pza. Santo Domingo; *Gran Hotel Velázquez* (☎ 1-575-28 00, fax 1-575-77 88) C/ Velázquez 62;.

● **Moderate** (7000-19,000 ptas per room): *Best Western Cortezo* (☎ 1-369-01 01, fax 1-369-37 74) C/ Dr. Cortezo 3; *Hotel Opera* (☎ 1-541-28 00, fax 1-541-69 23) C/ Cuesta de Santo Domingo 2; *Principe Pio* (1-547-08 00/80 00, fax 1-541-11 17) Cuesta de San Vincente 16.

Where to Stay (cont)

● **Moderate** (7000-19,000 ptas per room): *Rafael Piramides* (☎ 1-517-18 28, fax 1-517 00 90) P de las Acacias 40; *Regente* (☎ 1-521-29 41, fax 1-532-30 14) C/ Mesonero Romanos 9; *Regina* (☎ 1-521-47 25, fax 1-521-47 25) C/ Alcalá 19; *Trafalgar* (☎ 1-445-62 00, fax 1-446-64 56) C/ Trafalgar 35; *San Antonio de la Florida* (☎ 1-541-80 40, fax 1-559-09 51) P de la Florida 13.

● **Budget** (under 7000 ptas per room): *Cliper* (☎ 1-531-17 00, fax 1-531-17 07) C/ Chinchilla 6; *Hotel Europa* (☎ 1-521-29 00, fax 1-521 46 96) C/ Carmen 4; *Hotel Nuria* (☎ 1-531-92 08/07/06, fax 1-532-90 05) C/ Fuencarral 52; *Hotel Persal* (☎ 1-369-46 43, fax 1-369-19 52) Pza. del Angel 12; *Hotel Luis XV* (☎ 1-531-95 02, fax 1-521-43 94) Montera 47; *Felipe V* (☎ 1-531-00 49, fax 1-522-57 96) C/ Gran Via 15; *Chocolate* (☎ 1-543-83 23, fax 1-549-84 95) C/ Joaquín Maria López 29; *Hostal Olga* (☎ 1-429-78 87) C/ Zorilla 13; *Pensión Jaén* (☎ 1-429-48 58) C/Cervantes 5; *Posada del Dragón* (☎ 1-365-32 25) C/ Cava Baja 14.

Party Places

Madrid is a true party capital with streets livelier at 3 am than 3 pm. Bars and clubs stay open all night, encourage dancing and attract as eclectic a crowd as any city in Europe. City editions of the national newspapers *El Mundo* and *Diario 16* have listings information on Fridays. *El Pais* has a *'What's On'* section on Thursdays.

Best clubs include: *Teatro Kapital* at 125 Calle Atocha with a massive dance floor; *Nairobi* on Calle San Vincent Ferrer if you enjoy African trimmings; *Keeper* at 21 Calle Juan Bravo which attracts an older crowd; *Joy Eslava* on Calle Arenal in which it is probably impossible to have a dull night.

Of course, there are many other clubs worth visiting in Madrid. New venues pop up regularly. Another popular way to spend an evening is cruising the city's bars which are always lively and where one can warm up before tackling the bigger all-night clubs.

REST OF SPAIN
European City of Culture 2000: Santiago de Compostela

Santiago de Compostela, which is a UNESCO World Heritage City, is one of nine cities to be designated a **European City of Culture in the year 2000**. Compostela fought competition from Barcelona, Valencia and Salamanca to win the title which was

❏ **Millennium Festivals**

During the year 2000, three of Spain's better-known festivals will be given a millennial edge. El Carnaval – on 7 March 2000 – is a sort of Spanish Mardi Gras. While the celebration is staged all over the country, Cádiz and the island of Tenerife put on particularly good parties.

Holy Week, which will take place between 16-23 April 2000, is a religious festival which will gain added significance in the year 2000 and will be celebrated all over Spain. Finally, between 2-7 May 2000, the acclaimed Seville Fair takes place amid singing, dancing and drinking.

awarded in 1995. Each city is to base its millennium celebrations on a theme; in Compostela that theme is to be 'Europe and the World'. Year 2000 celebrations will follow on from the **Jubilee of St James** in 1999. Compostela has several plans to make lasting changes to the city to mark these two important years. A major programme of development will leave the city with: a new public common; a **University Park** which is to be cultivated in the Vista Alegere area; a **Centre for Advanced Studies**; a **School of Music**; a **Botanical Garden**; and a new **City History Museum**. An **environmental programme** will include clean-ups of the Sar and Sarela rivers.

Year 2000 events in Compostela will include: a **Great Festival of Music**; a series of **debates,** supported by UNESCO, which will tackle world questions as we approach the third millennium; a **Festival Celebration** of popular music; an **art exhibition** focusing on European and Latin American art in the year 2000; and two geographical exhibitions called **Faces of the Earth** and **Faces of the Gods** are to be staged in the city.

Tall Ships 2000 Finishing Point: Cádiz (4-7 May 2000)

The first leg of the trans-Atlantic Tall Ships 2000 (see p150) millennium race finishes in Cádiz. Crews will have raced from Southampton or Genoa and will set off again for Bermuda on 7 May. It is highly appropriate that Cádiz should be the launching point for the trans-Atlantic leg of the race. For 3000 years this famous port has been one of the most influential in Europe and is considered to be the continent's first gateway to America. Major festivities are planned at each of the Tall Ships 2000 ports. In Cádiz, fireworks, parties and events will be laid on for crew and spectators alike.

Museum for the Millennium: Bilbao

Bilbao, which is the capital of the northern Basque region of Spain, has crowned its programme of development for the year 2000 with the new Guggenheim Museum. Like its older sister in New York, Bilbao's Guggenheim is a mighty building. It could come to be seen as one of the most important buildings of this century.

Architect Frank Gehry has created an extraordinary structure which houses work by 20th century masters including Picasso, Matisse and Chagall and more recent artists such as Hirst and Koons.

Millennium Tour: Costa del Sol (26 Dec 99 – 2 Jan 2000)

Staying at Marbella, this seven-day millennium holiday from Maupintour includes accommodation at a seaside resort and a New Year's Eve 1999 party. The price has not been fixed but a US$850 per person deposit will guarantee a place. **Contact:** (☎ +1 800-255 4266).

❑ **Valencia Third Millennium Project**

The city of Valencia, UNESCO and ADC New Millennium have formed the Valencia Third Millennium Project which is a programme of reflection and debate about the past, present and future of humanity.

In 1997 the group held a similar event which attracted leading academics and politicians from 27 countries. The project organisers will also release an assessment of the past millennium on CD-ROM. Umberto Eco will help to produce the disk.

Contact: ADC New Millennium (☎ 6-579 5000, fax 6-579 5600).

England

Millennium-mania is beginning to build in Britain which is, after all, the home of time. New Year's Eve 1999 promises to be the biggest national party for 2000 years. A Commission has been set up to hand out funds to worthwhile millennium projects. As a result, Britain will be left with a lasting legacy as well as a nationwide hangover.

LONDON

London will literally lead the world into the third millennium which starts after midnight Greenwich Mean Time. The capital will be a match for any other city, with spectacular events planned from 31 December 1999 to the end of the year 2000.

❑ **ENGLAND**
Contacts
● **British Tourist Association/English Tourist Board** (☎ 0181-846 9000, fax 0181-563 0302), Thames Tower, Black's Road, Hammersmith, London W6 9EL
Average maximum temperature °C

	Dec	Jan
London	7	6

Capital: London
Flight times: to London from:
      LA – 11 hrs
      New York – 7 hrs 30 mins
      Sydney – 21 hrs 30 mins
Approximate exchange rates: Pound Sterling (£) – US$1=0.6, A$1=0.4
Time difference: GMT (+1 from last Sunday in March to last Sunday in October)
Country dialling code: ☎ 44

The Millennium Experience
Greenwich, London (31 Dec 1999 – 31 Dec 2000)

On New Year's Eve 1999 the Millennium Experience will open in the **Millennium Dome** on the Greenwich Peninsula in London with an opening ceremony and party. This will be the focus of millennium celebrations in Britain and the 'most spectacular millennial event anywhere in the world' according to the Millennium Experience Company.

The Dome, designed by the Richard Rogers Partnership, will be the largest such structure in the world and will cover 20 acres. It could house 13 Albert Halls. Instead, however, it will

---

❏ The Dome Debate

Former Deputy Prime Minister Michael Heseltine has called the Millennium Dome 'the biggest thing Britain has ever tried to do'. Virgin founder Richard Branson has labelled it 'the greatest white elephant of our time'. Health Secretary Frank Dobson has defied Labour Party managers by referring to the Dome as 'the biggest kite in history'. His boss, Tony Blair, calls it 'the most exciting thing happening in the world in the year 2000'.One thing's for sure: the Dome launch has been a spectacular PR disaster.

British people are cynical about the project. Any enterprise with a budget of more than £700 million deserves such scrutiny. But public feeling towards the Dome would doubtless be different if its launch had been better-handled. An air of secrecy has surrounded the scheme. There has been insufficient public debate. The Millennium Experience should have been inclusive from the start. It wasn't; and that's a shame, because the Dome deserves to be backed by the British public.

There's another problem: the Dome has a 25-year life-span. The British plan to celebrate 2000 years of human progress by putting up a temporary building. Many feel that an obelisk or column, something that has a fighting chance of lasting for another millennium, would be more appropriate. Perhaps when the Dome dies in 2025 it should be replaced by just such a lasting monument.

High-profile projects such as this rightly attract sceptical examination. The Millennium Experience is, however, a very exciting venture. When the Dome opens, it is likely that such criticism will be forgotten and the project's shaky start overlooked.

hold a giant person with a baby. The person – it is unclear whether it will be female, male or androgynous – will be 320ft long (the Statue of Liberty is 300ft high) and taller than Nelson's Column. Visitors will be able to get inside the figures where they will be treated to an innovative explanation of the entire cycle of life.

Details about the year-long Dome display have been very slow to emerge (to the chagrin of the British public) but there will be a 10,000-seat theatre surrounded by a ring of thirteen zones. The zones are: **The Mind**, exploring the creative talent in all of us; the **Body Zone**, see inside the 'human machine'; **Spirit Level**, a place for quiet reflection; **Licensed to Skill**, matching skills with work; **The Learning Curve**, dedicated to 'life-long learning'; **TransAction**, dealing with money and finance; **Dreamscape**, a surreal area devoted to a Dali-esque trip into your imagination; **Serious Play**, focusing on leisure and life; **Shared Ground**, a virtual journey around Britain; **Living Island**, an ecological zone; **Atmosphere**, a celebration of the wonders of the planet; **Time to Talk**, the future of communication and **uk@now**, what it means to be British now and in the next millennium. Other attractions are expected to include a display of the best British innovations and, possibly, Diana, Princess of Wales' dresses. There will also be an area of rainforest within the exhibition space.

Many other final features of the 'experience' have still to be decided. Prime Minister Tony Blair has famously stated that the Experience should pass the 'Euan test', meaning it should excite the likes of his teenage son. The Dome will be electronically

---

❑ **Greenwich: Party on the Prime Meridian**

If you trace a line through the north and south celestial poles via the cross-hairs of the Transit Circle telescope in the Meridian building at Greenwich, you get the Prime Meridian, 0 0' 0" longitude. Since 1884, this line has been the reference for measuring distance on Earth. A Millennium Countdown Clock has been installed above the meridian line. When it reaches zero, Greenwich Park will explode with celebrations – the first of the year 2000.

linked to other millennium sites around Britain. The site will be car-free. Visitors can get to it by Tube (the largest underground station in Europe is being built under the Dome) which will take 12 minutes from central London, boat (Park and Sail shuttles will run from central London), coach or bicycle. **Contact**: The Millennium Experience Company (☎ 0171 808 8200, Internet http://www.mx2000.co.uk).

New Year's Eve Party: Greenwich (31 Dec 1999)

A 24-hour global telecast and New Year's Eve party will be staged in Greenwich Park. A mixture of pop and classical music, pageant and spectaculars will be performed live and beamed around the world. Numbers will be limited to about 50,000. This will be the first party of the year 2000 – and one of the biggest. It is possible to hire the Old Observatory for private functions on

---

❏ Line Dancing

A brass line at Greenwich picks out 0 0' 0" longitude, the Prime Meridian. It is based on the calculations of the Astronomer Royal in 1851 and has served as the world's main reference point since 1884. How comforting to know that some things in life are unassailable. Times may have changed, but at least time itself is still measured from that brass strip at Greenwich. But is it?

According to Britain's *Daily Telegraph*, the Prime Meridian is not as immovable as it might at first appear. Prior to 1851, 0 0' 0" longitude had been placed in three other positions. One of these, the Bradley meridian, is still used today by the Ordnance Survey. It gets worse. Global Positioning Systems (GPS), which use satellite data to determine position, rely on the WGS84 grid which places the Prime Meridian 336ft east of the brass line at Greenwich. On 1 January 1998, WGS84 became the standard for air navigation. It has also been suggested that nautical charts be altered to follow the WGS84 system because GPS is so widely used in shipping.

So where does that leave Greenwich? Millennium celebrations will take place at the 1851 meridian. As party-goers watch the millennium countdown clock approach zero, most will be unaware that even that hallowed timepiece uses Universal Coordinated Time which is based on information from GPS satellites. Perhaps it's time the meridian line was dug up and moved once more.

> ❏ **Millennium Tours from the US: Greenwich**
> US-based travel company Maupintour is offering a chance to join
> the party at Greenwich (26 Dec 1999 – 2 Jan 2000). Prices are not
> yet available, but a refundable US$850 deposit will secure a place
> on the trip. **Contact:** Maupintour (+1 800-255 4266).

Countdown Days in the run up to the millennium. **Contact:** The
Old Royal Observatory, Greenwich, London SE10 9NF (☎ 0181-
858 4422, fax 0181 312 6632).

Greenwich and Docklands International Festival
London (31 Dec 1999)

A three-month summer festival will build up to major New
Year's Eve 1999 and New Year's Day 2001 celebrations in east
London. The emphasis is on mass-participation, and the New
Year's Eve party will feature live acts, fireworks and outdoor per-
formances around Greenwich – which is now a World Heritage
Site. Festival venues include: the Docks, Royal Arsenal, Trinity
Buoy Wharf, the Royal Naval College and on the Thames.
Contact: Greenwich and Docklands International Festival (☎
0181-305 1818, fax 0181-305 1188, e-mail greendock@global-
net.co.uk), 6 College Approach, Greenwich, London, SE10 9HY

New Year's Eve Party: London (31 Dec 1999)

An eight-acre dome (not to be confused with the Millennium
Dome) at the Woolwich Royal Arsenal Barracks near Greenwich
will welcome 18,000 people to a sit-down dinner and millennium
party on New Year's Eve 1999.

David Brason, party organiser, has asked several well-
known entertainers to 'sing for their supper'. He hopes to line up
26 international stars, and claims to be negotiating with, among
others, Elton John, Sting and Simply Red. The winner of the
1999 TV Masterchef series will oversee the dinner. Reserves of
vintage wine and champagne are being collected for the occasion. The temporary dome, which has yet to be built, has been
designed with no interior pillars so that everyone gets a good

view. Tickets will be available from ticket and booking agents. Brason is planning a high-profile launch. 'You will know when the tickets go on sale', he says. The price is high: £2000.

A similar party will be held on the island of Tenerife. Both will be connected by TV. A slightly different dome will be built on Tenerife at a secluded spot between the airport and Los Christianos. Tickets to the Tenerife party will include airfares and a week's accommodation. Price: approximately £2350.

Brason has access to the site for 15 weeks. He is planning several charity events over that period. However, the New Year's Eve party is a purely commercial venture – as was his decision to book 21,000 London hotel rooms for 31 December 1999.

New Year's Eve Party: Trafalgar Square (31 Dec 1999)
A spontaneous street party takes place in Trafalgar Square every New Year's Eve. Thousands are expected to gather there on 31 December 1999. It's also the most popular time and place to hold a reunion. But it might not be such a good idea to meet old friends in Trafalgar Square. With so many people expected, it will be hard enough finding Nelson.

There is, as yet, no official party planned at Trafalgar Square; so there will be no organised safety planning or crowd

---

❏ **London Club Scene**

London is cool. That's the verdict from fashion editors, music-makers and clubbers. This confidence has rubbed off on the city's club-life. Several clubs are planning millennium parties for New Year's Eve 1999: Most will be over-subscribed, so it will be worth trying to get tickets in advance. The following clubs claim to be planning something special for 31 December 1999: *Aquarium* (☎ 0171-729 9779) at 256-260 Old Street; *Electric Ballroom* (☎ 0171-485 9006) in Camden Town; *Equinox at the Empire* (☎ 0171-437 1446) in Leicester Square; *London Astoria 2* (☎ 0171-434 9592); *London Hippodrome* (☎ 0171-437 4311) in Leicester Square; *Ministry of Sound* (☎ 0171-378 6528) on Gaunt Street near Elephant and Castle; *Gardening Club and the Rock Garden* (0171-497 3154) on the Piazza off Covent Garden; *Subterania* (0181-961 5490) in Notting Hill.

control. If no group steps in to organise a party here, police recommend revellers avoid the area. **Uri Geller** intends to prevent the next millennium from reaching London. He wants to stand in front of Big Ben using his psychic energy to stop the hands from reaching midnight. If all goes to plan, thousands will join in by shouting 'stop!' simultaneously just before midnight.

The British Airways Millennium Wheel: London

At 150 metres the British Airways Millennium Wheel will be twice the height of the Statue of Liberty and will dominate central London. The world's biggest Ferris wheel will provide the capital with a remarkable spectacle, millennium landmark and much-needed vantage point rolled into one.

The Wheel will hang over the Thames opposite Westminster supported from just one side and will largely be powered by the River Thames. It sounds frightening, but in fact the 60 20-seat capsules will turn at a very sedate pace. During the 25-minute journey passengers will have the view explained to them through headsets. Rides will cost about £5.

Work has already started, and the Wheel should be up and spinning by summer 1999 – in time for New Year's Eve 1999 when competition for a ride is expected to be fierce. The Wheel will stay by the Thames for five years. There are plans to allow couples to hire a whole cabin to themselves on Valentine's Day in the year 2000. It has been suggested that the wheel's revolution be slowed down for that occasion!

❏ **New Millennium Brewing**

If you're worried about champagne supplies, you could toast the new millennium with beer. Dave Roberts of the Pilgrim Brewery (☎ 01737-222651) has brewed a **Millennium Ale**. He claims it follows a Victorian recipe and tastes just like the beer of 1899. The millennial pint will be an Indian Pale Ale.

Roberts plans to bottle the brew on 8 Jan 1999. But only 1999 bottles will be available – each selling for £19.99. At 6.5% the expensive tipple could help lubricate your New Year's Eve celebrations quite well. Although, let's face it, not as well as the ten pints of ordinary beer you could buy for the same amount.

❏ **Millennium Tour: London (30 Dec 1999 – 2 Jan 2000)**
A three-day millennium trip to London from Jetset Tours (☎ 0990-555 757) includes accommodation at a good quality hotel, a 'sights and lights' tour, a New Year's Eve gala dinner and party in the West End, a New Year's Day luncheon and an excursion to Leeds Castle. Price: £618 per person based on two sharing. (This does not include travel to London).

The Millennium Moment (31 Dec 1999)

Churches Together in England are asking that Jesus be remembered on 31 December 1999 through the Millennium Moment. The group wants people across the country to pause for a minute's silence at 11.58pm and to light a candle at 11.59pm. This simple act could potentially be rather moving if enough people decide to participate. It's hoped that party-planners will include the Millennium Moment in their arrangements.

Ringing in the Millennium: Nationwide (1 Jan 2000)

Britain greeted 1900 with the pealing of bells in churches across the country. There are three schemes gathering momentum which should allow every church in the United Kingdom to welcome the year 2000 in a similar fashion.

Ring in 2000 (☎ 01483-569 535) is a national bellringing recruitment drive which has joined forces with Celebration 2000. Celebration 2000 is a campaign to get every church to hold a new millennium service at noon on 1 Jan 2000. These services will take the form of 10 minutes of prayer preceded by five minutes of bellringing.

Another group, **Ringing in the Millennium** (☎ 01664-822 098), is an umbrella organisation which is helping churches to get their bells ready to sound on New Year's Day 2000. The idea came from St Remigius Church in the village of Long Clawson where, in 1893, a frame for eight new bells was installed for the turn of the century. At the time, however, the villagers could only afford five.

In 1993, with the help of villagers' goodwill and the Millennium Commission, the other three bells were added to the

❏ **Jubilee 2000**
Jubilee 2000 has a simple message: cancel third world debt. This church-led initiative hopes to allow third world nations to start the next millennium without the burden of enormous debt. Recipient nations would have to use this financial relief to fund health and education and to improve their economic environments. Supporters include former Prime Minister Lord Callaghan of Cardiff. The Jubilee 2000 Millennium Count-down Clock can currently be seen above the neon advertising boards of Piccadilly Circus.

frame in time for the turn of the millennium. The idea has quickly spread to other parishes and the project has become a major enterprise. Churches across Britain will install new bells or augment old ones by the end of the millennium.

Millennium Services (2 Jan 2000)

Formal State services, attended by the Queen and the Prime Minister, look likely to go ahead in each of the capitals in the United Kingdom on the first Sunday of the year 2000.

There are also plans to write Songs for the New Millennium which will lead to a book, CD and cassette. For information about that project, **contact:** Ann Richards (☎ 01482-445257), 37 Hymers Avenue, Hull, HU3 1LL.

The Prayer and Millennium Group will publish a resource pack to help smaller churches to present special millennial services over Christmas 1999, on the first Sunday of the year 2000 and over Easter and saints' days during the year 2000.

The Thames Festival: London (27-30 May 2000)

Free fireworks, theatre, art shows, entertainment and a torchlight procession will take place on the Thames and its banks between Westminster Bridge and Southwark Cathedral. There will also be a children's treasure hunt.

Thames 2000: London (Summer 2000)

Regattas, races, exhibitions and tall ships meetings will form the core of Thames 2000. The action will take place in the summer of 2000 around Greenwich, Blackwall, the Isle of Dogs, Royal Docks and Woolwich.

Portrait of a Century Millennium Exhibition
London (Oct 1999-Feb 2000)

One of the most enjoyable museums in London, the National Portrait Gallery (☎ 0171-306 0055, fax 0171-306 0058), will display a millennium exhibition featuring portraits of the most influential political, social and cultural figures from the 20th century.

The Biggest Birthday Party
Blackheath, London (21 June 2000)

A new charitable trust, A Child Is Born, is working on plans for a fundraising scheme which will reach a climax with an event at Blackheath. The idea plays on the theme of birthdays; the Blackheath event will be marketed as the world's biggest birthday party. For twelve months leading up to the mid-point of the year 2000, gifts will be gathered from around the world. These will then be redistributed to children across the globe on and after the birthday party on 21 June 2000.

Contact: A Child Is Born (☎ 0181-318 9233, fax 0181-463 0634) The Little House, 16 Belmont Hill, London SE13 5BD.

❏ **What is the Millennium Commission?**

The Millennium Commission uses National Lottery money to help fund projects which mark the end of the second millennium or celebrate the start of the third. A vast amount of money – around £1.6 billion – has been raised by the National Lottery, and the Millennium Commission has been able to help sponsor an impressive number of projects.

There are 14 flagship schemes which have been called Landmark projects. Landmark Projects not covered in this chapter are: **The Earth Centre**, Doncaster (☎ 0171-457 2020); **The Millennium Seed Bank**, Haywards Heath (☎ 0181-332 5607); **The Renaissance of Portsmouth Harbour**, Portsmouth (☎ 01705-834174); **Hampden Park Stadium**, Glasgow (☎ 0141-636 1390); **Bristol 2000**, Bristol (☎ 0117-909 6357); **International Centre for Life**, Newcastle (☎ 0191-226 1234); **New Technopolis**, Norwich (☎ 01603-212991).

Crystal Palace Mark 2

Developers London & Regional Properties are to finance a new Crystal Palace on the site of the old one which burned down in 1936.

The original Crystal Palace was built in 1851 as part of the Great Exhibition, an event with which the Millennium Experience has often been compared. Like the original, the new building will be constructed mainly from metal and glass. It will be ready by December 1999. Glass is a highly durable material, and it is hoped this new design could survive far into the next millennium – and possibly into the fourth.

This is one of very few major millennium-related projects to be sponsored entirely by private enterprise.

String of Pearls Millennium Festival: London (31 Dec 1999 – 31 Dec 2000)

A year-long millennium festival will take place along the Thames in the year 2000. Many of the most important buildings and institutions along the River, from the Tate Gallery in the west to the Design Museum in the east, will develop their own millennium events which will be a part of the String of Pearls. For example, the London Television Centre is developing plans to create a 'virtual journey' around the studio and an open day. So far, 'Pearls' are likely to include, among others, Lambeth Palace, Westminster Abbey, the Palace of Westminster, the National Gallery, the South Bank Centre, Metropolitan Police HQ, the National Theatre, the Museum of the Moving Image, London Television Centre, the Old Bailey, the Tate at Bankside, the

---

❏ **The BBC – What's On?**

Twentieth-century British history will be recorded in the voice of the people as part of the BBC's contribution to the millennium. Over 3000 hours of recordings will be made of people young and old talking about their lives in the 20th century. Most of this enormous archive will be presented in the Millennium Dome, but 500 hours will be broadcast on BBC local radio. The oral history is part of a larger project to present British history since the Romans.

Globe Theatre and the Tower of London. **Contact:** Dylan Hammond (☎ 0171-680 9286, fax 0171-702 0738).

Southwark Cathedral Millennium Project: London

Did you know that Southwark Cathedral is the oldest Gothic church in England and the oldest cathedral church in London? Southwark Cathedral, at the south end of London Bridge, has been somewhat ignored for a long time. Now the Millennium Commission has awarded over £3 million to the cathedral to finance a restoration, visitors' centre and floodlighting scheme. The cathedral has described the windfall as 'Cinderella's invitation to the ball'.

Tate Gallery of Modern Art Millennium Project: London

A new Tate Gallery of Modern Art is being built in the shell of the long-disused Bankside Power Station in London. The Gallery will display one of the most important collections of modern art in the world, including Abstract Expressionism, Surrealism and Pop, Minimal and Conceptual art.

Bankside Power Station, on the south side of the Thames opposite St Paul's Cathedral, is a remarkable building. It was designed by Sir Giles Gilbert Scott whose many other successful creations include the Battersea Power Station and the red telephone box. Swiss architects Herzon and de Meuron won an international competition to design the new gallery.

Their scheme includes a two-floor 'light beam' which will be added to the roof. This will fill the rooms below with natural light. There will be few other changes to the outward appearance

---

❏ **Solar-powered Pint**

A South London pub has been awarded £895,000 by the Millennium Commission to become the first solar-powered drinking den in London. The *Jolly Gardeners* in sunny Wandsworth will produce 50 per cent of its own electricity and will rely on the sun to keep its beer at the right temperature. It should work well; the warmer the weather, the cooler the beer.

of the old power station. This £130 million investment will seal Bankside's reputation as the 'new Left Bank'. March 2000 will see the new Globe Theatre open on Bankside. A Millennium Pedestrian Bridge – designed by architect Sir Norman Foster and sculptor Sir Anthony Caro – will link both these to the city. **Contact:** Tate Gallery (☎ 0171-887 8000, fax 0171-887 8007) Millbank, London SW1P 4RG.

Science Museum Wellcome Wing: London

In July 2000 the new Wellcome Wing will open at the Science Museum (☎ 0171-938 8000).

The £45 million wing will accommodate exhibitions on both the cutting-edge of contemporary science and science in the next millennium. A giant 3-D IMAX® cinema screen will help to animate the displays.

London Zoo Millennium Project: London

A new education centre will improve trips to London Zoo in the next millennium. The glass pavilion will house a mixture of interactive displays and animals and will focus on conservation of species and the environment.

Mayflower 2000: London to the New World

After 66 days at sea, the *Mayflower* arrived at Cape Cod on 21 November 1620 carrying the Pilgrim Fathers. That historic voyage will be re-enacted during spring 1999 as part of Britain's millennium celebrations.

A full-size replica *Mayflower* is being built at Chambers Wharf in London. The *Mayflower* will carry a crew of 20 and, possibly, around 15 passengers.

❏ **New Bank Holiday in the UK?**
There are plans afoot to create a new Bank Holiday in the year 2000. June 12 is the most likely possibility.

❑ LONDON – A BRIEF GUIDE

London is enormous. It would take a lifetime to explore every feature and experience every pleasure in this colossal capital. Since most millennial visitors will have days rather than years in which to enjoy London, here are some of the best sights in town.

What to See

Obviously you should visit **Greenwich**. The **Old Observatory**, which was built for the first Astronomer Royal in 1675, is now a museum. Outside, the Prime Meridian is marked by a line sunk into the concrete. At the turn of the millennium, the newest landmark in London – the **Millennium Dome** – will also be in Greenwich.

The New Year's Eve hotspot of London is **Trafalgar Square**, and it is equally enjoyable by day. From here, Nelson gazes down Whitehall from his 185-foot-tall column. Lions guard the fountain and pools in which brave, or deranged, revellers swim on 31 December.

Royalty draws millions to London. Keen royal-watchers should visit **Buckingham Palace** where the Changing of the Guard provides a free display of British pomp, the staggeringly opulent **Kensington Palace** and **Windsor Castle**, which has recently reopened after suffering terrible fire damage.

The Crown Jewels are on display at the **Tower of London**. Part palace part prison, the Tower is the most complete medieval castle in Britain. For a graphic foray into Old London, visit the gruesome **London Dungeon** where wax figures can be found at the sharp end of various medieval horrors.

A more aesthetic afternoon can be spent at one of London's galleries. The **Tate** at Millbank has a magnificent collection of international modern art from the Impressionists onward, and a display of British art from around 1600-1900. From March 2000 the new Tate at Bankside (see p122) will house an exhibition of modern art rivalling any other gallery. The **National Gallery** at Trafalgar Square has a vast collection of European art. Nearby, the **National Portrait Gallery** provides an even more entertaining hall of fame than **Madame Tussaud's**. There are some wonderful museums in London, most notably the **V&A**, **British Museum**, **Science Museum** and, everyone's favourite, the **Natural History Museum**.

Covent Garden is an excellent place to go for free entertainment. There are always buskers and street artists drawing crowds.

Be prepared to participate! **Leicester Square** and **Piccadilly Circus** are other energy hubs. Lively **Soho** and **Chinatown** fan out from Leicester Square. Piccadilly Circus is a good place from which to mount a long shopping campaign from **Regent Street** to **Oxford Street**.

Londoners will be listening out for the midnight chimes from **Big Ben** on 31 December 1999. The **Palace of Westminster** is the ornate home of British Government and a striking building in its own right. Visitors can watch the action in the Commons or Lords; go to St Stephen's Entrance.

Where to Stay

● **Expensive** (over £150): The *Savoy* (☎ 0171-420 2350, fax 0171-420 2360, e-mail info@the-savoy.co.uk), Strand, and the *Ritz* (☎ 0171-493 8181, fax 0171-493 2687), 150 Piccadilly, are two of London's most exclusive hotels. Rooms and tickets to the celebrations at both are in such high demand for New Year's Eve 1999 they propose to hold a draw. The names of all interested parties will be thrown into the hotels' respective hats and the winners picked out in 1998.

The *Four Seasons Hotel* (☎ 0171-499 0888, fax 0171-493 1895), Hamilton Place, will hold an event as will the *Grosvenor* (☎ 0171-834 9494, fax 0171-630 1978), Buckingham Palace Road; the *Dorchester* (☎ 0171-629 8888, fax 0171-409 0114), Park Lane, will base its New Year's Eve 1999 event on that of 1997. In 1997 the Dorchester held an impressive New Year's Eve Ball for £325 per person or dinner for £235 per person. There was also a dinner in the Dorchester Bar for £85. Two guests could stay at the Hotel for three nights and join the Ball for £1540.

The *Berkeley* (☎ 0171-235 6000, fax 0171-235 4330), Wilton Place, Knightsbridge, is arranging a special event; the modern *Royal Garden Hotel* (☎ 0171-937 8000, fax 0171-361 1991), 2-24 Kensington High Street, has yet to confirm details but has put a special Christmas Coordinator on the case; the recently-refurbished *Mandarin Oriental Hyde Park* (☎ 0171-235 2000, fax 0171-235 4552), 66 Knightsbridge, holds a New Year's Eve Ball and Dinner every year; the *Waldorf Méridien* (☎ 0171-836 2400, fax 0171-836 7244), Aldwych, will offer a two-night millennium deal with a gala dinner in the ballroom but there are, as yet, no prices; and a party is also being planned at *Le Méridien* (☎ 0171-734 8000, fax 0171-465 1631), 21 Piccadilly.

Where to Stay (cont)

● **Moderate** (between £60-150): ***Bonnington In Bloomsbury*** (☎ 0171-242 2828, fax 0171-831 9170), 92 Southampton Row; ***The Green Park*** (☎ 0171-499 9411, fax 0171-491 8971), Half Moon Street; ***Hospitality Inn Piccadilly*** (☎ 0171-930 4033, fax 0171-925 2586), 39 Coventry Street; ***Langham Court*** (☎ 0171-436 6622, fax 0171-436 2303), 31-35 Langham Street; ***London Ryan Hotel*** (☎ 0171-278 2480, fax 0171-837 3776), Gwynne Place; ***Regent Palace*** (☎ 0171-734 7000, fax 0171-734 6435), Piccadilly Circus; ***Rochester*** (☎ 0171-828 6611, fax 0171-233 6724), 69 Vincent Square; ***Rubens*** (☎ 0171-834 6600, fax 0171-828 5401), 39-41 Buckingham Palace Road; ***Strand Palace*** (☎ 0171-836 8080, fax - 0171-836 2077), Strand.

● **Budget** (under £60): ***Abbey Court Hotel*** (☎ 0171-221 7518, fax 0171-792 0858), 20 Pembridge Gardens; ***Central Club YWCA*** (☎ 0171-636 7512, fax 0171 636 5278), 16-22 Great Russell Street; ***Colliers Hotel*** (☎ 0171-834 6931, fax 0171-834 8439), 97 Warwick Way; ***Georgian House Hotel*** (☎ 0171-834 1438, fax 0171-976 6085), 35 St George's Drive; ***Marble Arch Inn*** (☎ 0171-723 7888, fax 0171-723 6060), 49-50 Upper Berkeley Street; ***Stanley House Hotel*** (☎ 0171-834 5042, fax 0171-834 7292), 19-21 Belgrave Road; ***YHA Highgate Village*** (☎ 0181-340 1831, fax 0181-341 0376), 84 Highgate West Hill.

British Museum Millennium Project: London

When Sir Robert Smirke designed the British Museum in the 18th century, he created an inner courtyard as its central feature. But in 1854 that space was covered over to form the Round Reading Room. The remaining space was used to store British Library books.

Now the British Library has moved its collection to a new building at St Pancras, and the British Museum is keen to make the inner courtyard its central focus once more. Sir Norman Foster and Partners have designed a new Great Court which will include the Reading Room, restored to its original 1857 appearance, a centre for education, exhibition space, bookshops and a restaurant. **Contact:** The British Museum (☎ 0171-636 1555) Great Russell Street, London WC1B 3DG.

❏ MILLENNIUM RAIL JOURNEYS
British Pullman New Year's Eve Party (31 Dec 1999)

British Pullman, the Orient-Express luxury train, will make a millennial journey to and from London via Tonbridge on 31 December 1999. The party starts with a champagne reception at the Grosvenor Thistle Hotel before passengers join the train at Victoria Station. A five-course feast will be served on board while serenading musicians stroll through the carriages. A piper will play in the New Year on Tonbridge Station. The price has not been confirmed, but will be at least £500 per person. A deposit will be required. **Contact:** Orient-Express (☎ (US) +1 800-524 2420, (UK) +44 171-805 5100, (Singapore) +65 392-3500).

The Venice Simplon Orient-Express has not yet announced its millennium plans, but is expected to retrace its original route from London to Istanbul.

Millennium Train Company Tour: London to Paris (29 Dec 1999 – 1 Jan 2000)

A Eurostar train will take revellers from London to Paris in time to celebrate the year 2000 at a New Year's Eve Ball at the Conciergerie on the Ile de la Cité.

The Millennium Train Company (☎ 01737-223 303, e-mail mtc2000.aol.com) tour starts with a champagne reception at Waterloo International Terminal and includes two nights in Paris. After shooting through the tunnel, the millennium train will emerge in France to be greeted by fireworks.

All-inclusive tickets cost £6500 for Platinum Class (first class train travel and 5-star hotel) or £4500 Gold Class (standard class travel and 4-star hotel).

REST OF ENGLAND
Eden Millennium Project: Cornwall

Cornwall is creating another world. The largest planthouse on Earth will be built at a disused clay pit near St Austell. This is, perhaps, the most exciting millennium project in Britain.

The Eden Project will create perfect Mediterranean, tropical and semi-arid environments in three enormous biomes. These giant greenhouses will be world-leading centres for research into conservation and sustainable farming. Each 'climate' will be

❏ **Total Eclipse 1999**

Cornwall is bracing itself for an influx of one million people on 11 August 1999 to see the first total eclipse of the sun to be visible in Britain since 1927. Chaos is on the cards as the county struggles to find a way to prepare for such numbers. Cornwall's narrow roads are easily blocked, and accommodation could sell out.

The track on which the eclipse will be visible leads from Cornwall across Europe and into Asia. It stops in India. Iran will see the longest eclipse at two minutes and 23 seconds. In Cornwall it will last just over two minutes and will occur at about 12.10pm. Royal Olympic Cruises are offering eclipse-watching voyages on the English Channel and the Black Sea. It will be 90 years before another solar eclipse occurs over Britain. But a 5-minute eclipse will be visible from Central Africa on 21 June 2001.

Never look directly at the sun; always project the image of the eclipse onto card using a telescope. Photographers should use a strong filter.

divided into: Arcadia, or wild areas; Shamba, showing hunter-gatherer cultivation; and Cornucopia which will be used to explore future cultivation methods.

A visitor centre will open in April 1999. Spectacular exhibitions are being designed to communicate the weird world of plants to an expected 750,000 visitors a year. Several restaurants will also be built at the site. These will offer exotic food from around the world.

This is a great millennium project; it combines entertainment with a useful legacy for the third millennium. **Contact:** The Eden Project (☎ 01726-222 900, fax 01726-844 600), Heligan, Pentewan, St Austell, Cornwall PL26 6EN

National Space Science Centre (NSSC) Millennium Project: Leicester

Leicester is counting down to the launch of a world-class British Space Centre in 2000. A hands-on exhibition centre will display the best collection of space hardware in Europe and will even have live links to its own satellite. After the Challenger disaster in 1986, the victims' families started to create Challenger Centres. These centres allow children to join simulated space flights and to deal with the types of problems that need to be solved on real missions. As part of the NSSC project, Leicester will build the first Challenger Centre outside North America. There will also be a planetarium. Education is to be of paramount importance at the NSSC.

The £46 million building follows a futuristic design by Nicholas Grimshaw and Partners. It is supposed to conjure an image of rocket and launchpad – although, in fact, it looks something like a see-through salmon jumping from the Atlantic. Entry tickets will cost about £6 per adult or £16 for a family ticket.

Contact: NSSC Project Office, University of Leicester (☎ 0116-252 2436, fax 0116-252 5000), University Road, Leicester LE1 7RH

Magna Millennium Project: Rotherham

An enormous exhibition space and visitor attraction is to be built on the site of a closed steel plant in Rotherham. The 40-acre site will become the fifth-largest exhibition area in Britain.

More exciting, perhaps, are the planned visitor attractions. These include: a simulation theatre, where visitors will be able to 'fly'; 'Professor Magna' interactive learning zones; a 'Ride of Steel'; and an adventure play area. Each of these attractions, and others, will play on the theme of industry. Magna will open in the year 2000.

Contact: Rotherham Industrial Development Office (☎ 01709-372099, fax 01709-837953), Reresby House, Bow Bridge Close, Templeborough, Rotherham S60 1BY

Tall Ships 2000 Starting Point: Southampton (20-23 April 2000)

The Tall Ships 2000 (see p150) trans-Atlantic millennium race will start from Southampton. Major celebrations and maritime events are planned to give the competitors an appropriate send-off. Southampton Harbour will be dominated by the festivities, and the ships themselves will make a wonderful sight.

Millennium Mystery Plays: York (22 June-20 July 2000)

From 22 June 2000 a cycle of 25 Millennium York Mystery Plays will be performed in the nave of York Minster. These plays started during the Middle Ages when each city guild would perform one part of the story of Creation. The whole story would then be performed on a procession of wagons which passed through the streets of York. Eventually the plays died out as Catholicism, with which the performances were associated, was oppressed. The plays were revived for the Festival of Britain in 1951. Fortunately, the original script still exists.

These plays, which feature local actors, will run for four weeks with no performances on Sundays or Mondays. Tickets will be on sale from autumn 1999. The York Early Music Festival, which is the most celebrated festival of early music in Britain, will coincide with the Millennium Mystery Plays. Joint tickets will be available. **Contact:** The Festival Office (☎ 01904-658338, fax 01904-612631, e-mail yemf@netcomuk.co.uk), PO Box 226, York, YO3 6ZU.

New Year's Eve 1999 Weekend: Cotswolds (30 Dec 1999 – 2 Jan 2000)

Set in the attractive village of Broadway, the Lygon Arms is one of the best hotels in the Cotswolds. As an old inn it has a welcome air of informality, but is, in fact, a celebrated hotel now owned by the select Savoy Group. The Lygon Arms is offering a tempting millennium package.

It starts on 30 December with a champagne reception and quickly gathers pace. After breakfast on New Year's Eve, a helicopter will carry party-goers off on a whistle-stop tour of the Cotswolds. That will be followed by a Scandinavian Smorgasbord lunch. A New Year's Eve Ball will later be held in the Great Hall. It promises to be an elegant affair with pipers playing in the new millennium and dancing into the early hours.

Guests will have little time to worry about their hangovers on New Year's Day, a champagne jazz brunch has been planned. Psychics will then be on hand to tell people what the next millennium has in store. 'Yes Mrs Smith...I can see...Alka Seltzer'. The price is £850 per person excluding VAT. A £250 non-refundable deposit is required to reserve a place. **Contact:** The Lygon Arms (☎ 01386-852 255, fax 01386-858611), Broadway, Worcestershire WR12 7DU

New Year's Eve 1999 Gourmet Feast: Cheltenham

If epicurean treats mean more to you than money, try this: the Chester Grosvenor Hotel (☎ 01244-324024) in Cheltenham is putting on a millennium feast for a hefty £1500 per head. Guests will gorge themselves on eight exquisite courses – each accompanied by a wine from a different decade of the 20th century. The post-dinner liquor will be an Armagnac from 1900.

Despite the price, staff at the Chester Grosvenor claim the millennial banquet is quite a bargain: one bottle alone, a 1921 Château d'Yquem Grand 1er Cru Sauternes, would put a £3500 dent in your bank balance – and that's if you could find a bottle. A £500 deposit will secure a place at the table of this 'Tribute to the 20th Century' dinner.

New Year's Eve 1999 Weekend: Warwickshire (30 Dec 1999 – 3 Jan)

Fancy seeing in the new millennium with Buddy Holly, Marilyn Monroe and Elvis? The Nailcote Hall Hotel is offering just such trite nonsense in a four-day millennium party package.

The revelry kicks off on 30 December with dinner followed by a 'Putting on the Ritz' party with the King Swingers band and a throng of bogus screen stars such as Charlie Chaplin.

Two parties are planned for New Year's Eve. 'Rock 'n' Roll in Rick's Bar' will feature a phoney Elvis and virtual Buddy

---

❏ **Mugs' Game**

Bookmakers William Hill have given some long odds on millennial bets according to the *Mail on Sunday:* Prince's '1999' to be number one when the millennium arrives – 12-1. NASA admits to finding alien life in 2000 – 66-1. Britain's throne to be occupied by King Charles and Queen Camilla by 2000 – 33-1. Elvis to turn up at a millennium party – 1000-1. This is a real long shot: an alien government to rule Earth at the turn of the millennium – 1,000,000 – 1. That's got to be worth a couple of quid!

Holly. At midnight, a piper will lead guests onto the terrace to watch a fireworks display. The other party will adopt a sixties theme complete with mock Beatles.

Price: £1450 per person including accommodation. Non-residents will be able to join the parties for between £160-290.
Contact: Nailcote Hall Hotel (☎ 01203-466174, fax 01203-470720, USA freefax 800-819 0027), Nailcote Lane, Berkswell, Warwickshire CV7 7DE

Croydon Skyline Millennium Project: Croydon
Office blocks have formed a 'mini-Manhattan' in Croydon. These functional buildings have earned the area an ill-deserved reputation for drabness. That will all change thanks to a fantastic idea from Croydon Council which will celebrate the millennium and leave the community a lasting legacy.

Croydon's key buildings will be lit up to create a dazzling skyline. This will be the single largest lighting project in the world. Apart from improving the area's image, the colourful Croydon Skyline project will be used for co-ordinated millennium celebrations.

New Year's Eve Party: Surrey (31 Dec 1999)
Professional party-planners CWA Associates are organising a Millennium's Eve dinner-dance in Guildford. Guests will find a jazz band, table musicians, a cabaret act and, later, more live music. The meal will be four courses with unlimited drinks and midnight will be marked by 'indoor pyrotechnics'. Tickets will cost between £125-150 per head. The venue has yet to be agreed.
Contact: CWA (☎ 01252-724888, fax 01252-724849), Charlton House, Searle Road, Farnham, Surrey GU9 8LJ

Millennium Point Project: Birmingham
Millennium Point is a centre for scientific entertainment and learning. It will be built in Digbeth, the historic heart of Birmingham, and will open during summer 2001.

Features include: the Discovery Centre, an interactive museum of the 21st century; the Technology Innovation Centre, a focus for technological research; the University of the First Age, a multi-sensory learning centre which will allow local children to communicate with other children across the world and even to run their own TV station; and the Hub. The Hub is a group of eating, drinking and entertainment venues which will form the centre of Millennium Point. **Contact:** Millennium Point Trust Company (☎ 0800-48 2000), The Council House, Victoria Square, Birmingham, B1 1BB.

The Lowry Centre Millennium Project: Salford

LS Lowry spent most of his life in Salford, where he documented industrial life in his paintings of 'matchstick men and matchstick cats and dogs'. Salford is set to honour its most famous son by naming a magnificent new cultural centre after him.

The Lowry Centre will house a 1650-seat theatre for opera, ballet and drama, a 400-seat community theatre, a children's gallery and, of course, the largest collection of Lowry paintings in the world. The children's gallery will be an interactive hands-on foray into the world of art. Children will be encouraged to join in with a strictly 'do touch' policy.

Linked to the Children's Gallery, but on an adjacent site, will be a National Industrial Virtual Reality Centre. Visitors will be able to explore virtual reality scenarios – even the moon. The more serious business of exploring the potential of virtual reality within academia and industry will be the Centre's main purpose. Entry to the Centre will be free, except for a small charge for the Children's Gallery. The £120 million project will open in 2000.

Contact: The Lowry Centre Project Office (☎ 0161-793 2486, fax 0161-793 2813), Chorley Road, Swinton, Salford M27 5BW.

'Billennium' Celebration: Stonehenge (31 Dec 1999)

An American group calling itself the Billennium intends to stage a worldwide celebration which will link various party sites by TV. The company has big plans but so far has not managed to set anything in stone. Well, except one of the party venues, which will – probably – be at Stonehenge. There is little more to report at this stage. **Contact:** Mark Mitten (☎ +1 773-327 2000, fax +1 773-327 1999, e-mail mitten@billennium.com).

Scotland

New Year's Eve is big in Scotland. The reason dates back to the Protestant Reformation of 1560. Protestant leaders cancelled the Christmas holiday because it was seen as too Catholic. New Year's Eve became the more significant celebration. Today, hogmanay is the excuse for enormous parties, particularly in Edinburgh and Glasgow.

EDINBURGH
Millennium Hogmanay 1999 (31 Dec 1999)
This north of the border bash will be the best street party in Europe – maybe even the world. Edinburgh's hogmanay has become a regular feature in the city's calendar. It is a feat of

---

❏ **SCOTLAND**
Contacts
● **British Tourist Association** (☎ 0181-846 9000, fax 0181-563 0302), Thames Tower, Black's Road, Hammersmith, London W6 9EL
● **Scottish Tourist Board** (☎ 0131-332 2433, fax 0131-343 1513), 23 Ravelston Terrace, Edinburgh EH4 3EU
Average maximum temperature °C

	Dec	Jan
Edinburgh	7	6

Capital: Edinburgh
Flight times: to Edinburgh from:
     LA – 11 hrs
     New York – 7 hrs 15 mins
     Sydney – 21 hrs 30 mins
Approximate exchange rates: Pound Sterling (£) – US$1=0.6, A$1=0.4
Time difference: GMT (+1 from last Sunday in March to last Sunday in October)
Country dialling code: ☎ 44

organisation. For four days, the Scottish capital is hijacked by circus performers, orchestras, rock acts, theatre companies, jazz bands, dancing troupes – in fact, just about every form of entertainment imaginable.

The main event is a mighty New Year's Eve street party. Concerts, parties and cutting-edge live acts are staged along Princes Street. During the 1996/97 hogmanay, some 400,000 people gathered in Princes Street alone. However, this proved to be too many, which is why the organisers have decided to make the Princes Street party a ticket-only event to control numbers. Tickets are free but limited.

Other core events include the Fire Festival, Hogmanay Carnival, Street Theatre Spectacular, Candlelight Concert in the Cathedral, New Year Revels and the Torchlight Procession. The organisers, Unique Events, are planning some surprises for the Millennium Hogmanay but will keep these main features. **Contact:** Edinburgh & Scotland Information Centre (☎ 0131-557 1700).

An alternative to the organised celebrations on Princes Street is a disorganised party at Arthur's Seat near Edinburgh. A growing number of revellers meet there every year. Don't expect an event; this is a popular but cold and unplanned way to see in the next millennium.

GLASGOW
Millennium Hogmanay 1999 (31 Dec 1999)

Glasgow also stages a great hogmanay celebration. Until now, though, this has been somewhat overshadowed by events in Edinburgh. The organisers hope to change that in 1999. Major outdoor stages will be set up at key points in the city centre and a street party will be held around George Square.

Hogmanay in Glasgow normally attracts between 20-35,000 revellers but is expected to bring in 150,000 party-goers on the eve of the year 2000. The organisers, UZ, want to create a 'major international event' which will compete with the celebrations in Edinburgh.

Contact: UZ (☎ 0141-552 6027, Internet: www.hogmanay.co.uk).

UK City of Architecture and Design: Glasgow (1 Jan–31 Dec 1999)

Glasgow has been named the UK City of Architecture and Design in 1999 by the Arts Council. It's a title Glasgow is taking seriously.

A series of exhibitions will take place throughout 1999. They include retrospectives on Frank Lloyd Wright and Mies van der Rohe, a study of the key moments in the cultural history of world cities since 1900, and lectures from some of the most important pacesetters in architecture and design.

The focus of the year-long event will be a cultural exhibition and education centre called The Lighthouse. This will be based in Charles Rennie Mackintosh's former Glasgow Herald building which is being converted for the purpose. A number of new public areas called Millennium Spaces will also be built around Glasgow.

An information centre has opened at The Terrace on Princes Street. **Contact**: Glasgow 1999 (☎ 0141-248 6994, fax 0141-248 8754) 62 Buchanan Street, Glasgow G1 3JE.

X-Site Science Centre Millennium Project: Glasgow

A state-of-the-art science museum will be built at Pacific Quay in Glasgow as part of Scotland's millennium celebrations. The X-Site Science Centre will boast an IMAX® cinema, an interactive library, a planetarium and, of course, exhibitions. A 100-metre tall Millennium Tower will also be built at the site as an observatory and gallery. **Contact:** Glasgow Development Agency (☎ 0141-204 1111, fax 0141-248 1600), Atrium Court, 50 Waterloo Street, Glasgow, G2 6HQ

ST ANDREWS
Open Golf Championship 2000 (20–23 July 2000)

The world-famous Royal and Ancient Golf Club at St Andrews will host an international open golf championship during July 2000. The top names in golf are expected to play this millennium tournament on the Old Course.

Contact: Royal and Ancient Golf Club (☎ 01334-472112, fax 01334-475483) St Andrews, Fife KY16 9JD.

❏ The Millennial Foundation and Yes 2000

The Millennial Foundation, one of the most enterprising millennium bodies in the world, is based in Glasgow. The Foundation has developed a simple scheme to celebrate the millennium and to raise funds for charity in the third millennium: it's called Yes 2000.

Yes 2000 is an umbrella group which will use satellite television to link 31 major millennium celebrations in every time zone across the world in a 24-hour telecast. Broadcasting companies in each of the 24 time zones will contribute one hour to the worldwide show. The telethon will start from Fiji and follow midnight as it progresses around the world to the Cook Islands on the other side of the International Date Line in the South Pacific.

The Foundation is also offering travel packages to many of these party sites (see relevant destination pages). Other fund-raising events, some of which will be joint Millennial Foundation/UNESCO 2000 projects, will take place throughout 1999 and 2000. Audrey Mason-Wadsworth, Chairman of the Millennial Foundation, says: 'the project is ambitious but necessary. When it's all said and done, won't it be wonderful to know that in addition to having a great party, we also served a great cause?'

Yes 2000 has the potential to raise a lot of money which will be donated to a number of projects from a Save the Children scheme in Rwanda to a UNESCO scientific programme in Kiribati. All sponsored projects will help either children or the environment.

Contact: The Millennial Foundation (☎ 0141-204 2000, fax 0141-248 1591) 10 Sandyford Place, Glasgow G3 7NB.

Millennium Link Project: Scotland

Canals are making a comeback. British Waterways has launched an £80 million redevelopment of the Forth & Clyde and Union canals. The re-opened Millennium Link (☎ 0345-952000) will be a coast-to-coast connection between Glasgow and Edinburgh.

Chairman of British Waterways Bernard Henderson says the scheme is about 'turning our heritage into our future'. Canals have been used to improve urban redevelopment in several ventures in England, but this is the first major canal restoration project in Scotland.

Wales

Wales will end the second millennium by hosting the Rugby Union World Cup in the new Millennium Stadium in Cardiff. The giant stadium will also be the venue for a party on New Year's Eve 1999.

Rugby Union World Cup: Wales (Oct-Nov 1999)

Rugby is a religion in Wales. From October 1999 the best sides in the world will descend on Cardiff to compete for the World Cup Webb Ellis Trophy. The new Millennium Stadium (see opposite) in Cardiff will see most of the action, including the final on 6 November. For rugby fans, there are few more enjoyable occasions than Cardiff on a big match day. Whether or not Wales makes the final, the city will be buzzing on 6 November. A closing ceremony and celebration will take place after the

---

❏ **WALES**
Contacts
● **British Tourist Association** (☎ 0181-846 9000, fax 0181-563 0302), Thames Tower, Black's Road, Hammersmith, London W6 9EL
● **Wales Tourist Board** (☎ 01222-499909, fax 01222-475322), Brunel House, 2 Fitzalan Road, Cardiff CF2 1UY
Average maximum temperature °C

	Dec	Jan
Cardiff	8	7

Capital: Cardiff
Flight times: (as for England, see p111)
Approximate exchange rates: Pound Sterling (£) – US$1=0.6, A$1=0.4
Time difference: GMT (+1 from last Sunday in March to last Sunday in October)
Country dialling code: ☎ 44

final. For travel packages to the World Cup, **contact**: Gullivers Sports Travel, (☎ 01684-293175, fax 01684-290093), Fiddington Manor, Tewkesbury, Gloucestershire, GL20 7BT.

The Millennium Stadium: Cardiff

It was with mixed feelings that the Welsh said goodbye to the Cardiff Arms Park rugby stadium. When the Welsh Rugby Union decided to auction the 'hallowed turf', they were inundated with offers. Rugby enthusiasts even paid good money for seats and struts from the old stadium! But something better is being built in its place. The Millennium Stadium, which will open in 1999 in time to host the World Cup, is to be a 73,500-seat arena with a retractable roof. This state-of-the-art stadium will host concerts and festivals as well as sporting events. The pitch will be suitable for a range of sports. An opening celebration will take place at the new £120 million stadium during June 1999. It will also be the venue for a major New Year's Eve 1999 party (see below).

New Year's Eve Party: Cardiff (31 Dec 1999)

The people behind the Millennium Stadium are plotting a mega-bash in the new arena on New Year's Eve 1999. This will be by far the biggest party in Wales. **Contact**: Lesley Thomson (☎ 01222-232661).

Wales Millennium Centre: Cardiff

Cardiff's docklands are in the process of massive regeneration. This project will be provided with a focus of international stature in the Wales Millennium Centre. This striking new building will become the home of Welsh art and culture. It will accommodate musicals, ballet and dance and will be home to the world-renowned Welsh National Opera. A museum, gallery, IMAX® cinema and shopping piazza will surround the 1900-seat theatre, under the same roof. The centre is scheduled to open in 2001. **Contact:** Wales Millennium Ctre Project (fax 01222-454304, e-mail wmc@cardiff-bay.co.uk), PO Box 2001, Cardiff, CF1 6YS

National Botanic Garden of Wales Millennium Project

Middleton Hall in Camarthenshire was once surrounded by one of the most impressive landscaped gardens of its time. The Hall

---

❏ **Millennium events in other parts of the UK**

● **Northern Ireland Odyssey** Over two million people a year are expected to visit the Odyssey Millennium Centre in Belfast. On completion in 2000, the Centre will be one of the biggest entertainment, leisure, sport and education centres in Europe. Shops, an IMAX® cinema (like architects, IMAX® are doing well out of the millennium!) an international science centre and an indoor arena will all be under the same roof.

● **New Year's Eve Party: Jersey (31 Dec 1999)** A luxury Millennium's Eve dinner and party will be held at the magnificent Elizabeth Castle on Jersey. The plans are well-advanced; a great menu has been fixed and various 'surprises' have been arranged to entertain guests throughout the evening. Price: approximately £150-190. **Contact:** Olaf Blakely (☎/fax 01534-888101) – Mr Blakely has yet to start taking reservations.

---

and gardens are now derelict. But that will soon change. Both are being restored in a highly ambitious scheme to create a leading botanic garden to rival any other.

Equal attention is being given to the aesthetic and the scientific – meaning that the gardens will be a beautiful attraction but also a centre for scientific research. An audio-visual Bioscope, a hands-on Bioverse education centre, glasshouses and a restaurant will be built at the gardens. **Contact:** The National Botanic Garden of Wales (☎ 01558-668768, fax 01558-668933), Middleton Hall, Llanarthne, Camarthenshire SA32 8HW

Iceland

REYKJAVIK

Reykjavik might not be the first place one would think of to hold a Millennium's Eve party. Well, think again. As a European City of Culture in the year 2000, and the venue for a Millennial Foundation party, Reykjavik could surprise you. A 'non-stop programme of festivities' has been promised by Reykjavik as a **European City of Culture** in 2000. The organisers have come up with the motto: 'Culture and Nature'. Other year-long festivals planned for the year 2000 include the Millennial Celebration of Christianity, the Millennial Celebration of the Discovery of America from Iceland and the Reykjavik Millennium Art Festival. The 50th anniversaries of the Icelandic National Theatre and the Icelandic Symphony Orchestra will also be celebrated. **Contact**: Tourist Information Centre (☎ +354 91-623 045), Bankastræti 2, 101 Reykjavik, Iceland

New Year's Eve Parties and Millennium Tours

The Millennial Foundation (see p137) will hold a New Year's Eve party at the Perlan Restaurant (☎ +354 91-620 200). This ultra-modern restaurant revolves every hour and is one of the most striking buildings in Reykjavik. The bash will be beamed around the world as part of a 24-hour millennium telecast. Drama, concerts and exhibitions will run throughout 1999 as part of the Millennial Foundation event. A six-day Millennial Foundation tour to Iceland will cost £1750. Arctic Experience (☎ +44 (0) 1737-218800) has a week-long tour to Iceland including a New Year's Eve party. Price: approximately £1000.

❏ THE LAST MILLENNIUM
The Year 1000 – Apocalypse postponed

Predicting apocalypse is an unfortunate vocation. Until now, at least, such pessimists have invariably been humiliated. The moment comes...and goes. Despite such frustrations, humankind has long had a penchant for expecting The End. Professor Richard Landes of Boston University explains that such thinking 'speaks to our most deeply-seated instincts -- the desire for justice, the need for meaning.'

The Coming of the Antichrist

The Church in Europe satiated that need for meaning by proclaiming that The End would be preceded by the Coming of the Antichrist. At the end of the eighth century the Coming of the Antichrist was thought to be close and omens began to appear. Professor Landes notes that the Roman Empire had fallen and the Pope expelled from Rome. Apocalyptic messages continued, even after the year had passed with the world still intact. (See overleaf).

The Last Millennium (cont)

A new End was needed, a date that was distant but comprehensible. The year 1000AD was chosen. There was no hiding that date, it was widely known and fairly well understood. Church leaders averted disaster in their own time but bequeathed their successors a date of alarming potency.

Portents of Doom

In the run up to the year 1000 several extraordinary events were interpreted as signs of doom. Halley's comet was seen, famines occurred and war and plague broke out. The problem was treated differently across Europe. In the Saxon Empire order remained largely intact, although the Saxon Emperor, Otto III, demanded a mass conversion to Christianity of the heathens.

The West grew more unstable in response to seemingly portentous signs, but mass reaction was not to panic.

The year 1000

The year 1000 was a catalyst for highly significant change. It was a leveller. Peace Councils were established and hundreds of simple white churches were built. Warriors were made to accept the rights of peasants and of the Church. Professor Landes describes the event as a 'social contract by public oath and acclamation'.

1033 – The End re-scheduled

Bad omens continued. Again, the apocalyptic prophets re-scheduled The End, this time for 1033 – the millennium of the resurrection. As Europe approached 1033, famine ravaged France. Again, mass response was to create evermore Peace Councils.

2000 – The End?

As we approach the year 2000 technology and science have, for many, replaced God. Few expect the Antichrist or The End of Time. We do fear the end of the world. Weapons of mass destruction, pollution and water shortages are real threats. If we want omens, there are plenty: the year 2000 computer crisis, fatal smog over South East Asia or even the death of Diana, Princess of Wales.

Our threats are new, and – largely – of our own making. Our omens are more easily explained. But still we fear for the world's future, and many plan to use the weight of the year 2000 to force changes which will improve life for those in the next century. Clearly, there are similarities between the mood now, as we approach the third millennium, and that of 1000 years ago.

THE CARIBBEAN

Since Cunard decided to send the QE2 on a millennial cruise to the Caribbean, other companies, including Celebrity Cruises and Disney, have been quick to make similar plans. Tour operator Abercrombie & Kent are also expecting the Caribbean to be a popular millennial destination and have devised several attractive packages. US Virgin Islanders are well prepared to welcome tourists for New Year's Eve 1999 but other islands, including Barbados, are catching up.

US Virgin Islands

Tourists are expected to head for the US Virgin Islands in big numbers at the end of 1999. Many Americans consider the island

---

❑ **US VIRGIN ISLANDS**
Contacts
● **USVI Division of Tourism**, PO Box 6400, Charlotte Amalia, St Thomas, 00804 (☎ 77-48784, fax 77-44390)
Average maximum temperature °C

	Dec	Jan
Tortola	29	29

Capital: Tortola
Flight times:
> Miami – 2hrs 40 mins
> London – 9 hrs 50 mins *to Miami*
> Sydney – 11 hrs *to LA*, 6hrs *from LA to Miami*

Approximate exchange rates: US dollar (US$) – £1=1.6, A$1=0.65
Time difference: GMT -4
Country dialling code: ☎ 1-809

❏ St Croix – What to See

This is the largest of the US Virgin Islands, although it is less developed and more laid-back than St Thomas. In fact, Cruzians (St Croix is a translation of Santa Cruz, the name given to the Island by Columbus) look down on St Thomas which they consider to be over-crowded.

There are some superb beaches on St Croix, and it is quite easy to find empty stretches. **Cramer Park**, the Islands' millennium party venue, is popular for snorkelling and gets very busy. Deep-sea fishing, windsurfing, snorkelling, sub-aqua diving, horse-riding, golf, tennis and waterskiing are all available.

The capital, **Christiansted**, is an attractive harbour town with a very Danish atmosphere. Denmark sold the Virgin Islands to America in 1917. Buildings like the **Customs House** and **Government House** reflect this colonial past.

St Croix was once the richest of the US Virgin Islands, with a well-developed farming industry. The plantations have left their mark. The **Whim Greathouse and Museum** is worth visiting for an introduction to the agriculture which dominated St Croix for hundreds of years. A more tempting exhibition can be found at the **Cruzian Rum Distillery**. A fascinating guided tour ends with a quick quaff at the bar.

of St Croix to be the easternmost point of the States – and so the first to see the sun rise on 1 January 2000. St Croix is all set to welcome millennial visitors.

New Year's Eve Party: Cramer Park, St Croix

Cramer Park, which is on the eastern tip of St Croix, is to be the venue for an elegant New Year's Eve party. Tourists are invited to attend the function which will feature dusk-'til-dawn dancing to local bands. Traditional Island delicacies will be delivered to the site by local restaurants. Cramer Park commands spectacular views over the Caribbean Sea.

New Year's Eve Fireworks: Point Udall, St Croix

Apart from the US territory of Guam, which is in the Eastern Hemisphere and so not counted by Virgin Islanders, Point Udall

❑ **British Virgin Islands, Grenadines and St Barts**

It has become something of a British Virgin Islands tradition to see in the New Year at *Foxy's* (☎ +1 809 49-59 258) on the Great Harbour of **Jost Van Dyke Island**. After midnight the party moves to the beach. Thousands are expected for 31 December 1999. On New Year's Eve hundreds of yachting people stop off at Foxy's too, so there should be quite a crowd. Foxy himself has promised top notch entertainment.

The Bitter End Yacht Club (☎ +1 809 49-42 746) on **Virgin Gorda** is another British Virgin Islands millennium party venue. Overlooking Gorda Sound, the Bitter End Clubhouse is an attractive and popular place. A party will also take place on **Anegada**, the northernmost British Virgin Island, to see the sun rise on the New Year, century and millennium. The Long Bay Beach Resort (in UK: ☎ 0800-898379) on **Tortola** will lay on an 11-day celebration over New Year 1999. Price: £1799. The British Virgin Islands Club (☎ +44 (0) 1932-247617) is offering that package with flights from Britain. Price: £4000.

Yacht Connections (☎ +44 (0) 1344 624897, fax +44 (0) 1344 626849, e-mail ac@yacht-connections.co.uk) are already offering a number of yachts for hire over New Year's Eve 1999. Yachts and catamarans are available from 60-82ft in length. Rates start at around the US$30,000 mark for 10-days' charter with room for 8-10 guests. Most of Yacht Connections' vessels are based in the British Virgin Islands but yachts in other parts of the Caribbean are also available.

According to Yacht Connections' David Schoonover, an old hand at celebrating New Year's Eve in the Caribbean, the only other places worth being when the clock strikes midnight on 31 December 1999 are *Basil's Bar* in Mustique (in the **Grenadines**) or *Gustavia* on St Barthélemy.

on St Croix is the easternmost point of the United States. As a result, resident revellers will enjoy a head start on the rest of America when it comes to celebrating the new millennium.

A spectacular fireworks festival has been planned at Point Udall. The display will be visible from Cramer Park, site of the Island's New Year's Eve party. The fireworks will start at midnight. Point Udall will be the focus of millennial celebrations on

❏ **Aquarius Rising**
Colorado-based prophet/futurologist Marshall Savage hopes to create a proto-space colony called Aquarius Rising on the island of St Croix.

the US Virgin Islands. Between now and the end of 1999 an extensive development programme is preparing the area for an expected surge in tourist numbers.

Sunrise Ceremony and Ships Parade: Point Udall
St Croix (1 Jan 2000)
When the first rays of the year 2000 appear over Point Udall, an interdenominational prayer service will be held. Local gospel groups will be invited to accompany the service. A parade of ships, visible from several positions on the islands but best seen from Point Udall, will conclude the all-night partying.

Barbados

Millennium Party: Sandy Lane Hotel
The famous Sandy Lane Hotel on Barbados will host the most extravagant celebration on the Island on 31 December 1999. A New Year's Eve party is held every year; it is thought to be the best on Barbados. But the Sandy Lane, whose list of famous guests reads like a 20th century roll of honour, is gearing up to a massive re-opening party on 31 December '99 having been closed for complete refurbishment.

Prices have yet to be fixed, but expect to pay *a lot*. Seeing in the 1998 New Year at Sandy Lane cost between US$880-2390 per room, per night. There was a minimum stay of 14 nights!

Contact: Sandy Lane (☎ +1-809 246 432 1311, fax +1-809 246 432 2954), St James, Barbados, West Indies

Millennium villa hire

Another way to see in the next millennium on Barbados is to hire a private villa. The following companies have villas available (UK offices listed): **Caribbean Centre** (☎ 0181-940 3399), **Caribbean Connection** (☎ 01244-355303), **Casa Caribe** (☎ 0161-486 9441), **Continental Villas** (☎ 0171-497 0444), **Douglas Holidays** (☎ 01242-235005), **Elderone** (☎ 0181-446 8122), **Elegant Resorts** (☎ 01244-897999), **Exclusive Villas** (☎ 0181-947 7300), **Meon Villas** (☎ 01730-266561), **Palmer & Parker** (☎ 01494-815411), **Worlds End Travel** (☎ 01582-481636).

Barbados Millennium Society

What started life as a reunion for a group of college friends has grown into a major millennial celebration complete with its own motto (*dum vivimus vivamus* – while we are alive, let us live), anthem and beach towel.

Rex Horning, an American banker and ex-Marine, formed the Barbados Millennium Society to arrange a millennium get-together for a group of friends from Oklahoma State University. Barbados was the preferred location because of its climate and proximity to the States.

On the evening of 31 December 1999 the BMS will sit down to a formal black-tie banquet which will be followed by a dance party. A 12-piece 'tropical show band' has already been booked. After a brief rest, jeeps will turn up to take the group to a remote spot on the east side of the island where a sunrise champagne breakfast and celebration has been arranged. Both the New Year's Eve party and accommodation will be at the Southwinds Beach and Racquet Club in Christ Church.

The BMS began as a private affair, but it is now possible for other like-minded party-goers to join the celebration provided they become associate members of the BMS.

Contact: Rex Horning, The Barbados Millennium Society (☎ +1 316-231 7276, e-mail barmsoc@fament.com).

❑ **Caribbean Millennium Tours (Abercrombie & Kent)**

Jamaica: 22 Dec 1999 – 5 Jan 2000. This two-week stay at the 45-room Jamaica Inn, which is set in six acres and has a private beach and pool, is likely to provide a peaceful start to the millennium. Full board. Price: £3522.

Young Island, St Vincent: 23 Dec 1999 – 3 Jan 2000. Accommodation on Young Island, which is just off St Vincent, is in separate wood-framed cottages. Sports facilities on offer include: a 44ft yacht, tennis court and windsurfing. Half-board. Price: £3166.

Barbados: 23 Dec 1999 – 3 Jan 2000. Cobblers Cove in St Peter, which offers complimentary watersports and an excellent beach-front restaurant, will be the venue for this millennium tour. Half-board. Price: £3508.

St Kitts: 28 Dec 1999 – 4 Jan 2000. This shorter break makes use of an old plantation house turned hotel, Rawlins Plantation, which commands great views of the sea and the mountain on which it sits. There is also a spring-fed swimming pool. Half-board. Price: £2215.

St Lucia: 22 Dec 1999 – 4 Jan 2000. Accommodation on St Lucia will be at the Mediterranean-style Windjammer Landing. Villas or rooms are available, making this a good choice for families. Room only. Price: £2329.

Abercrombie & Kent have based these prices on a similar trip in December 1996. The actual cost in 1999 is likely to be between 25-40% more. Final prices will be announced in September 1998. A £600 refundable deposit is required to reserve a space on an Abercrombie & Kent millennium trip. A further **non**-refundable deposit of £400 is required on 1 October 1998. The outstanding cost of the trip must be paid in full by 1 October 1999. **Contact:** Abercrombie & Kent (☎ +44 (0) 171-730 9600, fax +44 (0) 171-730 9376), Sloane Square House, Holbein Place, London SW1V 8NS, UK .

Bermuda

A laid-back start to the millennium will be on offer in Bermuda, where buildings are painted in pastel shades and business is done in shorts. A good time to visit will be June 2000, when the Island will welcome entrants in the Tall Ships 2000 race.

Bermuda's 150 islands, which are thrown together in a fish-hook shape, are among the most alluring anywhere in the world. They are famous for calm beaches, clear water, well-developed hospitality and, of course, golf.

Americans account for much of the islands' tourism because of its proximity to the States. British people also feel a certain bond with Bermuda which is a British Dependent Territory.

Hamilton, the capital, acts both as the administrative and cultural hub. This is the place for shopping and good food. Like most settlements on the islands, Hamilton is painted in pastel colours which give the impression of a toy town.

❏ **BERMUDA**
Contacts
● **Bermuda Tourism** (☎ +44 (0) 171-771 7001, fax +44 (0) 171-771 7037), 1 Battersea Church Road, London SW11 3LY, United Kingdom.
Average maximum temperature °C

	Dec	Jan
Hamilton	21	20

Capital: Hamilton
Flight times:
New York – 2 hrs 10 mins
London – 7hrs 45 mins
Sydney – 11 hrs *to LA*, then 5 hrs *to New York*
Approximate exchange rates: Bermuda Dollar (B$) – £1=1.6, US$1=1, A$1=0.6
Time difference: GMT -4
Country dialling code: ☎ 1-441

With some 150 shipwrecks scattered around its fringes, Bermuda is a centre for diving and offers several sub-aqua courses. Golf and horse-riding are about the only other strenuous activities available. For most visitors, though, that's perfect.

Bermuda will lure its usual blend of wealthy and romantic travellers to welcome the new millennium. To find out what's on in Bermuda, buy the *Bermuda Sun* newspaper on Fridays.

❏ The Tall Ships Race of the Century

To celebrate the new millennium, ISTA – the International Sail Training Association – has organised a series of races across the Atlantic called Tall Ships 2000.

There will be four legs: the first starting with two races to Cádiz in Spain, one from Southampton, England, the other from Genoa in Italy. Both will set off during April 2000. The second leg will be from Cádiz to Bermuda. Crews will have time to recover on a gentler cruise to Boston, Massachusetts from where racing will continue to Halifax in Nova Scotia. The final leg will be from Halifax to Amsterdam.

Each port of call will arrange entertainment for the crews and public events, such as firework displays, parades and fairs. ISTA arranges Tall Ships' races annually, and always draws a large crowd of spectators to each of its stages.

Part of the Tall Ships 2000 philosophy is to encourage young people to take part and to promote a friendly international competition. At least half of each crew must be between the ages of 15 and 25. The Tall Ships title is, in fact, something of a misnomer. While the great square riggers are welcomed, vessels as small as 9.14m LWL are also permitted to enter.

The Duke of Edinburgh, ISTA's patron, has said that for participants the event will be 'a great adventure and something to remind them of the turn of the century for the rest of their lives.'

Contact: Tall Ships 2000 (☎ 01705-586367, fax 01705-584661), 5 Mumby Road, Gosport, Hampshire PO12 1AA, England. Anyone hoping to find out how to join a Tall Ships 2000 crew should not contact the race organisers but should get in touch with their local sailing club or association. ISTA is not responsible for introducing would-be crew to participating ships.

New Year's Eve 1999 Party and Tour: Bermuda

The Millennial Foundation is offering a six-day tour to Bermuda which includes admission to the New Year's Eve party. The gala celebration will take the form of a traditional Scottish hogmanay. Visitors will stay at the first-class Southampton Princess Resort which sits in 100-acres of parkland and occupies the highest point on Bermuda. Price: £2500.

Contact: Millennial Foundation (☎ +44 (0) 141-204 2000, fax +44 (0) 141-248 1591, Internet: http://www.yes2000.co.uk), 10 Sandyford Place, Glasgow G3 7NB, UK .

Tall Ships 2000 Finishing Point: Bermuda
8-11 June 2000

Between 8-11 June 2000, entrants in the Tall Ships 2000 trans-Atlantic race (see opposite) will arrive in Bermuda after a gruelling voyage from Cádiz in Spain. Bermuda will greet her guests with fireworks, parties and parades. Thousands are expected to participate in the festival. Winners of this second stage in the race series will be given prizes at an awards ceremony. On top of the festivities, spectators will be treated to the wonderful view of the entrants' ships, many of which will be square riggers.

MILLENNIUM CRUISES

In 1982 the Tontine Club (see opposite) persuaded Cunard to take a deposit for 50 cabins on the *Queen Elizabeth II* over New Year's Eve 1999. Apart from guaranteeing its members a quality New Year's Eve, the Tontine did Cunard a favour: it set the Company thinking. Fifteen years on, Cunard is the best-prepared cruise company for the millennium – but there are others.

CUNARD

Cunard has five cruise itineraries on offer. The *Queen Elizabeth II* will sail from Southampton, England to Fort Lauderdale, Florida between 12 December and 4 January. Ports of call include: New York, Cozumel, Mexico, Limon, Costa Rica and Oranjestad, Aruba. Christmas Day will be spent at sea. Passengers will find themselves in Barbados on New Year's Eve.

The *QE2* itself is quite an experience. It has a reputation for outstanding comfort and style. Passengers will be well enter-tained throughout the voyage; there is even a range of 30 cham-pagnes on offer.

A 22-day cruise on board the *Royal Viking Sun* will set sail from Fort Lauderdale, Florida, on 19 December and will finish in San Francisco on 9 January. The ship will negotiate the Panama Canal before docking in Acapulco for New Year's Eve.

A third cruise, on the *Vistafjord*, starts in Genoa on 18 December and finishes in Mombasa on 8 January. The itinerary is a fitting one: Athens, Alexandria, Haifa and Jordan. New Year's Eve will be at Sharm el Sheik in Egypt. A lot of people are planning to visit the ancient areas of Egypt, Greece and Israel to greet the new millennium. This is one way to do it with real ele-gance.

The sister ships *Sea Goddess 1* and *Sea Goddess II* won't be seeing in the year 2000 together. A circular Caribbean route will take the *Sea Goddess I* to and from St Thomas between 22 December and 5 January by way of such attractive spots as

Grenada, Barbados and Martinique. New Year's Eve will be spent in the British Virgin Islands (see p145).

The *Sea Goddess II* is heading for Indonesia. Her cruise will start and end at Bali between 22 December and 6 January. Stops include: Sepa Island, Surabaya, Bau Bau and Palopa. New Year's Eve will be celebrated in Palua Naira.

Prices are still to be revealed but Cunard is operating a waiting-list reservation scheme. The required deposit is US$1000 or £750 per person. When Cunard announces pricing, cabins will be allocated to those with their names down first. Then a further deposit will be required. The original deposit will be refunded to those that either fail to get a cabin or change their minds.

Cunard, USA Suite 400, 6100, Blue Lagoon Drive, Miami, Florida 33126 USA or UK (☎ +44 (0) 1703-634 166) Mountbatten House, Grosvenor Square, Southampton SO15 2BF, UK.

❏ **The Tontine Club**

In 1982, David Banford set up the Tontine Club. A tontine is a sort of Victorian life insurance policy. Each member would pay a fixed sum into the group kitty every year for an agreed number of years. Along the way, of course, some members would die. When the final payment date was reached, the kitty would be shared out between the surviving members.

The Tontine Club runs on the same principle. In 1982, the Club booked 50 cabins on-board the QE2 for a yet-to-be-planned millennial cruise (at that time Cunard had not considered the millennium). The Club members agreed to go wherever Cunard decided to send the ship, each member paying a set sum into the Tontine bank account every year until 1999. Along the way, some of that money has been carefully invested, while some has been used to amass an enviable collection of wine and champagne for the trip. David Banford bought huge numbers of 1982 vintage Bordeaux back in 1984.

The wine and the investments have matured very well. That – and the fact that some members have, sadly, passed on – means the Tontine Club has a tidy sum to spend on celebrating the millennium in style. The original rules state that all Club money must be spent on seeing in the year 2000. The Cunard cruise is to Barbados.

ORIENT LINES

Two Antarctic cruises are on offer from Orient Lines: the Grand Millennium or the Millennium 2000. The first is a 32-day voyage on board the *Marco Polo* from 6 Dec 1999-6 Jan 2000.

Passengers will meet the ship in Cape Town before crossing the South Atlantic to South America. Ports of call include: Rio de Janeiro, Itajai, Montevideo, Buenos Aires and the Falklands. A New Year's Eve party will be held at Port Lockroy, 1500 miles from the South Pole. Prices start at £5995 per person.

Millennium 2000 passengers will join the *Marco Polo* in Buenos Aires. Shore landings will regularly be made using Zodiac landing craft. Antarctic experts will give lectures on board the ship. There is to be an open bar and a supply of complimentary wine. Prices for the Millennium 2000 cruise start at £4595 per person. **Orient Lines** (☎ +44 (0) 171-409 2500, fax +44 (0) 171-409 7525) 38 Park Street, London W1Y 3PF, UK.

ABERCROMBIE & KENT

Only 112 passengers will be able to join Abercrombie & Kent's two millennium cruises. From December 1999 to January 2000, the *Explorer* – which can carry 96 passengers – will make a millennial voyage to Antarctica. The price is estimated at £4642 per person. From 22 Dec 1999-4 Jan 2000, the beautiful *Alta*, a three-masted schooner, will carry just 16 passengers to the Galápagos Islands in the Pacific. The price will be approximately £3340 per person. **Abercrombie & Kent** (☎ +44 (0) 171-730 9600, fax +44 (0) 171-730 9376), Sloane Square House, Holbein Place, London SW1V 8NS, UK.

CELEBRITY CRUISES

A small deposit is needed to secure a place on Celebrity Cruises' waiting list: £175 or US$250. The Company is planning five voyages using their *Galaxy*, *Century*, *Zenith*, *Horizon* and new *Mercury* ships.

Exact itineraries have yet to be finalised, but the cruises are likely to be in the Caribbean and around the coasts of Mexico and Alaska. Celebrity Cruises' waiting list deposit is refundable. Things change quickly, however, and you should ensure that your deposit is still refundable when you put it down. **Celebrity Cruises** USA (☎ 001 305-262 6677) 5201 Blue Lagoon Drive, Miami, Florida, 33126 USA or UK (☎ +44 (0) 171-355 0606) 17 Old Park Lane, London W1Y3LG, UK.

PRINCESS CRUISE LINE

This company will accept deposits of US$200 per person. Again, the deposit is refundable. Would-be passengers can expect to wait until 12-18 months prior to departure before receiving prices or itineraries. **Princess Cruise Line** UK (+44 (0) 171-800 2468).

ROYAL CARIBBEAN CRUISE LINE

All RCCL ships will have a millennial itinerary but the same conditions apply as for the Princess Cruise Line: a refundable US$200 deposit is required to find a place on the waiting list. Again, final details won't be revealed until 18 months prior to sailing. **Royal Caribbean Cruise Line** UK (☎ +44 (0) 1932-820210).

MARINE EXPEDITIONS

For a longer stint at sea, Marine Expeditions has devised a 114-day 'expedition cruise' from November 1999 to March 2000. The cruise will take its intrepid sailors to seven continents and seven seas for US$8888 per person. A US$2500 deposit is required. **Marine Expeditions** (☎ +1 416-964 9069), 30 Hazelton Avenue, Toronto, Ontario M5R 2E2, Canada.

SEABOURN CRUISE LINE

Two of Seabourn's small 270-berth ships will cruise the Caribbean between 27 December and 12 January. The voyages will be round trips from Fort Lauderdale. New Year's Eve will be spent at Charlotte Amalie in the US Virgin Islands where a gala celebration is being arranged. **Seabourn Cruise Line**, 3921 Long Meadow Road, Downers Grove, Illinois 60515, USA.

DISNEY

This familiar name is new to cruise ships. The *Disney Magic* liner is still being built. However, its maiden voyage will take place in 1998. A family-orientated millennium cruise will set sail for the Bahamas in late December 1999. Various packages are on offer, including add-ons at Disney theme parks before and after the cruise. **Disney Cruise Vacations** (☎ +1 407-566 3500), 210 Celebration Place, Suite 400, Celebration, Florida 34747-4600.

CARNIVAL
Three- or four-day millennium cruises require a refundable deposit of £100, or £165 for a week-long cruise. **Carnival** UK (☎ + 44 (0) 171-240 3336), USA (☎ +1 305-599 2600).

FRED OLSEN
Millennium cruises to the Canary Islands. A no-deposit-required register of interest is open. **Fred Olsen** UK (☎ +44 (0) 171-931 8888).

Holland America
Accepting deposits of £330 for week-long cruises. Longer cruises require a deposit of £650. **Holland America Line** UK (☎ +44 (0) 171-729 1929), or USA (☎ +1 305-947 3411).

P&O
No details yet, but the Company is accepting a refundable £500 deposit. **P&O** (☎ +44 (0) 171-800 2222).

MEDITERRANEAN SHIPPING CRUISES
Accepting deposits of £50 on cruises which are likely to be to the Indian Ocean and Caribbean. **Mediterranean Shipping Cruises** (☎ +44 (0) 171-637 2525).

FESTIVAL CRUISES
Accepting deposits of £70. **Festival Cruises** UK (☎ +44 (0) 171-436 0827).

❑ **Rex Travel** in the US are millennium cruise specialists on the Internet. Contact Rex Travel through the company web-site at http://www.rextravel.com

SOUTH AMERICA

The only way to celebrate the millennium in South America is to organise a party of your own or join a millennium tour. Brazil, Chile and Argentina are likely to hold celebrations but nothing definite has been arranged yet – with the notable exceptions of a free party on Copacabana Beach in Rio de Janeiro, and a six-day celebration in Costa Rica.

New Year's Eve 1999 Party: Brazil (31 Dec 1999)
One of biggest free parties in the world is scheduled for New Year's Eve 1999 on Copacabana Beach in Rio de Janeiro. The eight-mile-long stretch of sand will be filled with an expected 2.5 million revellers and a giant carnival. Fireworks, music stages and a mass-millennial countdown are planned.

Milenio: Costa Rica (27 Dec 1999-2 Jan 2000)
Together with the United Nations, the Costa Rican Government is organising a peace conference and millennium celebration. Peace conference delegates, including Nobel laureates, environmentalists and world leaders, will gather to reflect on the past and to discuss ways to further peace in the next millennium. The cel-

❏ **Panama Canal returns to Panama**
At noon on 31 December 1999, Panama will get its canal back. James Bryce described the Panama Canal as 'the greatest liberty man has ever taken with nature'. It was built by the United States between 1904-1914, after an unsuccessful attempt by the French, and links the Caribbean and Pacific Oceans. The States acquired the canal and the Canal Zone from Panama in 1903. After an anti-American backlash in the seventies, the US agreed to give both back on Millennium's Eve. Panamanians aren't shy when it comes to partying; with two good reasons to celebrate, Panama will be a great place to be when the millennium arrives.

ebration on 31 December 1999 will be broadcast around the world and the climax will be a giant fireworks display. It will be based around several stages featuring live music and performance. **Contact:** Milenio (☎ +1 415-206 0262, fax +1 415- 206 9620), 163 Fairmount Street, San Francisco, Ca 94131, USA.

South America Millennium Tours (Travcoa)
● **Rio de Janeiro (28 Dec 1999 – 11 Jan 2000)** New Year's Eve in Rio de Janiero plus an Amazon River Cruise and a trip to Manaus. Price: US$7795.
● **Peru and Galápagos (20 or 28 Dec 1999 – 7 Jan 2000)** Includes: La Paz, Lake Titicaca, Cuzco, Machu Picchu, Lima, Quito, Otavalo and a Galápagos Islands cruise (over New Year's Eve). Price: US$5495-8995

South America Millennium Tours (Maupintour)
US-based travel firm Maupintour (☎ +1 800-255 4266) has millennium trips to Machu Picchu (26 Dec 1999-2 Jan 2000), Rio de Janeiro (26 Dec 1999-2 Jan 2000) and the Galápagos Islands (26 Dec 1999-4 Jan 2000) on offer. A deposit of US$850 is required to secure a place. Final prices are not yet available.

Millennium Tour: Easter Island (dates flexible)
Chilean travel company Azimut 360 specialises in tailor-made tours. A millennium trip to Easter Island is available for approximately US$600 per person. That price is an estimate and does not include international flights. The exact details and dates of the trip are flexible.
  Contact: Azimut 360 (☎ +56 2-735 8034, fax +56 2-777 2375, e-mail azimut@reuna.cl), Montecarmelo 180, Dpto 36, Providencia, Santiago, Chile.

❏ SOUTH AMERICA FOR THE INDEPENDENT TRAVELLER

It is frustrating that so few millennium plans have been hatched in South America. But when the time comes independent travellers are likely to find the continent welcoming and celebratory. Tourist boards and party-planners in South America have assured *The Millennium Guide* that parties and fiestas will take place. There are many beautiful, exciting and appropriate places in South America in which to welcome the year 2000. Here are some of the best:

Argentina

From the cosmopolitan buzz of capital Buenos Aires to the spectacular scenery of Patagonia, Argentina offers staggering diversity and beauty. **Buenos Aires** will definitely celebrate the millennium – it's just that the authorities currently have no idea how! Argentina's capital might resemble Paris, but its heart is unmistakeably Latin. The intense but sophisticated locals (*Porteños*) will make good company on New Year's Eve 1999. The international airport is at Ezeiza. Bus transfers will cost about $10. Internal flights land at the more convenient Aeroparque Jorge Newbury, which is a 10-minute taxi trip from town. Long-distance buses, which serve Buenos Aires well, arrive at the Estacin Terminal de Omnibus.

If you can find a hotel room, you will be able to greet the future at one of the most astounding natural sights anywhere in the world: the **Iguazú Falls**. Around 300 separate falls make up one incredible and deafening cascade. Getting there by bus is the best value option, but the journey from Buenos Aires to Iguazú will take about 20 hours.

In Patagonia the independent reveller will find several tempting places in which to celebrate, but – arguably – none more attractive than **Bariloche**. If you do head here, be prepared to mingle with a strange mix of wealthy Brazilians and European jet-setters. This is an up-and-coming place. Bariloche could hardly be better placed, with great views of across Patagonia and up into the Andes. The bus ride from Buenos Aires takes around 20 hours. There are regular two-hour flights from the capital to Bariloche, however, which has its own airport.

Bolivia

Millennial travellers should head for two places in Bolivia. **Tiahuanaco** is the most important archaeological site in the country. It is not as impressive as Machu Picchu, but it is fascinating.

Bolivia (cont)

Built by the Aymara before they were defeated by the Inca, Tiahuanaco is a partially-excavated series of temples, gates and monoliths. The best way to get here is by car, but it can be done by bus from La Paz (50 miles).

The most beautifully-positioned town in Bolivia is **Coroico** in **Los Yungas**. Surrounded by plunging valleys, waterfalls and lush vegetation, Coroico really is in its own Eden. There will be celebrations in the town, but competition for hotel rooms is expected to be fierce. It takes just three hours to get to Coroico by bus from La Paz (about US$10).

Brazil

Visitors to Brazil are often overwhelmed by its vast size and staggering diversity. This diversity is nowhere more obvious than in the comparison between Rio de Janeiro and the Amazon. The first is a sprawl of urban hedonism; the second a sprawl of largely untamed wilderness. There will be a colossal party in **Rio de Janeiro** on Copacabana Beach (see p157). Other celebrations will undoubtedly spring up all over this city which prides itself on its ability to have a good time. Most international and domestic flights arrive at Galeão International Airport. Take an airport bus into town (US$5).

If you would rather escape the urban jungle and see in the next millennium in the **Amazon**, try visiting Belém, Manaus or Santarém. Each is a convenient base from which to make excursions into the enormous forest. There are daily flights between each of these towns and other major cities in Brazil.

Chile

Averaging just 110 miles in width, there is nowhere else to go in Chile but north or south. North will take you to the world's driest desert; head south and you will reach the Antarctic.

Viña del Mar, not far from the capital Santiago, is a playboy's paradise. The bikini-clad girls, flash casinos and ultra-smooth nightlife would make 007 feel at home. The city is always in party mood and it will be an exciting if expensive millennial destination. Regular bus services link Viña del Mar to Santiago's Universidad de Santiago station.

Book ahead if you intend to reach the mysterious **Easter Island** in time to greet the next millennium. With idyllic beaches and a rugged interior littered with baffling *moai* stone statues,

Easter Island is an obvious millennial location. The island has an atmosphere of frightening isolation, but it is served by regular flights from Santiago. Expect to pay at least US$1000 for a return flight.

Columbia

It is a shame that to so many people Columbia is known only as an exporter of drugs. The country is one of the friendliest and most beautiful in South America. Head for **Cartagena** on the magnificent Caribbean Coast. This laid-back and under-developed paradise is a world away from the urgency of Bogotá. Buses and 'planes connect Cartagena with the capital.

Ecuador

Quito, the capital of Ecuador, is one of the best-kept secrets in South America. It is an energetic city of over a million people. The climate is wonderful; equatorial but comfortable because of the city's altitude. The Old City is a stunning labyrinth of colonial elegance and ancient streets which UNESCO has named a World Heritage Site. After dark stylish clubs and bars dominate the New City. The international airport is the Aeropuerto Mariscal Sucre which is well served by American Airlines and Continental. Taxis to the town centre cost between US$5-10.

A more popular millennium destination will be the remarkable **Galápagos Islands** which lie some 600 miles off the coast of Ecuador. Tourism in these remote and highly volcanic islands has boomed over the last 30 years. Several tour operators and cruise companies are planning to take millennial tours to the islands. The animal life here is extraordinary. Indeed, Darwin used his observations in the Galápagos Islands to prove his theory of evolution. Return flights from Quito cost between US$400-600.

Peru

Go to Machu Picchu or Iquitos and you will not be alone. Peru will attract thousands of millennial travellers. The Land of the Incas is both exceptionally beautiful and wonderfully varied.

There can be no doubt that **Machu Picchu** and its environs will be swamped by would-be revellers. This ancient Inca city was left untouched until the early years of this century when it was re-discovered by an American explorer. It is the most important – and impressive – archaeological site in South America.

Peru (cont)

At Machu Picchu, the combined effect of monumental Inca architecture and a truly staggering view across the Andes is almost overwhelming. It is unlikely that any gatherings will be allowed at Machu Picchu itself, but expect to find hundreds of like-minded travellers staying at **Cuzco**. A train line connects Machu Picchu to Cuzco and the outside world. Cuzco is another imposing place – albeit a 'live' city rather than a 'lost' one. It is a mutant blend of the culture and architecture of the Inca and subsequent Spanish empires. It is advisable to fly to Cuzco from Lima rather than endure the two-day bus trip.

Lima itself is the sort of city which makes a big impression on its guests. It is certainly engaging: this is one place where it is probably impossible ever to be bored. But poverty, crime and over-population are rife. The airport is about 10 miles from the city. Expect to pay between US$15-20 for a taxi transfer.

A better New Year's Eve location is **Iquitos** in the heart of the Peruvian rainforest. This is a welcoming oasis of calm in one of the most untamed areas of the world. One can make various excursions into the jungle from Iquitos and it is an attractive port town in its own right. Stay at one of the many jungle lodges in the area for a good chance of cheap accommodation. The remoteness of Iquitos is brought home when trying to get there. Flying is the only option. Scheduled flights run from Lima and Miami.

Venezuela

There are plans afoot to celebrate the millennium in **Caracas** in some style. What will happen is anyone's guess but Venezuala's exhilarating capital is a great city in which to party. Caracas is often compared to Miami. With good beaches and even better clubs, the reputation is well earned. If you do head here for Millennium's Eve, make sure you make the trip to the awesome **Angel Falls** which can be reached by air from Caracas for around US$250. This is the tallest waterfall in the world (3212 feet) and it is breathtaking. Visitors to Venezuela will arrive at the Simón Bolívar International Airport. Pay for the 40-minute taxi ride to Caracas in advance at one the taxi kiosks.

NORTH AMERICA

USA

At the end of a century which has been called the American Century, it should come as no surprise that from the White House downwards events are being planned to welcome the year 2000. Americans love to think big. The new millennium is just such an opportunity.

❑ **USA**
Contacts
● **New York Convention & Visitors Bureau** (Internet: http://www.nycvisit.com), 2 Columbus Circle, New York, NY 10019
● **New Orleans Metropolitan Convention & Visitors Bureau Inc.** (☎ 504-566 5011, fax 504-566 5046), 1520 Sugar Bowl Drive, New Orleans, LA 70112
● **Huntington Beach Conference & Visitors Bureau** (☎ 714-969 3492, fax 714-969 5592, e-mail Hbvisit.aol.com), 101 Main Street, Suite 2A, Huntington Beach, CA 92648
Average maximum temperature °C

	Dec	Jan
Los Angeles	19	18
New Orleans	19	18
New York	6	4

Capital: Washington DC
Flight times: (to New York) from:
Â Â London – 7 hrs 30 mins
Â Â Sydney – 20 hrs 30 mins
Approximate exchange rates: US Dollar (US$) – £1=1.6, A$1=0.65
Time difference: East Coast: GMT -5; West Coast: GMT -8
Country dialling code: ☎ 1

NEW YORK CITY

New York is hoping to become the millennium capital of America by adopting a very catholic approach to its party plans. It is succeeding: on New Year's Eve 1999 New York will be one of the most exciting cities in the world. A massive event will take place in Times Square and a number of top venues and hotels are also planning parties.

Global Celebration: Times Square, New York (31 Dec 1999 – 1 Jan 2000)

New Yorkers hate to be outdone, which is why on 31 December 1999 Times Square will become the venue for one of the world's biggest millennium bashes.

The square will be surrounded by giant TV screens which will beam pictures of parties from each of the world's 23 other time zones to New York's revellers. The city will celebrate the arrival of the year 2000 24 times. It's a two-way thing. Smith-Hemion Productions have been drafted in to create a 24-hour-long show to broadcast to the rest of the world. New York's screens will flicker into life at 7am Eastern Standard Time.

As is traditional on New Year's Eve in Times Square, confetti will be thrown, the ball dropped and *Auld Lang Syne* sung. The lowering of the ball (which glitters with 12,000 rhinestones, 180 halogen lights and 144 strobes) from Number One Times Square happens every New Year's Eve at midnight. On this occasion, Times Square will be 17 hours into its party by the time the ball drops. There will also be a laser light show.

Contact: Times Square 2000 (☎ 212-768 1560, fax 212-768 0233, Internet http://www.times-square.org/index2.html), 1560 Broadway, Suite 800, New York, NY, 10036

First Night New York: New York City (31 Dec 1999)

First Night New York is an annual series of family-orientated dancing and theatre events across the city. Several shows and celebrations are being arranged for New Year's Eve 1999, but there are, as yet, no specific details. **Contact:** Grand Central Partnership (☎ 212-922 9393, fax 212-661 4384).

❏ **Times Square**

Times Square has been variously labelled 'The Great White Way', the 'Crossroads of the World' and the 'New Year's Eve Capital of America'. More recently such superlatives have given way to an unenviable reputation for sleaze, sex shops and drug-dealing. That image is being reversed by an extensive programme to sanitize and regenerate this famous cultural hub. Porn cinemas are slowly being replaced by offices, and criminals are suffering from the city's effective zero-tolerance policing approach. The atmosphere around this centre of Broadway theatreland is changing once again – this time for the better.

New Year's Eve 1999 will be a triumphant moment for the Times Square Business Improvement District which has worked hard to restore the Square to its former glory. Nothing will be left to chance, and visitors can confidently assume that by 31 December '99, Times Square will be a perfectly safe place in which to welcome the year 2000. Times Square will, once again, be able legitimately to claim that it is the New Year's Eve Capital of America.

New Year's Eve 1999 Weekend: RIHGA Royal Hotel (31 Dec 1999 – 2 Jan 2000)

The RIHGA Royal Hotel (☎ 212-307 5000, fax 212-765 6530) is offering a luxury New Year's Eve 1999 weekend for couples. On Friday 31 December 1999 guests will find a limo ready to take them from the airport to their hotel, which overlooks Central Park and the Hudson River. There they will check in to one of the sumptuous Grand Royal Penthouse Suites which feature a sitting room, living room, dining room, kitchen, marble bathroom and master bedroom.

New Year's Eve itself will be spent at the Rainbow Room (see 168) where a millennium dinner dance is planned. New Year's Day will start with breakfast in bed and will end with a Broadway show. Limos will be on hand to ferry passengers around New York all weekend. And the price? A modest US$10,000.

New Year's Eve Party: Marriott Marquis Hotel
New York City (31 Dec 1999 – 1 Jan 2000)

If you want to witness the spectacle of Times Square on 31 December 1999 (see 164), but hope to be cocooned in luxury, try the Marriott Marquis Hotel's (☎ 212-398 1900, fax 212-704 8930) famous New Year's Eve party.

Every year the Marriott Marquis, which is in Times Square, stages a magnificent New Year's Eve event. The new millennium will see a better-than-ever bash. A black-tie gala for 1200 people is being planned in the Hotel's 8th and 9th floor atrium lobby. After dinner and dancing, the climax of the laser light show will be 20,000 balloons falling from the top of the 37-storey atrium – the world's tallest; other surprises are also being planned. Guests will be able to enjoy the Marriott's party and watch the events outside in Times Square. Prices have not yet been announced but

---

❑ Arts Projects in the Big Apple

As part of the American Government's millennium plans, the **National Endowment for the Arts** is helping to finance a wide range of interesting projects for the year 2000. New York City has gained support for 13 initiatives. They include: a **Masterworks of 20th Century American Choreography Festival** and national tour from 1998 to 2003; a **New York City Ballet** tour to all 50 states in America between 1998 and the year 2000; a five-year project will help towns across America to copy the example set by the **Boys Choir of Harlem** in New York City; a **Musical Celebration of the Millennium** through a collaboration between Chamber Music America, composers and over 100 jazz and chamber groups; and a **Millennium-mobile** which will tour the States during 1999 capturing video images of the nation. The result will be a giant TV portrait of America at the end of the second millennium. Money has also been awarded to projects at: The **New York Library for the Performing Arts** ; the **José Limon Dance Foundation**; the **New York City Public Theater**; the **New York Shakespeare Festival**; the **Whitney Museum of American Art**; and New York's celebrated **Museum of Modern Art** (MOMA) has also been awarded money which it will use to support a survey of modern art and to stage 25 new exhibitions. Each exhibition will be accompanied by public information projects and several will tour America

there is a mailing list. Only one guest has managed to book a suite. In 1983, a man from upstate New York had the foresight to make a reservation, the first for 31 December 1999 in the city. Marriott have rewarded his patience by offering him a suite with a Times Square view.

New Year's Eve Party: World Trade Center

Windows on the World is to stage a quarter-of-a-mile-high party at the top of the Two World Trade Center in Lower Manhattan. It will take revellers 58 seconds to reach the 107th floor where the action takes place. The backdrop to the 31 December 1999 celebration will be a view of the Big Apple from its tallest building.

Chicago Special Performance (31 Dec 1999)

Seats are available now for a special New Year's Eve 1999 performance of the Broadway hit *Chicago* at the Shubert Theatre. Tickets can be purchased through Tele-Charge (☎ 212-239 6200 or 800-432 7250 from outside the New York metro area).

Celebration 2000 New Year's Eve Party
Jacob K Javits Center, New York City

A group of business people with a background in finance, advertising and entertainment have formed Celebration 2000. They have devised a programme of millennium events leading to what looks set to be a sensational New Year's Eve 1999 party at the Jacob K Javits Convention Center in New York.

The party will begin at 6pm with a cocktail reception. Top acts will entertain revellers and a gourmet meal will be served. While countless party organisers are promising 'top acts', Celebration 2000 have a very good chance of securing top class entertainment; one of the founding members of Celebration 2000 is a big wheel in the music business.

At midnight a firework display will take place over the Hudson River. TV screens in the Center will show other celebrations from across America and beyond. Celebration 2000 itself will be televised.

The Jacob Javits Center offers a staggering 900,000 square feet of space and is built on 1.8 million square feet of land overlooking the Hudson River. It is one of the world's largest buildings and will play host to one of the world's largest millennial parties. Apart from the fact that this will be a great party, there's another good reason to go: Celebration 2000 have formed an alliance with Save the Children. Together, Celebration 2000 hopes to raise a substantial sum to benefit the world's children.

Contact: Celebration 2000 (☎ 212-644 8900, fax 212-688 1883), 155 East 55th Street, New York, NY 10022. **Internet:** http://www.celebration2000.com.

New Year's Eve Party: The Rainbow Room
New York City (31 Dec 1999 – 1 Jan 2000)

This recently-refurbished restaurant is one of the finest in New York. Situated on the 65th floor of the Rockefeller Center, it commands an outstanding panorama of the Manhattan skyline and offers a stylish dining experience within its glass, bronze, silk and crystal interior.

There will be a New Year's Eve function at the Rainbow Room (☎ 212-632 5000), but competition for a table will be fierce. There are already 211 reservations and 900 names on the waiting list. The management plans to make a further 600 seats available.

Apparently, the Rainbow Room is likely to attract some unusual guests to its New Year's Eve '99 party. A 95-year old man has made a reservation because he thinks the thrill of waiting for the big night will keep him alive long enough to see the year 2000. One couple have booked a table for themselves, their daughter and her husband. The catch is that the daughter is 18-

---

❑ **Call to Start from Scratch**

An American couple are leading a campaign to scrap the year 2000 and call it the year zero instead. Alan and Lori Dechert (fax 503-350 0758) want to break the link between religion and the calendar to 'promote cooperation between nations'. A year zero calendar is already on sale. There is a problem with this high-minded idea: the calendar will not change, it will simply start again. It will have been zeroed on the 2000th anniversary of Christ – so, in a sense, it will still be based on the Christian tradition.

years old and with no husband in sight. So if you're a young, single guy and too late to make a reservation of your own...

New Year's Eve Cruise: New York City (31 Dec 1999)

One hundred guests will have the opportunity to spend New Year's Eve 1999 drifting past the sparkling Manhattan skyline aboard Custom Cruises' motor yacht, the *Diplomat*. Passengers will enjoy a five-star feast from the galley of the 135ft vessel. Champagne will, of course, be handed out liberally and there will be after dinner dancing to live music. If you're interested, don't waste too much time in contacting ☎ 914-381 8077 as space is very limited.

❏ Catalyst for Change

While the world prepares to party on 31 December 1999, many groups and individuals plan to use the millennium to raise public awareness of some of the more sobering issues facing us as we enter the next century. **Catalyst**, the brainchild of Royce Bernstein and Christopher Murray of Georgetown University, is one such group.

Catalyst is organising an event in June 1999 which will bring together thousands of young people from different countries to discuss the future and to allow tomorrow's leaders to meet one another and to create an action plan for the future. To join the meeting, a young person must first give a 'millennial gift' in the form of a positive contribution to his or her community.

Bernstein and Murray are motivated by what they see as an alarming range of growing problems which need to be tackled if the world is to avoid dire consequences. They are concerned by the fact that a fifth of the world's population shares over 80% of the world's income; they are equally keen to address environmental issues such as the staggering statistic that 50,000 species become extinct every year. Catalyst is convinced that young people must be made aware of these issues. After June, Catalyst's action plan, which will have been devised by young people from all over the world, will be presented to the Parliament of World Religions and to the meeting of international civic leaders at Thingvellir in Iceland in the summer of 2000.

Contact: ☎ 202-986 6523 or e-mail: catalyst@bulldog.goergetown.edu

❏ NEW YORK – A BRIEF GUIDE

New Yorkers are among the most diverse and stylish citizens of any city – and that confidence and panache rubs off on every aspect of the Big Apple. In New York, one has the feeling of being at the centre of events.

What to See

There is a long list of 'must-see' sights in New York but there are two ways to get an overall impression of this vast city: from the viewing platforms of either the 420-metre-tall **World Trade Center** or the magnificent 381-metre-tall **Empire State Building**. The Empire State Building is one of most instantly recognisable buildings in the world – thanks to King Kong – but the real symbol of New York is the **Statue of Liberty**. Designed to celebrate the 100th anniversary of the United States, it does indeed represent the city.

Another great view of the city can be enjoyed by floating past the glittering Manhattan skyline on a boat – particularly at night. The **Staten Island Ferry** offers a cheap way to see this spectacle. Few other American experiences – except, perhaps, shooting under the twin towers of the Golden Gate Bridge in San Francisco – make you feel more like being in a movie.

Fifth Avenue, in mid-town Manhattan, is quintessential New York. This is where the forest of sky-scrapers is at its most dense and where extravagant spending is at its most intense. Famous jewellers such as Tiffany and Van Cleef entice the well-heeled from their opulent apartments in **Trump Tower**.

Broadway, the heart of theatre-land and home of **Macy's**, runs into **Times Square**. This recently-sanitized centre of New York excess is worth a visit, not least because it is to host a massive New Year's Eve 1999 party (see p164). **Central Park**, the city's lung which lies between Fifth and Eighth Avenues, is a great place to go to watch New Yorkers at play. One recent addition to the park is a team of mobile roller-blade workers which is charged with the task of encouraging roller-blading in the park by lending out the gear and giving instruction.

The city's **Museum of Modern Art** (MOMA) is one of its gems. It houses perhaps the world's greatest collection of modern art and shouldn't be missed by any visitor. Other world-class cultural centres include the **Metropolitan Opera House** (the 'Met'), the enormous **Metropolitan Museum of Art** and Frank Lloyd

Wright's magnum opus, the **Guggenheim**. The Guggenheim, on Fifth Avenue, is outstanding; here a fabulous art collection is housed in one of the most important buildings of the 20th century.

Of course, there is far more to New York than jaw-dropping art collections and architecture. In this city one can encounter a cross-section of cultures simply by strolling from one block to the next. The fact that New York City is so diverse makes it a wonderful place in which to usher in the next millennium.

Where to Stay

Hotels in the Big Apple are generally better prepared for the millennium than other cities. Several are taking bookings already, and many will be offering special packages and parties.

● **Expensive** (over $170): Two upmarket hotels, the *RIHGA Royal* and the *Marriott Marquis*, are planning elaborate New Year's Eve 1999 parties. See p165 for details. The *Manhattan East Suite Hotels* Group (☎ 212-465 3700 or, in America, 800/ME-SUITE) operates nine hotels in New York. These hotels are quite expensive but good value. Each is accepting names on a millennium mailing list. A team has been created to plan millennium festivities and 'surprises' at the hotels.

The *Crowne Plaza Manhattan* (☎ 212-767 7720, fax 212-977 5517) at 1605 Broadway has started a mailing list. In November '98 people on that list will be sent rate information and a reservation card. The card must be returned with an as yet undisclosed and non-refundable deposit by 1 December 1998. From January 1999 rooms will be allocated. The *New York Hilton and Towers* (☎ 212-586 7000) is accepting group reservations but not individual bookings until late December 1998 or early January 1999. Two hotels have tempting names for millennium travellers:

The *Millennium Broadway* (☎ 212-768 4400, fax 212-768 0847) at 145 W 44th Street, which boasts particularly impressive views, and the *Millennium Hilton* (☎ 212-693 2001, fax 212-571 2316) at 55 Church Street.

● **Moderate** (between $90-170): The *Days Hotel* (☎ 212-581 7000, fax 212-974 0291) at 790 8th Avenue will start taking reservations on 1 Jan 1999 – as will the *Hotel San Carlos* (☎ 212-755 1800). Earlier reservations, from October 1998, will be accepted by the *Gershwin Hotel* (☎ 212-545 8000). At 100 W 58th Street, the *Helmsley Windsor Hotel* (☎ 212-265 2100, fax 212-315 0371) will begin taking reservations from 1 June 1998.

Where to Stay (cont)

The *Howard Johnson Plaza Hotel* (☎ 212-581 4100, fax 212-974 7502), a good-value option with some 300 rooms, will take reservations from 1 Jan 1999. *The Mayflower Hotel on the Park* (☎ 212-265 0060) will start to accept reservations around mid-1998 as will the *Roger Smith Hotel* (☎ 212-755 1400).

● **Budget** (under $90): Try the well-appointed *New York International Youth Hostel* (☎ 212-932 2300) at 891 Amsterdam Avenue or the *YMCA* (☎ 212-755 2410) at 224 E 47th Street. The *Banana Bungalow* (☎ 1-800-6-HOSTEL or 212-769 2441, fax 212-877 5733) in the Upper West Side of Manhattan is inexpensive and conveniently located.

Party Places

For listings, buy the *New York Magazine*, Sunday's *New York Times*, Friday's *New York Newsday*, the *New Yorker* or the *Village Voice*. New York City is a clubber's paradise. Entertainment in the Big Apple ranges from hardcore club-kids' hang-outs to Broadway via a fantastic live-music scene. It is also a famously dynamic scene – clubs come and go with the seasons.

At the time of going to print, the following are some of New York's most fashionable clubs: *Sound Factory*, 618 W 46th Street, is becoming very popular – in fact it's pretty hard to get in after midnight. There are water fountains around the club so you need not buy bottles of over-priced water; the *Palladium* on 3rd Avenue and 14th is one of the largest clubs in New York. These days it attracts a mixed gay/straight crowd and plays some of the best dance music in town; *Life* at 158 Bleecker Street is less fashionable but has a friendly and easy-going atmosphere; one of the more trendy venues is *Flamingo* on 2nd Avenue; a younger crowd heads for *Cheetah* at 12 W 21 Street, although the dance floor is a bit cramped; *Carbon* at 605 W 55th Street plays great music but it can be hard to get in; *Twilo*, at 530 W 27th Street; in Queens, try the *Metropolis* at College Point, a large and popular club. Expect to pay around US$15-20 to get into most of these places. After that, drinks are around US$5 for a beer or US$7 for a short.

For comedy check out *The Original Improvisation* at 358 W 44th Street. This comedy showcase is where many of New York City's most famous stand-ups first raised a titter. For live music, try *The Bitter End* at 147 Bleecker Street or the *Village Vanguard* (jazz) at 178 7th Ave South. Both are New York institutions.

❑ MILLENNIUM TOURS TO NEW YORK

Millennium Tour: New York (29 Dec 1999 – 2 Jan 2000)

One way to secure a place in Times Square on New Year's Eve 1999 is to join a millennium tour to New York from Maupintour. The US tour operator is offering a four-day trip which can be reserved with a US$850 per person deposit. Prices will not be available until December 1998. **Contact:** (☎ 800-255 4266).

Millennium Party and Tour: New York City (30 Dec 1999 – 4 Jan 2000)

This ex-UK tour from Jetset (☎ +44 0990-555 757) includes flights from Britain, transfers, accommodation, a New Year's Day lunch party and tickets to a top Broadway show. New Year's Eve is free. The price is an excellent £999 per person. A Florida add-on will cost an extra £1200 per person.

New Year's Eve 1999 Gala Party and Tour: New York (28 Dec 1999 – 3 Jan 2000)

The Millennial Foundation (see p137) has arranged a six-day tour and New Year's Eve extravaganza in New York City.

Accommodation will be at the Pierre Hotel and the price includes access to the celebration on New Year's Eve. Price: £2500. **Contact:** The Millennial Foundation (☎ +44 (0) 141-204 2000, fax +44 (0) 141-248 1591, Internet: http://www.yes2000.co.uk), 10 Sandyford Place, Glasgow, G3 7NB, UK .

Millennium Tour: New York

UK's Travel for the Arts (☎ +44 (0) 171-483 4466) is to offer a four-night millennial break in New York with four-star accommodation, a New Year's Eve dinner and opera at the Met. Price and dates have yet to be announced.

Celebration 2000 20th Century Collectibles Exhibit: New York City (26 Dec 1999 – 1 Jan 2000)

On first impressions, this is a strange idea. Celebration 2000, organisers of what is likely to be one of America's best New Year's Eve parties, are taking over an entire floor of the Jacob K Javits Center to host an enormous collectibles exhibition. Memorabilia from the worlds of music, sport, fashion, photography, computers, architecture and finance will be on view. If it's collected, it will be there. Perhaps it isn't such a weird idea. The exhibition will be a fairly comprehensive retrospective of the past 100 years and will reflect the changes in our culture over that period. So, if you want to dig out that elusive first edition of *Batman* or that 1954 Matchbox Jaguar, this could be your chance for a happy end to the second millennium.

Opsail 2000 Tall Ships Sail Parade
New York City Harbour (4 July 2000)

Opsail 2000 (see p184) are to stage the fifth tall ships gathering in New York Harbour since 1964. A 4 July Sail Parade and International Naval Review will be the climax of a week of maritime festivities and new millennium celebrations. As the flotilla of tall ships steers its millennium parade from the Verrazano Narrows Bridge, a fleet of some 30,000 vessels from over 50 countries is expected to line a 10-mile stretch of the harbour in salute. The United States Coast Guard bark *Eagle* will lead the Tall Ships Armada. Opsail hopes to attract millions of spectators. On the same day, and in collaboration with Opsail, the United States Navy will stage the Fifth International Naval Review.

❑ **New York's New Museums for the Millennium**

Architect Peter Eisenmann has designed a new museum for the **Staten Island Institute of Arts & Sciences** (SIIAS) to be built at the Staten Island Ferry Terminal in St George. The museum, which will exhibit changing displays relating to art, science and history, will have some 60,000 square feet of exhibition space, a restaurant, classrooms, archive rooms and a 200-seat library. SIIAS will have to compete with the New York Historical Society to open the city's first museum of the new millennium. The Staten Island museum is expected to cost US$40 million and will open between the year 2000 and 2001.

A US$7.5 million grant from the Henry Luce Foundation has enabled the New York Historical Society to build a state-of-the-art **Henry Luce III Center for the Study of American Culture**. The Society has collected around 60,000 American paintings, sculptures and artifacts, most of which relate to New York's history. The new Center's display will be diverse, including George Washington's presidential coach and the world's largest collection of Tiffany lamps. **Contact:** ☎ 212-873 3400.

NEW ORLEANS

If any city has the right to call itself the Party Capital of the world, it's New Orleans. In America only New York will rival the Big Easy for sheer hedonism on 31 December 1999.

Throughout 1999 Louisana and, in particular, New Orleans will be celebrating **Francofête '99** (the Louisiana Tricentennial 1699-1999) with a comprehensive programme of festivals and cultural events.

New Year's Eve Party: Jackson Square, New Orleans (31 Dec 1999 – 1 Jan 2000)

Jackson Square is the heart of New Orleans' lively French Quarter. Jazz bands, mimes, jugglers and artists animate the Square all year round.

It is a New Orleans tradition to head for Jackson Square to see in the New Year. On 31 December 1999 the Square will be full of revellers. The crowd will be entertained by fireworks and bands. Following tradition a lighted ball will drop from Jackson Brewery at midnight.

At the centre of the Square, the statue of General Andrew Jackson, who won the Battle of New Orleans, will watch over party-goers. Another interesting aspect of Jackson Square is St Louis Cathedral which overlooks it from the west.

New Year's Eve Party: New Orleans (31 Dec 1999 – 1 Jan 2000)

New Orleans' Windsor Court Hotel, which is considered to be one of the best hotels in the world, is offering a New Year's Eve 1999 party and two-night package. The Time Machine Party will be a typical N'Awlins-style dinner and celebration held in the Grill restaurant and Polo Club lounge which will be decorated in the style of different decades of the 20th century. Before the party

❑ **Further Information**
New Orleans Metropolitan Convention & Visitors Bureau Inc.
(☎ 504-566 5011, fax 504-566 5046), 1520 Sugar Bowl Drive, New Orleans, LA 70112

gets going on New Year's Eve, guests will be invited to bury a time capsule in the Hotel's grounds. The two-night stay, which will cost US$2000, includes the dinner and party, a suite, breakfast, limousine service to and from the airport and the movie of HG Wells' *The Time Machine* for in-room entertainment.

A deposit must be put down by 2 August 1999 to reserve a place. That deposit is refundable, but – to avoid a fee – cancellations must be made at least 2000 hours (or 83 days!) before the event. **Contact:** Windsor Court Hotel (☎ 504-523 6000 or, in America, 800-262 2662, fax 504-596 4513), 300 Gravier Street, New Orleans, Louisiana 70130.

❏ **The French Quarter and Mardi Gras**

Many visitors to N'Awlins never get beyond the French Quarter (or Vieux Carré – Old Square) which is the label given to the crescent-shaped old-town area which fans out for several blocks around **Jackson Square** – the scene of an annual New Year's Eve street party. The French Quarter is home to a never-ending party which is why New Orleans is an apt city in which to enjoy the biggest celebration for 1000 years.

Despite trying just a bit too hard to woo tourists, it is easy to love the endless jazz sounds, lively cafés and happy atmosphere of the Quarter. This is where jazz was invented – and they won't let you forget it! **Bourbon Street** is virtually a living museum to it and is also home to the **Voodoo Museum** which illustrates how Christian and pagan African beliefs fused to form a bizarre cult in the city. The attractive **Ruelle d'Orleans**, or Pirate's Alley, is famed for its street artists and is a good place to relax before tackling the frenetic **French Market**. The Market has managed to retain a real function for the people of N'Awlins, as well as making a wonderful spectacle for visitors. Junk and gems sit side by side and food stalls offer spices and strong local coffee.

Carnival season starts on the Feast of Epiphany, 6 January, but **Mardi Gras** (or Fat Tuesday) takes places on Shrove Tuesday. Since the middle of the 19th century, Mardi Gras in New Orleans has been a byword for legendary and often decadent revellery. Parades and floats cram the roads while costumed and masked participants wander the Mardi Gras route tossing beads and trinkets to the crowd. The party ends abruptly at midnight on Shrove Tuesday when the streets are quickly cleared for Ash Wednesday.

New Year's Eve Party: New Orleans
31 Dec 1999 – 1 Jan 2000

This is a great venue for a party: a new millennium celebration will be held at Gallier House in the French Quarter. Gallier House was designed in the 19th century by New Orleans' best-known architect, James Gallier Jr. It was his family home – and a beautiful example of an opulent Creole town house.

Gallier House has since been turned into one of the city's more interesting museums. From the typically ornate balconies one can enjoy a great view across the Vieux Carré. The party will be connected to a series of others across the globe by the Millennial Foundation (see p137). In fact, the Millennial Foundation are offering a six-day tour to New Orleans.

New Year's Eve Party and Tour: New Orleans

Tickets for the New Year's Eve party at Gallier House (see above) are included in the Millennial Foundation's six-day pack-

---

❏ **Millennial Money-Spinners**

Enterprising American companies are hoping to cash in on the millennium by producing such useful gifts as the CountDown™ Watch. The watch, which costs US$79.95, counts down to the millennium – or whichever date one enters – and is available from Branco International (☎ 516-544 4604).

Another indispensable piece if millennial equipment is the MTC2000™ Time Capsule Kit available from Millennium Celebrations Inc (☎ 630-573 2944). The kit, which costs US$59.95, is made out of heavy duty plastic and includes a certificate of origin and a special sealant to make sure the capsule's contents remain safe. Like several other US firms, Millennium Celebrations Inc have bigger plans for the millennium than simply producing plastic time capsules. Skip Kitchen, the fantastically-named Company President, sees the millennium as the biggest advertising opportunity of all time. He is looking for sponsors to provide the capital for a mega-New Year's Eve celebration which would act both as a party and a giant commercial.

The Billennium (☎ 773-327 2000) has similar plans for an enormous celebration/sponsorship deal and has produced a range of millennial products including a time capsule and countdown clock.

❑ **NEW ORLEANS – A BRIEF GUIDE**

New Orleans (pronounced N'Awlins, never Noo Orleens) is a giant among party capitals. The city will lure thousands of millennial revellers in 1999. There isn't even a closing law! Since its malaria-ridden and swampy start in 1718, life in the 'Big Easy' has never been dull. N'Awlins has been French, Spanish and American and has strong links to Africa and the Caribbean.

This cultural diversity, together with a reputation for wild parties, Mardi Gras and a humid climate gives the 'city that care forgot' an exciting edge unlike any other. Since the turn of the century, life in New Orleans has been set to a **jazz** score which was pioneered by local heroes such as Jelly Roll Morton and Louis Armstrong. Hungry party-goers are sustained by **Creole** and **Cajun** cooking.

What to See

Orientation in New Orleans depends not on the compass but on waterways. Visitors will find themselves directed to 'downriver' (downtown), 'upriver' (uptown), 'lakeside' (towards Lake Pontchartrain) and 'riverside' (towards Old Man River). The **French Quarter** (see box), which fans out from **Jackson Square** (see p175), and **Mardi Gras** (see p176) are the city's biggest draws.

Downriver from Jackson Square is the **Old US Mint**, now part of the Lousiana State Museum with fascinating jazz and Mardi Gras exhibits.

Canal Street, N'Awlins' major shopping strip, divides the French Quarter from the Central Business District. Historically, Canal Street partitioned the Americans from the Creoles, and is still referred to as the 'neutral ground'. **Streetcars**, which have been trundling through New Orleans for 150 years, **paddlewheel steamboats** and jazz cruises are part of the New Orleans experience. A newer attraction is the **Aquarium of the Americas**.

Where to Stay

● **Expensive** (over $170): The *Windsor Court Hotel* (☎ 504-523 6000 or, in America, 800-262 2662, fax 504-596 4513) in the CBD is offering an extravagant New Year's Eve 1999 package for US$2000 (see p175); *Fairmont Hotel* (☎ 504-529 7111, fax 504-522 2303), also in the CBD area, is one of America's oldest luxury hotels; the enormous *Hyatt Regency* (☎ 504-561 1234, fax 504-523

0488) is a luxury AAA rated hotel; *Le Meridien* (☎ 504-581 3111, fax 504-586 1543) on Canal Street has a European feel and the *Château Sonesta* (☎ 504-586 0800, fax 504-586 1987) overlooks Bourbon Street in the French Quarter.

● **Moderate** (between $90-170): The *Pontchartrain Hotel* (504-524 0581, fax 504-524 7828) in the Garden District boasts a fantastic restaurant; The *Bienville House Hotel* (☎ 504-529 2345, fax 504-525 6079), *Hotel de la Poste* (☎ 504-581 1200, fax 504-523 2910), the *Bourbon Orleans Hotel* (☎ 504-523 2222, fax 504-525 8166), *Le Richelieu* (☎ 504-529 2492, fax 504-524 8179) and the *Place D'Armes Hotel* (☎ 504-524 4531, fax 504-581 3802) are all excellent and well-priced hotels in the French Quarter.

● **Budget** (under $90): Try the *YMCA International Hotel* (☎ 504-558 9622, fax 504-523 7174) on Charles Street; *Prytania Inns* (☎ 504-566 1515, fax 504-566 1518) five-minutes from the French Quarter; *Madame Julia's Boarding House* (☎ 504-529 2952, fax 504-568 1390) on Julia Street or the *Famous Plaza Inn* (☎ 504-455 9300, fax 504-454 6199) close to the airport.

Party Places

Jazz is what New Orleans does best. If you want to hear the music of jazz stars such as Kid Ory, Louis Armstrong or Charlie Parker in its most appropriate setting (dark bars and smoky clubs) try the following: the *Famous Door* at 339 Bourbon Street which has been in business since 1934; *Maxwell's Jazz Cabaret* at 615 Toulouse Street; *Preservation Hall*, an almost legendary jazz venue, at 726 Saint Peter Street; *Fritzels* at 339 Bourbon Street; *Snug Harbor* at 626 Frenchman Street; *Tipitana's* at 501 Napoleon Avenue (a favourite of local star Harry Connick Jr) or catch the *Creole Queen Paddlewheeler* which offers jazz dinner cruises.

If you need to get away from all that jazz, try *City Lights* at 310 Howard Avenue which is one of New Orleans' few full-on dance clubs. Other nightclubs include: the *544 Club* at 544 Bourbon Street; *Pete Fountain's Night Club* at the Hilton Hotel; *Rhythms* at 227 Bourbon Street or *Razzoo* at 511 Bourbon Street. The *Old Absinthe House* at 240 Bourbon Street is a great bar which has welcomed celebrity drinkers from Mark Twain to Mick Jagger. The opening bar scenes in Oliver Stone's *JFK* were shot in *The Napoleon House* at 500 Chartres Street. The Napoleon House was built as a hideaway for Napoleon after his exile to St Helena.

age to the Home of Jazz. Accommodation will be at the Royal Sonesta Hotel which is in the French Quarter and boasts an oyster bar named *Desire*. Price: £2500. **Contact:** The Millennial Foundation (☎ +44 (0) 141-204 2000, fax +44 (0) 141-248 1591, Internet: http://yes2000.co.uk), 10 Sandyford Place, Glasgow G3 7NB, UK.

Millennium Tour: New Orleans
(28 Dec 1999 – 2 Jan 2000)

This five-day trip to New Orleans from US tour operator Maupintour will include accommodation and a New Year's Eve

❑ **Supersonic into the Next Millennium**

A St Louis-based tour operator, **Intrav**, is offering an 18-day around-the-world millennium spin on Concorde. The supersonic sortie will set off from the States on 24 December 1999 and will take in Hawaii, Sydney, Hong Kong, Delhi, Kenya and Cairo before touching down in America again on 10 January 2000. Christmas will be spent in Honolulu and New Year's Eve in Sydney. The cost is a cool US$75,000. Air France is to lease one of its Concorde aircraft to Intrav. **Contact:** Intrav (☎ 1-314-727 0500, fax 314-727 9354), 7711 Bonhomme Avenue, St Louis, MO 63105-1961.

Another Air France Concorde has been booked by **Concorde Spirit Tours** in Florida. They plan a mad dash across the globe to and from Paris between 28 December 1999-8 Jan 2000. The *Millennium IV* flight will leave Paris at midnight on 31 December 1999 and will arrive in Kona, Hawaii a few minutes later – local time – having stopped in Canada on the way.

After four nights at the Waikoloa Village in Kamuela, *Millennium IV* will set off for Acapulco in Mexico where accommodation has been arranged at the Westin Las Brisas resort. Flying at speeds of 1350 mph between landings, *Millennium IV* will meet midnight four times.

Unfortunately, Concorde Spirit Tours are hoping to sell every place on the trip to one corporate sponsor but if they fail to do that seats will be sold to the public. **Contact:** Donald L Pevsner (☎ 407-449 0882, fax 407-449 0883), Concorde Spirit Tours, 1765 East Riviera Drive, Merritt Island, Florida 32952.

party. A US$850 deposit is required to reserve a place. The price has yet to be announced. **Contact:** (☎ 800-255 4266).

New Year's Eve Party: New Orleans
(31 Dec 1999 – 1 Jan 2000)

O'Flaherty's Irish Channel Pub (☎ 504-529 1317) in the French Quarter is planning a 'Rising of the Moon' New Year's Eve 1999 party with live Irish folk music and all the usual trappings of a traditional Celtic celebration. A cover charge of around US$10 includes some champagne.

New Year's Eve Party and Dinner: New Orleans
31 Dec 1999 – 1 Jan 2000

A New Year's Eve 1999 dinner will be held at the Bizou Restaurant at 701 St Charles Avenue. A special millennial *prix fixe* menu is being devised by chef Daniel Bonnot. **Contact:** Judy Hubbard (☎ 504-524 4114, fax 504 522 1679).

❏ **The Second Coming?**

According to a recent poll conducted by Associated Press, over 26 million Americans expect Jesus to arrive in their lifetimes. The same poll suggests that 40% of American Christians expect Jesus to arrive in 21st century or at the turn of the millennium. The San Diego Union Tribune reports that, of those, over 21 million feel a pressing need to convert others before He comes.

During October 1997 a group called the End-Time Handmaidens met at the Sheraton Washington Hotel for its annual convention. The Handmaidens are millennialists; they believe the Second Coming of Christ will coincide with the millennium – despite Jesus' advice that 'no one knows the hour'. For the Handmaidens (and many other more conventional American evangelists) 2000-year periods have great religious significance.

Other groups follow the Book of Revelation, which predicts a dismal future for anyone who fails to get things straight with God. Apparently, one third of the world will burn. Then one third of the survivors will be killed by angels after an horrendous term of torture. Such prophecies mirror people's worries at the turn of the last millennium (see p141). Ted Daniels, an American cult authority, has found 1500 cults with millennialist leanings.

❏ HOLIDAYS IN SPACE

Space tourism is about to make the giant leap from science fiction to science fact. Holidays in space could be available early next millennium.

Government space agencies, including NASA, are generally supportive of space tourism but are not directly involved in its development. Private business is leading the new space race. With tourism now the world's largest industry, the rewards for the first to offer a weekend break beyond the upper atmosphere are likely to be great.

The X-Prize Foundation

Peter H Diamandis, President of the X-Prize Foundation, has triggered the final sprint of the space tourism marathon by offering US$10 million to the first team to project someone into space on two consecutive flights within a fortnight. Like the Orteig Prize in 1927, which tempted Charles Lindbergh to make his famous flight across the Atlantic, the X-Prize has caught the imagination of several independent rocket scientists.

One of these is Steven Bennett of the Starchaser Foundation in Britain. Bennett believes the prize is within his reach. He has already launched rockets to 20,000 feet and soon hopes to propel a completely reusable, three-stage rocket called Lexx to a height of 15 nautical miles. It will even carry a 50-kilo payload. Other entrants include ex-NASA scientists and aerospace experts. Most plan to pilot their spacecraft themselves.

Space Tourism Society

California's Space Tourism Society, of which Apollo 11 astronaut Dr Buzz Aldrin is a governor, believes space tourism is not only feasible but potentially a massive market. After all, how many of us have watched in awe as pictures of Earth have been beamed back to us by successive Shuttle crews and thought, 'if only *I* could visit space'? The first firm to supply a safe trip to space for civilians will be swamped with interest – whatever the price.

Space Hotel

A well-established architectural practice which specialises in the design of tourist resorts, Wimberly Allison Tong & Goo, is developing a scheme to build a space hotel. It may sound incredible, but

WAT&G are convinced their cosmic retreat could be circling 200-miles above Earth by 2017. External fuel tanks will be salvaged from Shuttle missions to be used to launch the space hotel.

Guests will enjoy hydroponically-grown food and will experience weightlessness. For the inevitable sufferers of space-sickness, one room will have artificial gravity. Games will be organised to prevent visitors' muscles from atrophying. Howard Wolff, Vice-President of WAT&G, says he hopes to 'strike a balance between an out-of-this-world experience and providing some creature comforts'.

Zero Gravity Tours

Zero gravity tours are already available to space tourists. Parabolic flights, which are used to prepare astronauts for weightlessness, are flown from Space City in Russia by a company called ZERO-G.

It's also possible to take a trip to 'the edge of space'. An American company called Space Adventures flies civilians to the very edge of the Earth's atmosphere in MiG-25 fighter aircraft. Travelling at twice the speed of sound, and reaching 70,000 feet, the passenger is entertained by a view of the Earth's curvature.

Sub-orbital Flights

Space Adventures are also taking deposits for sub-orbital flights, such as the winner of the X-Prize might be able to offer. The flight will cost around £60,000, but £4000 is enough to secure a place on the waiting list.

There are several retired astronauts on Space Adventure's team, which is not building its own spaceships but will make an agreement with whoever is first to operate such a vessel.

Space Cruises

John S Spencer, founder of the Space Tourism Society and space architect, is convinced that space travel will be accessible to ordinary travellers – with deep enough pockets – sooner than most people think. Spencer wants this burgeoning business to model itself on the cruise line industry, with spacecraft shuttling guests to space cruisers in constant orbit. And why not? The technology is out there.

❏ **Opsail 2000**

John F Kennedy founded Opsail in 1961 to promote sail training and 'goodwill among nations' through the international sailing community. Sadly, Kennedy didn't survive to see the maritime event he had created.

Since 1961, Opsail has organised tall ships gatherings on 4 July in 1964, 1976, 1986 and 1992. Each took place in New York Harbour. Tall ships will meet in San Juan, Puerto Rico, on 25 May 2000 where they will participate in the opening ceremony of Opsail 2000 and the Puerto Rico Regatta 2000.

After sailing parallel to the East Coast of America, joining various maritime events along the way, the ships will congregate in New York Harbour in time for a week of festivities leading up to 4 July. **Contact:** Kay Banks, Opsail (☎ 202-862 2484, Internet http://www.opsail.org), 1333 New Hampshire Avenue NW, Suite 700, Washington, DC 20036. The International Sail Training Association has also organised a Tall Ships 2000 race (see p150).

EASTERN USA
Tall Ships 2000 Start Point: Boston (12-16 July 2000)
The penultimate race in this four-stage contest will start from Boston, Massachusetts and finish in Halifax, Nova Scotia. Tall Ships 2000 (see p150) is a major international event and the race organisers expect large crowds to join the celebrations in Boston.

Millennium Tour: Washington DC
(28 Dec 1999 – 2 Jan 2000)
This package includes special performance at the Kennedy Center and Ford's Theatre. **Contact:** Maupintour (☎ 800-255 4266).

New Year on South Beach: Miami (31 Dec 1999)
South Beach in Miami will be lined with stages and multi-media entertainment on 31 December 1999. An all-night orgy of live performance will break at midnight for a choreographed fireworks display.

❑ **First Night Celebrations**

In 1976 First Night organised the finale of the bicentennial celebrations in Boston. The group has grown rapidly, and now acts as an umbrella organisation for New Year's Eve celebrations across the United States and Canada. On 31 December 1997, 164 First Night events were held in the States and 18 in Canada. More communities are hoping to participate for the millennium.

First Night celebrations are alcohol-free community parties which use visual and performing art to provide a sober but lively start to the New Year. Typically, the celebrations include parades, music, mime, storytelling and theatre and conclude with a countdown to midnight and fireworks display. **Contact:** Zeran Earls (☎ 617-357 0065) First Night President, to find out how to start your own First Night celebration, to find the nearest party or for general information.

COLORADO
New Year's Eve 1999 Weekend: Colorado Springs (30 Dec 1999-2 Jan 2000)

The Broadmoor Hotel in Colorado Springs is offering a three-night millennium package. It kicks off with a champagne reception followed by a 'roaring twenties' dinner and casino evening on 30 December 1999. Two live acts will booked for New Year's Eve so that two parties can run side by side in the International Center and Colorado Hall. An indoor laser light show will be followed by fireworks around the lake at midnight. Price: $5000 per couple (all-inclusive). A $1000 deposit is required during 1998 to reserve a place.

Contact: The Broadmoor (☎ 800-634 7711 or 719-471 6132, fax 719-577 5802), One Lake Avenue, Colorado Springs, Colorado 80906.

New Year's Eve 1999 Ball: Boulder

Another Colorado hotel, the Boulderado in Boulder, has plans for a New Year's Eve Ball and accommodation package but the price has not yet been decided. For more information **contact:** The Boulderado (☎ 303-442 4344).

CALIFORNIA

With a voracious appetite for spectacle and a world-beating entertainment industry, one would expect California to host bigger and better bashes than any other state in America. There are events planned in Los Angeles and San Francisco (both cities know how to throw a party) and the City of Angels is building the first cathedral of the third millennium.

New Year's Eve 1999 Party and Tour: San Francisco

A New Year's Eve 1999 mega-party which will be connected by TV to 30 others by the Millennial Foundation (see p137) is planned for San Francisco. The Millennium Foundation is also offering a six-day trip to join the party. Accommodation will be at the Grand Hyatt in Union Square, which is the centre of the city's shopping district. San Francisco is the most attractive and entertaining city in California and will no doubt celebrate the millennium in its own inimitable style. Price: £2500.

Contact: The Millennial Foundation (☎ +44 (0) 141-204 2000, fax +44 (0) 141-248 1591, Internet: http://yes2000.co.uk), 10 Sandyford Place, Glasgow G3 7NB, UK.

❏ **Cyber-Celebrations**

There's a limit to how many people any one party can hold – or is there? Call them sad or call them visionary, some people plan to celebrate the eve of the next millennium with just their computer and the ever-growing Internet for company. Potentially, Internet parties can accommodate many millions – which is more than can be said for the average New Year's Eve venue.

Arthur Cassidy, who can be reached by e-mail (how else?) at hotwired@mail.enterprise.net, has confirmed that on New Year's Eve 1999 a 24-hour chat party will be held on the Internet. It will span time zones and continents and will probably be the nearest thing to a global party that happens.

Another group, the Electronic Millennium Project, is developing an Internet millennium celebration and a giant multi-lingual, multi-cultural public information web-site to which individuals will be able to contribute. For more information about that, e-mail John Nicholson at john.nicholson@ukonline.co.uk or visit EMP's website at: http://emp2000.ukonline.co.uk

Millennium Tour: San Francisco
(28 Dec 1999 – 2 Jan 2000)

Maupintour has devised this five-day trip to see in the new millennium in San Francisco, with accommodation at the lavish Westin St Francis Hotel on Powell Street and a New Year's Eve dinner party included. A US$850 deposit will secure a place. **Contact:** (☎ 800-255 4266).

New Year's Eve Party: Los Angeles (31 Dec 1999)

Each salon in the Queen Mary liner, which is permanently moored in Long Beach Harbour, will be decorated in the style of a different decade of the 20th century for the ship's Millennium's Eve party. There will also be live entertainment, fireworks and other 'surprises'. The Queen Mary is now a luxury hotel. A one-night stay on 31 December 1999 – together with the party – will cost US$1999 per person. Tickets to the party only are on sale for US$199 per person. **Contact:** The Queen Mary (☎ 562-435 3511), 1126 Queens Hwy, Long Beach, Los Angeles, Ca 90802.

New Year's Eve Party and Tour: Beverly Hills

Both the Gala Party, which will be broadcast to the world by the Millennial Foundation (see p137), and the accommodation for this six-day trip will be at the Regent Beverly Wiltshire Hotel which faces Rodeo Drive in Beverly Hills. The party is bound to be glamorous at this famous hotel which is regularly patronised by stars, and has featured in several movies, including *Pretty Woman* (with Richard Gere and Julia Roberts). Price: £2500. **Contact:** The Millennial Foundation (☎ +44 (0) 141-204 2000, fax +44 (0) 141-248 1591, Internet: http://yes2000.co.uk), 10 Sandyford Place, Glasgow G3 7NB, UK .

Odyssey 2000 Around-the-World Bicycle Ride: Los Angeles-Los Angeles (1 Jan – 31 Dec 2000)

It's a drastic way to fight the post-Christmas flab, but nearly 300 people have registered interest in an epic year-long around-the-world cycle ride to see in the new millennium. Tim Kneeland & Associates of Seattle have devised a route which takes in over 50 countries and covers 20,000 miles. It's called Odyssey 2000. The journey starts and finishes in Los Angeles, and progresses in an easterly direction. Odyssey 2000 has yet to finalise the exact itinerary because of the changing political situation in some countries *en route*. But an approximate itinerary has already been very well researched. Everything from luggage transportation to accommodation and medical aid will be provided. Despite covering over 70 miles per day, the organisers claim that participants need not be hardcore athletes. Indeed, a woman in her seventies hopes to join the ride.

Odyssey 2000 will cost an enormous US$36,000 – or around US$99/day. A US$500 registration fee will secure a place. A fund-raising option is available, but it will be difficult to find enough sponsorship to cover the trip and make a healthy donation to charity.

Contact: Tim Kneeland & Associates Inc (☎ 206-322 4102, fax 206-322 4509), 200 Lake Washington Blvd, Suite 101, Seattle, WA 98122-6540 .

The First Cathedral of the Third Millennium
Los Angeles (Dedication Ceremony 4 September 2000)

Los Angeles will see its new Roman Catholic cathedral, the Cathedral of Our Lady of the Angels, dedicated on 4 September 2000. The US$50 million development will be built on the 5.5-acre site of a disused parking lot in downtown LA. Los Angeles

---

❑ **World Millennium Snapshot**

The idea behind this project is to encourage people around the world to record on film the arrival of the third millennium – something which will probably happen anyway. Thousands of these images will then be collected and added to a database which, it's hoped, will form a sort of model of the whole world at the turn of the millennium. This database (or world 'holomorph' as it has been labelled) will be available on the World Wide Web and on CD Rom. The project is certainly an interesting one, but requires further sponsorship if it is definitely to go ahead. The organiser, Greg Wright, is also the man behind the South Pole Sweepstakes Project. **Contact:** Gregory Wright (☎ 818-784 0325, fax 818-981 6835, e-mail greg@newciv.org).

has the largest Roman Catholic archdiocese in the States, but has been without a cathedral since the Cathedral of St Vibiana was destroyed by an earthquake in 1994. Spanish architect Jose Rafael Moneo has won the competition to design the cathedral with a striking and ultra-modern scheme.

New Year's Eve 1999 Events: Huntington Beach (31 Dec 1999)

Councillors in Huntington Beach, the attractive Orange County community which played a big part in introducing surfing to California, are working hard to make the city a magnet for millennial tourism. Events have been organised at the **Waterfront Hilton Beach Resort** (☎ 714-960 7873), the **Huntington Harbour Yacht Club** (☎ 714-840 2373), **Seacliff Country Club** (☎ 714-536 5358), **Meadowlark** (☎ 714-846 1364) and the **Huntington Beach Holiday Inn** (☎ 714-891 0123). Each event has been coordinated so that no two functions are too similar and to make it possible for people to attend more than one party on the same evening.

New Year's Eve Party: Tustin Marine Corps Air Facility (31 Dec 1999)

Former Disneyland executives Jack Lindquist and Steve Clark have put forward plans to hold a Disney-esque party for 25,000 people at a specially-designed Millennium Park at the Tustin Marine Corps Air Facility in Orange County. With backing from the Orange County Business Council, the project is almost guaranteed to be as big as Linquist and Clark hope. **Contact:** Huntington Beach Conference & Visitors Bureau (☎ 714-969 3492).

New Year's Eve 'Party 2000': Southern California 30 Dec 1999 – 1 Jan 2000

A Los Angeles-based group called Party 2000 is planning what it claims could be the 'biggest concert ever held'. The three-day New Year's Eve mega-party is scheduled to take place on a 4000-acre site in Southern California close to the Arizona border. Party 2000 hopes to attract top acts to its five stages which will form the core of the 24 hour-a-day party. Revellers will be expected to camp; there will be four campgrounds and 500 barbecues. The party organisers expect to book some 50 big-name bands.

Ticket prices are high and vary depending on when they're bought. Before 1 Jan 1998 – US$330; 31 Dec 1998 – US$445; 30 June 1999 – US$600; after 30 June – US$850. A deposit can be put down now, but tickets must be paid for in full by 15 February 1999. Be warned: the deposit is non-refundable. When a project is this ambitious, there is always a real chance that the actual event will fall short of expectations. Party-goers must be at least 17 years old.

Contact: Mark Henry, Party 2000 (☎ 816-461 9116 or, in America, 888-PARTY 2000, Internet http://www.party20 00.com), 8033 Sunset Blvd, Suite 238, Los Angeles, Ca 90046, USA.

❏ COMPUTER CHAOS

We have a problem. The information technology industry has betrayed an astonishing lack of foresight by leaving time-bombs ticking in computer systems the world over.

The Problem

Quite simply, many systems and software packages are unable to recognise the year 2000. Computer memory was very limited during the early years of the technological revolution. To save space, programmers allowed only two digits to store dates. '1984', for example, would be written as '84'.

This became something of a standard convention, and it works – this century. But the practice means the year '2000' will be stored as '00'. Computers will see '00' as less than '99', and so will assume '00' means '1900'. The potential chaos this seemingly simple bug could cause is almost incalculable.

The Consequences

Date-dependent computer systems are used in nearly every sphere of modern life. Less serious inconveniences could include computer-controlled cars failing to start, elevators stopping, or food orders written-off as out-of-date. More worrying is the unpredictable effect this cyber-strife could have on finance and government. Potentially it could be life-threatening in areas such as aviation or medicine. It sounds dramatic, but a mass collapse of computing systems could lead to civil unrest. How long would order be maintained if cashpoints refuse to release money, interest is wiped off accounts and food supplies fail?

Governments and business leaders are becoming aware of the issue, but time is running out. Many organisations need to plan beyond 2000 and are already suffering. Some programming professionals believe problems could start sooner than most expect. The highest number in a 4-digit sequence is 9999. In programming, that figure has often been used to represent infinity or as an error code. As a result, systems could crash on 9 September 1999.

The Cost

Information technology analysts *Gartner Group* say the global cost of fixing the problem could be as much as US$600 billion. Despite the extraordinary costs, however, experts believe businesses cannot afford to ignore the so-called 'Millennium Bug'.

What to do about it

According to the **Computing Software and Services Association (CSSA)**, the representative body of Britain's IT industry, managers should waste no time in adopting a structured approach to dealing with the problem.

CSSA advice includes performing a vulnerability check, establishing a year 2000 programme and creating an inventory of systems before actually tackling the problem. More detailed guidance can be found on the CSSA web-site at www.cssa.co.uk or by calling ☎ +44 (0) 171-405 2171.

In the United States try the **Information Technology Association of America (ITAA)** on ☎ 703-284 5340. Concerned computer managers in Australia could try the **Australian Information Industry Association (AIIA)** on ☎ +61-6-282 4700.

It is ironic that a century which has witnessed such staggering scientific advances should end in technological turmoil. Whether one views the problem as a timely reminder of our fallibility or just inevitable teething troubles, the message is clear: do not underestimate the Millennium Bug.

ALASKA
New Year's Eve 1999 Party and Tour: Alaska

The Millennial Foundation (see p137) has organised this six-day millennial trip to the best-known party site in Alaska. The Alyeska Prince Hotel, which is 40 miles outside Anchorage and set in one of the best ski resorts in Alaska, is famous for its spectacular New Year's Eve extravaganzas. On 31 December 1999, the Millennial Foundation will use TV to connect the gala party at the Alyeska to 30 other party sites. The Alyeska boasts seven restaurants, an 18-person whirlpool and great views of Mount Alyeska. Price: £2500.

Contact: The Millennial Foundation (☎ +44 (0) 141-204 2000, fax +44 (0) 141-248 1591, Internet: http://yes2000.co.uk), 10 Sandyford Place, Glasgow G3 7NB, UK.

HAWAII
Millennium Tour: Hawaii (26 Dec 1999-5 Jan 2000)

Hawaii has already attracted a lot of attention from millennium party-planners. Despite the fact that celebration details are sketchy, hotels and resorts are filling up fast. Maupintour (☎ 800-255 4266) are offering a luxury 10-day tour to Hawaii which includes good quality accommodation, a New Year's Eve party and a helicopter sightseeing trip.

❏ **Beacon Millennium Project: Tonga to Hawaii**

A chain of beacons (which can mean fires, lights, lasers, illuminations, pyrotechnics, arena scoreboards or flares) will be lit across the globe at midnight local time on New Year's Eve 1999.

Starting in Tonga, the chain of light will lead across New Zealand, Australia and several other countries before arriving at Greenwich in time for midnight GMT. Then it's on to Canada and back across the Pacific to Hawaii where the final fire will be lit on Honolulu. Bruno Peek of the Beacon Project says the global event will 'launch the dawn of the new millennium and celebrate the 2000th anniversary of the birth of Christ'.

Contact: Bruno Peek (☎ +44 (0) 1502-580670) in Britain or Martin Robertson (☎ +1 416-766 675, fax +1 416-766 9675) in Canada.

Mexico

Americans have long been in love with the romance of Mexico. In many ways, this fascinating country has a similar hold to Las Vegas over the American imagination; it's an exciting place to escape to for a snatched weekend or a week's retreat from the daily routine.

There is no doubt that Mexico will welcome large numbers of American visitors looking for somewhere out of the ordinary to see in the third millennium. Unfortunately, the Mexicans have so far been slow to capitalise on this fact. That will change, eventually. At this stage, three areas look set to steal the lion's share of millennial tourism.

ACAPULCO

On New Year's Eve 1999 Acapulco will fill up with the usual mix of people in search of a good time in Mexico's most famous resort. It might not be quite what you expect; yes, the clubs are cool and beaches long and sandy, but Acapulco is still a working port. Don't expect the unadulterated paradise so often portrayed on the silver screen; indeed, you will quickly discover that adultery is one of the resort's most profitable trades – for genuine Mexican gigolos, that is. This is where wealthy middle-aged American women go to escape from their husbands for a weekend.

Nevertheless, despite its seedier side, Acapulco Bay is irresistible and will be rocking when the millennium comes round. Acapulco is easy and cheap to get to from Mexico City. Buses run around the clock; the journey lasts about seven hours.

BAJA CALIFORNIA

Baja California is many visitors' first encounter with Mexico. On first sight it is an unimpressive start as the dry and, for many miles, featureless landscape is hardly inspiring. But Baja

California has a devoted following among American travellers, many of whom plan to party here when the millennium arrives. There are quiet, secluded Pacific beaches and an attractively rugged interior. The beachy resorts of San Blas and Mazatlán are well-known among young American – and particularly Californian – travellers. Both will be backdrops to serious partying on New Year's Eve 1999. Buses regularly serve this entire coastal route from Tijuana or Nogales to Mexico City.

YUCATAN

Those hoping to see in 2000 surrounded not by beer-swilling surfers but by the Maya might want to stay at the village of Pisté near **Chichén Itzá**. This is the best-preserved of all Mayan sites, and it is truly stunning. Although the history of Chichén Itzá is a hotly-disputed subject, it seems likely that the site was at its most successful at the end of the first millennium. It's easy to reach and is well served by buses from Mérida and Cancún.

Another popular Mayan site is **Palenque**. It's smaller but more beautiful than Chichén Itzá. The pyramid tomb and intricate palace are amazing. However it's the location of Palenque that makes this such a spectacular place; jungle-coated hills crowd the site. Beyond that, the endless Yucatán plain stretches to the horizon. Most of the site dates from the seventh century. Stay at the nearby Palenque Village which is most easily reached by bus from Villahermosa.

Finally, **Uxmal**, in the south-east corner of Mexico, is another magical and ancient site which is expected to attract a lot of interest on Millennium's Eve. This site is a beautiful example of *Puuc* architecture and is at least as impressive as any other in the area. One of the great things about Uxmal is the *son et lumière* spectacle which is put on most nights. It is hoped that this long-running attraction will feature as part of a millennium ceremony at the site. Uxmal is a 50-mile bus journey from Mérida.

Canada

Canada was quite slow to start planning for the millennium but is quickly catching up. Vancouver, Toronto, Montréal, Calgary, Halifax and Newfoundland are all planning major millennial parties and celebrations.

Most Canadians appear to be against wasteful celebrations and are keen to see their millennium money spent on useful legacies as well as a good time.

❏ **CANADA**

Contacts

● **Centre Infotouriste (Montréal)** (☎ 514-873 2015 or, in North America, ☎ 1 800-363 7777, Internet http://www.cum.qc.ca /octgm), 1001 Square-Dorchester, Montréal H3B 4V4

● **Greater Québec Area Tourism & Convention Bureau** (☎ 418 692-2471/651-2882, Internet http://www.quebec_region.cuq.q c.cq), 60 rue D'Auteuil, Québec G1R 4C4

● **Tourism British Columbia** (☎ 250-387 1642 or, in North America, ☎ 1 800-663 6000), PO Box 9830, Stn. Prov. Govt, Victoria BC V8W 9W5

Average maximum temperature °C

	Dec	Jan
Montréal	-3	-6
Vancouver	7	6

Capital: Ottawa

Flight times: (to Vancouver) from:
LA – 3 hrs
London – 10 hrs
Sydney – 19 hrs

Approximate exchange rates: Canadian Dollar (C$) – £1=2.35, US$1=1.43, A$1=0.9

Time difference: Toronto: GMT -5; Vancouver: GMT -7

Country dialling code: ☎ 1

NEWFOUNDLAND
New Year's Eve 'First Light' Party (31 Dec 1999)
Cape Spear on the tip of Avalon Peninsula in Newfoundland is the easternmost point in the North American continent. The Millennium Council of Newfoundland and Labrador (☎ 709-722 4003, fax 709-576 6031) is organising a big bash there with plenty of champagne to toast the first dawn.

NOVA SCOTIA
New Year's Eve Party: Halifax (31 Dec 1999)
Halifax will combine millennium celebrations with its 250th birthday party on New Year's Eve 1999. Outdoor parties are planned in the downtown area on the evening of the 31st, preceded by a series of cultural events. **Contact:** Halifax 2000 (☎ 902-420 4724, fax 902-490 5950).

QUEBEC
New Year's Eve Jazz Festival Party: Montréal
The organisers of the Montréal International Jazz Festival (☎ 514-523 3378) will stage a millennium jazz party on 31 December 1999. Major stars from the world of Jazz are expected to lead Montréal into the 21st century from outdoor stages and indoor venues across the downtown area.

Montréal Millennium Jazz Festival (28 June-9 July 2000)
The Montréal Millennium Jazz Festival will be the biggest jazz festival in the world. It takes place every year and attracts top stars and some 1.5 million jazz-lovers. Music oozes from bars, clubs and outdoor stages all over Montréal. This will be the 21st festival.

Contact: Festival International de Jazz de Montréal (☎ 514-523 3378 or 514-523-FEST).

TORONTO
New Year's Eve 1999 Celebration (Toronto 2000)
A gala New Year's Eve 1999 celebration is being planned for Toronto but the organisers have yet to announce any details. For information about that and other events planned for Toronto

(including a 6-month Exposition of the Future) **contact:** Toronto 2000 (☎ 416-777 2000, fax 416-862 8111), 1 Yonge Street, Suite 2000, Toronto, Ontario M5E 1N4

Millennium Eve Vigil: Toronto

A mass-Millennium Eve Vigil will be held in central Toronto from noon on 31 December 1999 to noon the following day. Participants will be encouraged to 'grieve for the horrors of the last 1000 years' until midnight when 'the gift of life' will be celebrated.

On New Year's Day the tired and, perhaps, bored vigil-keepers will ask poets and artists to help conjure images of the future. For more information contact the organisers (e-mail millenniumvigil@hcol.humberc.on.ca).

❏ Have You Written a Will?

Natasha Van Bentum, founder of the Millennium Foundation of Canada (MFC) which is based in Vancouver says: 'you could say we're anti-celebration'. Her view, which contrasts with that of *The Millennium Guide*, is that millennium festivities are a waste of scarce resources at a time when the world should be debating how to be less wasteful.

The MFC is concerned by the prospect of millions, possibly billions, of dollars 'going up in smoke on 31 December 1999 in the form of fireworks and the like'. To Van Bentum, 'to contemplate such waste at this point in humankind's evolution is unthinkable'.

But the MFC does intend to mark the millennium with two projects: the Earth Legacy Project and Wills for the Earth. The first is a scheme to encourage people to make a bequest to an environmental group. Wills for the Earth hopes to raise awareness of the fact that seven out of ten people have not yet written wills. Van Bentum believes that many of those people might be inclined to leave a legacy to an environmental charity. Not the cheeriest of thoughts for the new millennium, but a practical one.

Contact: Natasha Van Bentum, The Millennium Foundation of Canada (☎ 604-708 3474, e-mail nvbentum@cyberstore.ca, Internet http://www.millennia.org), 330 East 7th Avenue, Suite 104, Vancouver, British Columbia V5T 4K5.

❏ **Drumming in the New Millennium**

Drumming is indigenous to every culture and has been used for communication since the Stone Age. That's why two groups are promoting a global 'drum in' of the next millennium. Susan Ferrier Mackay of **Rhythm of the Earth**, based in Canada, came up with the idea of a world drum-in to 'send a message to the Earth: that we care what happens to her'. She wants people from different communities to join the drum-in through her website. Her 'millennium rhythm', which is based on a human heartbeat, can be downloaded from the site. **Contact:** Susan Ferrier Mackay, Rhythm of the Earth (☎ 905-468 4668, fax 905-468 5153, e-mail bhdrum@vaxxine.com or phillb@mclellangroup.com, Internet http://www.mclellangroup.com/rhythmoftheearth/contents.html).

Another group, **All One Tribe**, will hold a similar world drum session for the millennium. The organisers are looking for area coordinators to expand the drumming network as far as possible. There are plans to link sites by live satellite TV. All One Tribe hold drumming festivals every year. **Contact:** All One Tribe (☎ 800-442-DRUM, e-mail beat@allonetribedrum.com, Internet: http://www.soulzone.com/millenum/index.html)

ALBERTA
New Year's Eve 1999 Party and Tour: Lake Louise

This six-day trip to Lake Louise in the Canadian Rockies includes accommodation at the Château Lake Louise and entry to the Hotel's Gala New Year's Eve 1999 party. Several surprises are planned including a torchlight procession of 2000 skiers at midnight. The Hotel is huge and offers a good range of activities. It also commands beautiful views of Lake Louise and is close to the pistes. Price: £2500.

Contact: The Millennial Foundation (☎ +44 (0) 141-204 2000, fax +44 (0) 141-248 1591, Internet: http://yes2000.co.uk), 10 Sandyford Place, Glasgow G3 7NB, UK

New Year's Eve Festival: Calgary
(31 Dec 1999 – 2 Jan 2000)

A three-day millennium festival will dominate downtown Calgary from New Year's Eve 1999. Final plans are still unavail-

❑ **Millennium Vancouver 2000! Celebration Society**
Thanks to the Millennium Vancouver 2000! Celebration Society
(MV2000! for short), Vancouver will be the liveliest city in Canada
when the year 2000 arrives. The group is a non-profit making
umbrella body which is helping to plan and publicise millennium
celebrations all over the city.

Apart from coordinating millennium events, MV2000! hopes
to make money which can be left as a community legacy. After
2001, the money will be distributed to community and arts projects
around Vancouver. **Contact**: Thomas C Esakin, President and
General Manager MV2000! (☎ 604-618 5825, fax 604-684 6888,
e-mail millennium@vancouver2000.bc.ca), PO Box 48381, 595
Burrard Street, Bentall Centre, Vancouver, British Columbia V7X
1A2.

able but the community-wide festival will include live performances, cultural events and a countdown party.

Contact: Calgary 2000 (☎ 403-268 2000, fax 403-268
5245, e-mail itstime@cadvision.com), PO Box 2100, Station M
Calgary, Alberta T2P 2M5

VANCOUVER
On New Year's Eve 1999, the third-largest city in Canada,
Vancouver, will become the country's millennium capital thanks
to a well-prepared organising team and some bright ideas.

New Year's Eve Events: Vancouver (31 Dec 1999)
MV2000! (see above) are creating a series of pre-millennium
countdown events, starting with a party in August 1998, which
will culminate in an enormous city-wide celebration on New
Year's Eve 1999.

An all-night street party is planned in the city-centre with
the cooperation of bars and clubs in the area. Big-screen TVs will
be mounted at strategic locations in the Downtown district. These
will show footage of other millennium events around the world.
Midnight will be marked with fireworks and a laser light show.
Passports to the Millennium' will be on sale before New Year's

Eve. Revellers can have their passports stamped at each event, a memento of the big night. Other planned celebrations include: a Millennium Eve Costume Ball, a Millennium Eve Gala in which the Vancouver Symphony Orchestra and Vancouver Opera are likely to participate, a party for 20-35 year olds only and a multi-faith Service of Celebration.

A Festival of Nostradamus and a Festival of Time are set to take place in the year 2000, before a ceremony on 1 January 2000 to welcome the 'real' arrival of the third millennium.

Countdown Clock and Time Capsule: Vancouver

A countdown clock and time capsule scroll will be taken on a tour round town between now and New Year's Eve 1999 in an effort to encourage support for the city's millennium plans. The clock will eventually find a permanent home in Canada Place. Anyone will be able to sign the scroll which will be deposited in the time capsule. The capsule will be sealed at a ceremony on 31

❑ VANCOUVER – A BRIEF GUIDE

Everything works in Vancouver. The streets are clean, the crime rate low and transport efficient. This multi-cultural Pacific city is easy to enjoy, if rather predictable. Vancouver also packs a surprising amount into a relatively compact space.

What to See

A strong Asian community has created a magnificent **Chinatown**. **Vancouver Aquarium**, to the east of **Stanley Park**, is the attractive home of some friendly Beluga whales. Stanley Park is itself well worth visiting, with a beautiful forest and a well-maintained series of paths and trails. Another park, **Vanier**, contains the **Vancouver Museum** which is notable for its fascinating displays on Native Canadian life.

Shopping life revolves around **Broadway**, **Commercial Drive** and **Robsonstrasse**. The latter makes every effort to appear as European as it sounds. Vancouver also boasts a number of beaches. While it might be too cold to swim on New Year's Eve, **Kitsilano** ('Kits'), **Sunset** and **Jericho** Beaches make welcome retreats from city-life. In fact, a visit to Jericho is a well-known Vancouverite hang-over cure.

Where to Stay

● **Expensive** (over $180): *Hyatt Regency Vancouver* (☎ 604-683 1234) on Burrard Street; *Coast Plaza at Stanley Park* (☎ 604-688 7711, fax 604-685 7210) which is two blocks from Stanley Park and English Bay; *Pacific Palisades Hotel* (☎ 604-688 0461, fax 604-688 4374) with great views across the city, mountains or the harbour; *Metropolitan Hotel* (☎ 604-687 1122, fax 604-643 7247) on Howe Street; *Four Seasons Hotel* (☎ 604-689 9333, fax 604-684 4555) in the centre of shoppers' paradise on West Georgia Street; the well-positioned *Pan Pacific Hotel Vancouver* (☎ 604-662 8111, fax 604-685 8690); the excellent *Sutton Place Hotel* (☎ 604-682 5511) on Burrard Street; the *Landmark Hotel* (☎ 604-687 0511) is the tallest in Vancouver.

● **Moderate** (between $90 and $180): *Best Western Chateau Granville* (☎ 604-669 7070, fax 604-669 5579); the *Holiday Inn Vancouver Downtown* (☎ 604-682 5566, fax 604-684 4736) is verging on the expensive but is only minutes from Stanley Park; the *Sandman Hotel* (☎ 604-681 2211) is quite good value. Also try *Days Inn Vancouver Downtown* (☎ 604-681 4335); *The Inn at False Creek* (☎ 604-682 0229); *Sylvia Hotel* (☎ 604-681 9321) on English Bay.

● **Budget** (under $90): *HI Vancouver Downtown* (☎ 604-684 4565, fax 604-684 4540); *Vincent's Backpackers Hostel* (☎ 604-682 2441); *YMCA* (☎ 604-681 0221, fax 604-681 1630); the *YWCA* (☎ 604-895 5830, fax 604-681 2550) is well equipped and welcomes families; the *St Regis Hotel* (☎ 604-681 1135) is good value and has recently been renovated; *Washington Hotel* (☎ 604-689 7857, fax 604-689 7857); *Barclay Hotel* (☎ 604-688 8850) on Robson Street.

Party Places

Most clubs are in the Downtown or West End areas. Places to try include: *Graceland* at 1250 Richards Street; *Hard Rock Café* at 686 W Hastings Street; *Mardi Gras* at 1015 Burrard Street; *The Roxy* at 932 Granville Street for regular rock acts; trendy *Mars* at 1320 Richards Street or *Level 5* at 595 Hornby Street. In Central Vancouver try: *Big Bam Boo Club* on 1236 W Broadway or *Kits on Broadway* at 1424 Broadway.

For free entertainment listings pick up *AF Magazine* or *Georgia Straights*.

December 1999. It will also be possible to buy MV2000! personal capsules into which Vancouverites will be able to stash away messages to their descendants.

Millennium Medal of Merit

Vancouverites are being asked to nominate the person or people they consider to have given most to the city over the last 200 years. An independent panel of academics will sift through the suggestions to find 2000 winners of the Millennium Medal of Merit. The award can be given posthumously.

SOUTH PACIFIC (EAST)

Western Samoa

Western Samoa is the closest island group to the International Date Line – but on the eastern side. So the islanders will have to be content to hold the last party of 31 December 1999.

Samoan marketeers are undeterred, offering visitors such slogans as 'Your last millennium experience' or 'Samoa: where time ends'. And why not? There's a lot to be said for prolonging the moment by being among the last to see in the New Year.

Western Samoa is the largest Polynesian country with a population of over 160,000 – 90% of whom are full Samoans. It is rightly known as the Heart of Polynesia. Two islands dominate Western Samoa: Savai'i and 'Upolu. Millennium celebrations will be based on 'Upolu.

❑ **WESTERN SAMOA**
Contacts
● **Western Samoan Visitors' Bureau** (☎ 20-878, fax 20-886, e-mail samaowsvb@pactok.peg.apc.org), PO Box 2272, Apia
● **Internet:** http://www.pise/-orbit/samoa/welcome.html
Average maximum temperature °C

	Dec	Jan
Apia	29	30

Capital: Apia
Flight times: from:
       LA – 11 hrs
       London (connect in Sydney, Auckland or LA) – 27 hours
       Sydney – 4 hrs
Approximate exchange rates: Western Samoan *Tala* or Dollar (WS$) – take US Dollars
Time difference: GMT-11
Country dialling code: ☎ 685

❏ WESTERN SAMOA – WHAT TO SEE

'Upolu

Apia, the capital of Western Samoa and centre for millennium celebrations, is situated roughly in the middle of the north shore of 'Upolu, the country's second largest island. 'Upolu is much more densely populated than its larger neighbour, Savai'i, although development mainly follows the coast.

There is a National Park on the island, **O le Pupupu'e**, and the slightly more easily pronounced **Mt. Vaea Scenic Reserve**. The former is a cross-section of the island, stretching from the coast to the mountains. The latter is an attractive area, great for hiking, which has the peak of Mt. Vaea as a focal point.

Robert Louis Stevenson and his wife, Fanny, are buried at the top of Mt. Vaea. Stevenson's wish to be buried there required a hand-built road to be cut into the mountain. It was named **'The Way of Loving Hearts'**, revealing the Samoans' affection for the *Tusitala* or 'teller of tales'.

The **Robert Louis Stevenson Museum** at Vailima is located in the writer's beautiful home. The property also serves as the official residence of the Samoan Head of State.

Savai'i

After New Zealand and Hawaii, Savai'i is the largest island in Polynesia. But it is sparsely populated with big areas of unspoilt wilderness and a strong traditional culture. This lack of development can be off-putting to travellers in search of luxury but is ideal for anyone looking for 'real' Polynesia.

Divers, **surfers**, **snorkellers** and **ramblers** will love Savai'i, but those short of time or those who are easily bored might prefer 'Upolu.

There are a lot of sites of archaeological interest on Savai'i, most notably the biggest ancient monument in Polynesia: **Pulemelei Mound**. This 12-metre tall pyramid is shrouded by jungle, so only intrepid travellers are likely to want to visit it.

Those who enjoy hunting hidden ruins should visit the **Tafua Savai'i Rainforest Reserve** which occupies a bulge in Savai'i's south-eastern corner. Pristine rainforest surrounds an extinct crater now inhabited by flying foxes. A lovely stretch of lava coast is another good reason to explore the reserve.

❏ **Rugby in Western Samoa**
South Pacific nations, particularly Fiji, have contributed a steady stream of world-class players to the great game of Rugby Union. Western Samoa is certainly no exception. Local stars such as Vai'ga Tuigemala, Michael Jones and the Bachop brothers are literally giants of the game – all of whom, like many South Pacific islanders, also played for the famous New Zealand 'All Blacks'.

Rugby fans would be well advised to hang around after the millennium party is over. On 7-8 January 2000 there's the **National 10-a-Side Rugby Tournament**. Two weeks later, on the 21 and 22 January, the **Rugby Union National Provincial Sevens** will show-case some of Samoa's finest. Then on 4 and 5 February 2000 the **Polynesian Airlines/Marist International Sevens** take place. In Western Samoa, rugby fans can start the new millennium as they mean to go on.

Millennium Celebrations in Western Samoa

Western Samoa's millennium celebrations are centred around the Government Plaza in Apia on the island of 'Upolu although events will also take place elsewhere.

Throughout 30 December 1999 Western Samoa will confirm its friendly reputation through a 'meet and greet' programme at all points of entry. At 6am the **New Year's Eve** celebrations will start with a morning devotion and thanksgiving service at the Apia Government Plaza

A float parade will follow at 9am, winding its way from Vasigano Women's Centre to the Apia Government Plaza.

During the day, several other celebratory events are planned. Millennium messages of welcome will be delivered at the Government Plaza. A millennium carnival will take place – the venue as yet unknown – and other millennial entertainment will be put on across the country.

The evening programme begins at 6pm with a millennium collegiate showcase at the Government Plaza. From 9pm there will be a millennium band jam session and concert to entertain the crowd at the Plaza. Millennium blessings and thanksgiving will then be conducted by candlelight from 11.45pm. Western

Samoa will start a nationwide millennium countdown at 11.59pm, and at midnight traditional church bells will ring out in a climax that will also include a long fireworks display.

The party will continue throughout the night, with several Samoan bands taking to the stage. Party-goers will be able to celebrate until the last dawn of the first day of the year 2000 lights the islands.

Cook Islands

The Cook Islands are among the most attractive in the South Seas. Rarotonga, the largest of the Islands, is planning a New Year's Eve 1999 party to be held in Avarua City. The celebration will be called 'Symphony of Drums – the South Pacific Call'. It will feature a continuous Mardi Gras-style street party along Avarua's one-kilometre main road.

Enthusiastic millennium planning is in progress in the Cook Islands, and many hotels and resorts hope to hold their own parties. **Contact:** Tourism Cook Islands (☎ +682 29-435, fax +682 21-435, e-mail tourism@cookislands.gov.ck or visit the Islands' new web site at http://www.cookislands-tourism.com), Head Office, PO Box 14, Avarua, Rarotonga, Cook Islands.

❏ **Letter to *The Times***

Sir, I beg you to publish no more tedious, pedantic letters, such as
the two you print today, from those who want us to postpone celebrating the millennium until we have seen 2000 safely to its end.
They prate of numeracy, but know not the joy of numbers.

It is not an anniversary that we shall be celebrating, because
nothing whatever happened at either the beginning or the end of 1
BC (certainly not the birth of Jesus). What we are all getting excit-
ed about is that *all the numbers will change*.

It is like seeing 99,999 turn into 100,000 on the car milometer.
That's what it's all about.

Yours sincerely
Dr ML West *FBA*
All Souls College, Oxford OX1 4AL
January 26

INDEX